THE FRENCH ACTRESS AND HER
ENGLISH AUDIENCE

For centuries English and French theatrical conventions have had an uneasy relationship with one another: mutual admiration, mutual envy, mutual distrust. Just as the fascination of difference lies in the potential for sameness, so these opposed traditions have observed each other at close quarters and invited each other back home. In an unusually detailed and carefully illustrated book, John Stokes explores the reception of the French actress by English audiences from the early nineteenth century to the middle of the twentieth – a period when the relationship between England and France was transformed and re-defined. Mlle Mars, Sarah Bernhardt and Edwige Feuillère are among the many actresses invoked; prominent English spectators include William Hazlitt, Charles Dickens and Oscar Wilde. The result is a vivid coming together of theatre history and cultural studies that will appeal to scholars of English and French literature as well as to students of acting.

JOHN STOKES teaches at King's College London where he specialises in the history of drama. He is a regular contributor to the *Times Literary Supplement* and other journals. His previous books include *Oscar Wilde: Myths, Miracles and Imitations* (1996), and, with Michael Booth and Susan Bassnett, *Bernhardt, Terry, Duse: The Actress in Her Time* (1988) and *Three Tragic Actresses: Siddons, Rachel, Ristori* (1996), all published by Cambridge University Press.

THE FRENCH ACTRESS
AND HER ENGLISH
AUDIENCE

JOHN STOKES

CAMBRIDGE
UNIVERSITY PRESS

PUBLISHED BY THE PRESS SYNDICATE OF THE UNIVERSITY OF CAMBRIDGE
The Pitt Building, Trumpington Street, Cambridge, United Kingdom

CAMBRIDGE UNIVERSITY PRESS
The Edinburgh Building, Cambridge, CB2 2RU, UK
40 West 20th Street, New York, NY 10011–4211, USA
477 Williamstown Road, Port Melbourne, VIC 3207, Australia
Ruiz de Alarcón 13, 28014 Madrid, Spain
Dock House, The Waterfront, Cape Town 8001, South Africa

http://www.cambridge.org

First published 2005

Printed in the United Kingdom at the University Press, Cambridge

Typeface Adobe Garamond 11/12.5 pt.   *System* LATEX 2$_\varepsilon$ [TB]

A catalogue record for this book is available from the British Library

ISBN 0 521 84300 6 hardback

For Peter and Valerie Mendes
Oh, les beaux jours

Contents

Illustrations

Acknowledgements

I have been fortunate, first at the University of Warwick and more recently at King's College London, to work with people who share my fascination with the theory and practice of performance. I have learned from them all. Four friends I first encountered when they were graduate students have greatly enhanced my understanding of the history of the actress. They are Elaine Aston, Maggie Gale, Gail Marshall and Joanna Robinson.

Over the years librarians in London and Paris have been unfailingly helpful but I should mention, in particular, the staff in the Study Room at the Theatre Museum for whom nothing theatrical is too much trouble.

Jane Sacchi generously gave me access to papers relating to her late mother, the actress Margaret Rawlings. Rosemary Geddes has kindly approved my use of a letter from the late Sir Alan Bates.

At Cambridge University Press, Vicki Cooper has once again proved herself to be the most sympathetic of editors.

Faith Evans began improving my French in the winter of 1962 'sous le ciel de Paris'. She has been doing so – and much else besides – ever since.

*

An earlier version of '"Peacocks and Pearls": Oscar Wilde and Sarah Bernhardt' was delivered at the '1890s' Conference at the University of Newcastle in 2001. Thanks to Professor John Batchelor for inviting me to speak.

I am grateful to the editors and publishers of the following for permission to reprint material:

'Rachel's "terrible beauty": an actress among the novelists' in *English Literary History* (Johns Hopkins University Press), vol. 51, Winter 1984, pp. 771–93.
'Memories of Plessy: Henry James restages the past' in *Women, Theatre and Performance: New Histories, New Historiographies*, ed. Maggie B. Gale and Viv Gardner, Manchester University Press, 2000, pp. 81–101.

'Déjazet/déja vu' in *Women and Theatre*, Occasional Papers 3, 1996, pp. 30–52.

'The modernity of Aimée Desclée' in *New Theatre Quarterly* (Cambridge University Press), vol. 6, no. 24, November 1990, pp. 365–78.

'"A kind of beauty": Réjane in London' in *Themes in Drama* (Cambridge University Press), vol. 6, 1984, pp. 97–119.

Figures 2, 3, 4, 5, 8 and 9 are reproduced by permission of V&A Images / Victoria and Albert Museum; figures 1, 7 and 14 by permission of the British Library; figures 6, 10, 15, 16 and 20 by permission of the Bibliothèque Nationale de France; figures 13, 18 and 19 by permission of the Mander and Mitchensen Theatre Collection; figure 17 by permission of the Bettmann Archive, Corbis.

Introduction: The golden age of acting

> It *paid* apparently, in the golden age of acting, to sit through interminable evenings in impossible places – since to assume that the age *was* in that particular respect golden (for which we have in fact a good deal of evidence) alone explains the patience of the public.
>
> Henry James[1]

Sometimes the most beguiling face of the Other belongs to our closest neighbour. That, at any rate, has usually been the case with the tangled relations – mutual admiration, mutual envy, mutual distrust – that have always existed between the English and French theatres. Just as the fascination of difference lies in the potential for sameness, so these opposed traditions have observed each other at close quarters and invited each other back home. There were French actors in London as early as 1629; Charles II, who had spent time in Paris, patronised French troupes in the 1660s and 1670s, and although royal hospitality inevitably waned during subsequent reigns, further visits to London took place throughout the 1720s and 1730s. In 1738 there were violent protests when a French company was given permission to open at the Haymarket, and a rather similar situation occurred in 1749 when another French company, backed by David Garrick, tried to establish itself at the same theatre. Again there were riots. Those very first visits had prompted some disquiet at the presence of female performers; later the reasons for protest were economic and political. But continuously volatile relations between two cultures, as well as the financial insecurities typical of all theatre business, only make the number of trips in both directions look all the more impressive.

   The eight chapters that make up this book encompass an extended phase in the protracted dealings between theatrical practices that have always been notorious for their formal contrasts. They do so by focusing, in quite precise ways, upon a number of French actresses who appeared in England between the early nineteenth century and the middle of the twentieth: a period of time that saw the emergence, the triumphs and the transformations, the

I

eventual demise of the great Romantic performer, a dynastic line far more narrowly defined than any English tradition, a theatrical transmission that has, in fact, no English equivalent at all. The consistency of theatrical conventions and of play texts were clearly factors, but the Romantic period in France exhibited a complex set of political attitudes at the same time as it mapped out an aesthetic. The Romantic actress became an active vehicle for the expression of history, by turns a contemporary phenomenon, a vision or parody of the past, the living embodiment of lost chances and social cost.

Consequently I pay little or no attention to those other French *artistes* – singers, dancers – who fascinated English audiences over the decades, and I make few attempts to offer broad generalisations about Anglo-French cultural relations. Theatrical reception is always made up of disparate inter-pretation. If, on the French side, my emphasis is mainly upon the theatrical conditions that determined their initial appearances, on the English one it is upon the way the actresses were seen and felt by individuals, particu-larly by writers and artists. These responses were, inevitably, extremely various and I have no wish to force a pattern on a whole range of subjective interpretations, allowing simply for a shared historical moment.

On the few occasions when journeys in the reverse direction are invoked, by the English to France, it is usually for reasons of context.[2] Only rarely were the cross-channel visits reciprocal exchanges and there were distinc-tive and recurring concerns on both sides that were neither intellectually balanced nor historically synchronised. However, the frequency of trips in both directions certainly did increase significantly throughout the nine-teenth century. Writing in 1899, Clement Scott, a conservative critic who nonetheless considered himself an advocate of internationalism,[3] was able to announce that, in addition to legendary visits to London by the Comédie-Française in 1870 and 1879,

without setting foot in Paris, it has been possible for English playgoers, in a course of years, to become familiar with such varied and special talent as that of Rachel and Sarah Bernhardt, Regnier and Lafont, Bressant and Delaunay, of Lacressionère and Geoffroy, of Ravel and Berton, of Dupuis and Baron and Leonce, of Got and Coquelin. Without even visiting the Boulevards, we have been able to discriminate between Aimée Desclée and Fargueil, and Schneider and Chaumont, and Blanche Pierson and Bartet, and Leonide Leblanc and Pasca, and Granier and Judic, and Jane Hading and Réjane, and who shall say how many more representatives who have their little day and disappear?[4]

Arranging these seasons was never straightforward, as Scott well knew. Despite his appreciation of the number of those French performers who, within recent memory, had been welcomed in England, he wondered how many playgoers

who, though perfectly familiar with the French play seasons at the old St James's, at the old Princess's, at the defunct Holborn, at the Opéra Comique, at the Gaiety, at the Royalty and the Adelphi, illuminated by Sarah Bernhardt and Coquelin, are aware that in the year 1848 one of the most important companies in Paris, came to London to play 'Monte Cristo' at Drury Lane, and was literally hissed and hooted off the stage by a body of roughs and enthusiasts, who came fully persuaded that English art would be ruined at once and irretrievably if French plays were ever to be permitted at any theatre save the St James's, where they were to be graciously tolerated, but there and there alone. (Scott, 2, 437)

This refers to a salutary moment in 1848 when the Théâtre-Historique had been booed off the stage at Drury Lane and pamphlets had been distributed enjoining Britons 'to stand by the British Drama'.[5] The French, it was undeniable, had long made their presence felt simply by virtue of the number of their plays that had ended up, in one form or another, upon the English stage. Yet, as Michael Booth has pointed out, the fact that 'many plays of the time, whether comedies, farces, or melodramas, were taken from the French', does not necessarily mean that the English theatre was moribund or had no identity of its own.[6] The range of dramatic material on offer was wide, the acting often vibrant, and performances must always be related to the local milieu, the expectations of experienced audiences. These make it apparent that the French influence was not always stultifying. The most famous joke against the French neo-classical tradition – Mr Curdle's definition in *Nicholas Nickleby* of the unities as 'a kind of universal dovetailedness with regard to place and time – a sort of general oneness' – occurs alongside Nickleby's own praise of a French piece he has been asked to translate for its 'abundance of incident, sprightly dialogue, strongly-marked characters'.[7] It is true that Dickens had little time for Rachel and the kind of tragedy that she represented, but there were plenty of other French performers whose art he enjoyed immensely.

Performers interpreting their own repertoire in their own language make different and probably greater demands upon an audience than plays which have been translated and adapted for local conditions; and, in any case, my primary concern here is not with plays so much as with players, and very specifically with actresses. (I retain the word 'actress', incidentally, rather than the currently preferred and supposedly neutral 'actor', not because the women lacked power – they were often in control and always influential – nor because they were sexually provocative in ways unknown to men – obviously both sexes can be attractive on stage, and to both sexes – but because of the language used about them, and the traditions to which they belonged. Performing women were compared with other women, rather than with men.)

It is also true that actresses have suffered from prejudice and even from persecution as well as having been the beneficiaries of occasional privilege.[8] They have been vilified and outlawed for the supposed immorality of their profession; they have been acclaimed for reasons having little to do with their talent; they have had freedoms thrust upon them that other women have been denied – and have then been made to pay a price for an independence they may not have sought. Women on stage have been observed in prurient ways and simultaneously honoured for their uniquely inspirational power. This was overwhelmingly the case with the great French actresses of the seventeenth and eighteenth centuries: a distinguished line of brilliant women courted by writers, admired by their peers, and often scapegoated by their religion. Champmeslé,[9] Lecouvreur,[10] Clairon:[11] it was a uniquely eminent list that had immediately entered legend and to which most later French actresses have had to relate.

Yet for all the achievements of individuals, the English have always been aware that in comparison with their own traditions French acting, both gesture and declamation, appears rigidly codified and ponderously oratorical. This has made heavy demands upon English audiences whilst causing them to be peculiarly sensitive to discrepancies and changes whenever they occur. Add the fact that the same types (*emplois*) recur throughout the classic French repertoire in a quite unEnglish way – *soubrettes, ingénues, grandes coquettes* and so on – and the challenge of difference becomes that much greater. It is difficult to determine the ease, or otherwise, with which English audiences, even in quite recent times, could grasp alexandrines delivered at high speed or catch the drift of Parisian *argot*, could recognise some subtle variation in character or respond to rhetorical and gestural emphases. In the nineteenth century there was a good deal of cynicism about these interpretative abilities from those who admitted to not possessing them,[12] though translations were sometimes made available at theatres and the professional critics, at least, do seem to have been remarkably well equipped.

All of which ensured that visits by French actresses were anticipated, scrutinised and analysed with unique intensity. Their charismatic influence upon English culture, by no means confined to those who had a professional investment in theatre, has never been appreciated as the long-lasting phenomenon that it undoubtedly was. The actresses provided stimulus for novelists, poets, essayists, artists of every kind, for whom comparisons between past and present, as well as between contemporary performers, were irresistible.[13] And while these oppositions could sometimes work to restrict meaning, and to stimulate an unhealthy appetite for supposed rivalry between women, a spectator sport of a quasi-voyeuristic kind, they could equally generate flashes of insight and shape new definitions, as one dazzling performance lit up another. Together the French actresses constitute a myth of a golden age of acting – a myth for which we have, as Henry James might say, 'a good deal of evidence'.

NATIONAL SPECULATIONS

Underpinning the cross-channel journeys, alongside a wish to entertain, to inspire, and to impress, there was invariably the hope of financial profit and political advantage.[14] We begin in the post-Revolutionary, post-Napoleonic period, when mutual curiosity was exceptionally lively, but even then there were still strong precedents lingering on from the previous century.[15] On the two occasions (1751 and 1763–4) when he had made extended stays in France, David Garrick had been anxious to meet with the great of the literary and theatrical worlds, an ambition he had achieved. And while he may have felt ambivalent towards French theatre, this did nothing to prevent him from planning for reciprocal arrangements between London and Paris, collaborating with Jean-Louis Monnet of the Opéra-Comique in 1749. Monnet made an initial arrangement with John Rich of Covent Garden for two performances a week. This fell through when Rich backed off, fearing the degree of anti-French sentiment in London. At Garrick's suggestion, Monnet then moved to the Haymarket. What followed was determined more by matters of politics than of theatrical taste: a divided audience made up of pro- and anti-French factions, accusations of disloyalty directed at an MP who had supported the project, fighting in the streets, the intervention of the Lord Chamberlain bringing the season to a halt, eventually Monnet's arrest.[16] Nevertheless, the friendship between Monnet and Garrick survived these disasters and Monnet is to be seen as a pioneer. More than a century later, in 1911, he was being invoked as 'an early impresario, a fore-runner of those cosmopolitan managers who have, since his day, led troupes of comedians from Paris to London, New York and the ends of the world'.[17]

Just as Garrick, with his distant French ancestry, was probably bi-lingual and unquestionably well read in the history and theory of French theatre, Hippolyte Talma, his opposite number in terms of theatrical reform, could claim to have been brought up in partly in London.[18] As a boy, he visited London theatres and acted with an amateur company composed of French residents. In the 1780s Lord Harcourt, his friend and benefactor, even mooted the idea of a London branch of the Comédie-Française that would specialise in the classic French repertoire. This came to nothing but it did give Talma an entrée into Parisian theatrical circles and he eventually joined the Comédie himself in 1787, later becoming a determining figure in its complex fortunes during the revolutionary and Napoleonic periods.

Prolonged hostilities inevitably put a halt to any further plans for exchanges between England and France, although there was a short break in 1802, following the Peace of Amiens, when it was possible to visit the continent once more.[19] After Waterloo, French performers were back in London in relative strength, though they were for most part culled from popular Parisian theatres such as the Vaudeville. There were regular weekly events organised by aristocratic ladies at the Argyll Rooms, where short plays – farces, one-act comedies, the occasional Molière – would be delivered in the original before music and the dancing of waltzes and quadrilles that went on until one or two o'clock in the morning. These subscription evenings, attracting a Society clientele, were extremely well attended: on one evening in 1819 some '400 fashionables' were reported to be present.[20]

By comparison with the Argyll entertainments, the series of recitations from French classics eventually given by Talma and Mlle George at the King's Theatre in the summer of 1817, though brief, stands out as a special event. The pair were not only famous stars but they had led highly charged political careers, which made their presence in London notable as a symptom of changing diplomacy as well as a matter of theatrical interest. Despite the considerable courtesies paid them (private boxes for John Philip Kemble's *Macbeth*), the times were still felt to be sensitive. Invited to speak at Kemble's grand farewell banquet Talma, in the heat of the festive moment, proposed a toast wishing 'success to the British Nation, and to the British Stage', a gesture much appreciated by those present – although he had subsequently to explain it away to his compatriots.[21]

At the same moment as a changing political climate allowed French performers to come to London so the English, as Fanny Kemble was to put it, began 'as they have since continued, in increasing numbers, to carry amazement and amusement from the shores of the Channel to those of the Mediterranean, by their wealth, insolence, ignorance and cleanliness'.[22] Naturally, when in Paris the English headed for the theatres. Sir Walter Scott, in the capital in 1815, declared that 'he never received greater pleasure from any theatrical exhibition' than from a performance by Mlle Mars.[23] William Charles Macready, there in 1822, also delighted in Mars: 'Nor was her voice her only charm: in person she was most lovely, and in grace and elegance of deportment and action unapproached by any of her contemporaries.'[24]

Although there were French actors in London in the 1820s and, although seeing Mlle Mars continued to be one of the recommended experiences for English tourists in Paris, it was not until late in the decade that she eventually appeared in London, at the King's Theatre in 1828. She returned in 1832, this time to Covent Garden, brought over by an adventurous but badly organised actor now turned manager, Pierre Laporte, but there were rows about money and Laporte apparently ended up out of pocket.[25] In general, both English managers and French *artistes* would look to make a sound profit from a London season,[26] although the possibilities inevitably reflected organisational changes on the French theatrical scene.

Earlier in the century a licensing system operated in Paris whereby individual theatres were allowed to specialise in particular forms. So, for example, at various times the Variétés, the Vaudeville, the Gymnase and the Palais-Royal were permitted to stage vaudevilles, while the Porte-Saint-Martin, the Gaîté and the Ambigu-Comique offered melodrama. In time these rigid demarcations broke down and the eventual abolition of the licensing system in 1864 led at first to a burst of classic plays in boulevard theatres, but this was short-lived: 'as even the Comédie-Française was discovering at the time, there were more lucrative works waiting to be put on than the classics'.[27]

Inevitably business fluctuated, despite the general increase in theatrical activity. A commentator writing in 1889 compared the present situation in Paris which, despite the large number of theatres, seemed to be lacking in energy, to 1832 when, although there were only five state-supported and eight commercial or boulevard theatres, the sheer quantity of plays staged was overwhelming.[28] A modern historian notes the overall growth that followed 1864: 'by 1882 the eleven theatres operating in Paris in 1828 had grown to twenty-three, and the total revenue had risen from 4,789,000 francs to 20,168,000 francs'.[29] The figures are complex and hard to judge but it does seem clear that the Parisian theatres saw a steady increase in profits in the course of the century, some of it due to the tourist trade, and that this bottomed out in the early 1880s. That same pattern of growth and slump may be reciprocally reflected in the regular appearances of French performers in London; stars could easily find material ripe for export among all the diverse theatrical activities of their home town and turn to their London seasons as a useful source of additional earnings in the event of a downturn.[30]

The first figure to make major profits through the wholesale importation of French performers was John Mitchell, a Bond Street ticket agent, whose clients included Queen Victoria herself.[31] Mitchell's entrepreneurial skill lay in his creation of a stylish Society event. In 1842 he took possession of the St James Theatre in King Street, an elegant new building that had been raised on the site of an ancient inn some seven years earlier. Even before Mitchell's time the programme at the St James had had a French inflection: a new farce, *The French Company*, staged in 1835, had a character purporting to be a star of the Comédie-Française and in 1836 Jenny Vertpré, already a popular London performer, was in residence with a permanent company that invited established French stars to join it for short engagements. The repertoire included *Tartuffe* and *Le Mariage de Figaro*. Success with more home-grown products was limited: *The Village Coquettes*, a comic opera by Charles Dickens and John Hullah, ran for a mere twenty nights, and in the later 1830s there was even recourse to the kind of animal acts which had proved so successful at Drury Lane. But French ballet and German opera did well and when Mitchell took possession of the theatre he capitalised on this precedent by inviting more foreigners and by instigating a series of annual seasons that ran for some twelve years, causing the St James sometimes to be known simply as 'The French Theatre'. Among French actresses, Plessy, Rachel (who had made her English début at Her Majesty's in 1841 but who appeared for Mitchell throughout the 1840s right up until her last London performance in 1855), Déjazet, Vestris, Doche, Rose Chéri, all starred at the St James; among French actors: Perlet, Bouffé and Lemaître.

Mitchell's French seasons took place early in the year and such was his theatre's prestige that they attracted a formidable Society audience. As the *Morning Post* was able to proclaim in 1845:

Here fashion plumes its wings for more enlarged re-unions – the coteries, freed from the confined limits of the *salons* of the country mansion, now rejoice at the sight of the painted canvas – the real now gives place to the artificial – and fine ladies and fine wits, and MPs and captains on leave, breathe more freely in the gas-freighted atmosphere of the theatre, than in the halls decked with freshest flowers – the wit of the stage and *l'esprit* of the actors save the necessity of personal effects – and infinite is the profit of the exchange. The announcement of the French Plays is to London what the dove was to the ark – the various orders essay to leave their hum-drum domesticity, and rush to Mitchell's Library to secure stalls and boxes. Bearded precursors, like the pioneers of the Imperial army, precede the *troupe*, and give 'note of preparation'; while fresh relays of myriad bonnet-boxes rejoice the various streets and outlets of St James's Square.

Even the limited capacity of the St James proved to be an asset:

Its size secures its exclusiveness, and imparts to it rather the air of a distinguished family performance than that of a public theatre – and we confess that when we weigh the large sums paid to the *artistes*, and the innumerable contingent expenses of such an establishment, so confined in its limits, we are greatly astonished at the courage and perseverance of the manager. The programme is singularly rich in names of Parisian dramatic celebrity; the company has been selected with great judgment, and the appearances of the stars have been so arranged that a succession of variety is secured. As each of the *celebrities* has a peculiar style, and the dramas have been written for their especial interpretation, a positive excellence in the principal character and in the ensemble may be with safety reckoned upon.[32]

That same year, 1845, Mitchell arranged for Macready and Helen Faucit to appear in *Hamlet* in Paris, and for a time he had plans to establish there a sister theatre to the St James, though these never materialised. The Rachel seasons remained his greatest triumph; so proud was Mitchell of his association with the actress that he presented the Comédie-Française with a portrait of her to hang in its galleries.[33] In 1854 Mitchell retired from the St James, but foreign entertainers and French companies continued to appear at theatres through into the 1870s, including one run by Raphael Félix, Rachel's brother. At the turn of the century the St James prospered under the patrician rule of the actor-manager George Alexander before becoming notable for a time as the home of thrillers and other more lightweight diversions. It is at least historically apt that it should have been there that, more than a century later, in 1951, the Renaud-Barrault Company would take up a brief but impressive residency featuring Edwige Feuillère, and in 1953 that the same theatre would host a visit from the Comédie-Française. My final chapter places the great success of Feuillère amidst a renewed bout of francophilia brought on by the cultural deprivations of a European war in which the French had been seen as allies.

Following on from Mitchell's pioneering stint at the St James, the most ambitious manager in the business of importing French stars in the latter half of the century was John Hollingshead, who ran the Gaiety Theatre (itself based on the Théâtre Lyrique in Paris) between 1868 and 1886. Once again, it was a highly entrepreneurial venture, as Hollingshead makes quite clear in his various autobiographies, where he likes to refer to 'speculations' that were his own 'and no one else's'.[34] The Paris Commune of 1871 had caused some members of the Comédie-Française to flee to London, where they had made a substantial impression; Hollingshead's greatest coup was to bring the company over in its entirety in 1879. Even if the visit did fire an idealistic movement for an endowed theatre in England, the 1879 negotiations 'were conducted in a purely commercial spirit. Whatever worship of art there may or may not have been in the transaction was discreetly kept in the background on all sides'.[35] Hollingshead's invitation was at first resisted by the then Director of the Comédie, Emile Perrin, who feared that if the company left Paris it would jeopardise its state payment of some £10,000 a year. In the event, Perrin was able to accept because its Paris home needed large-scale redecoration, which would in any case involve closure of the theatre. The London season therefore suited everyone. Perrin, 'a gentlemanly merchant', says Hollingshead, was obviously a skilled bargainer and he demanded that the company be paid in advance week by week over the six-week season. Hollingshead recouped by doubling the normal seat prices; he could at least be sure of a full house on the evenings when Sarah Bernhardt was due to appear. These were so popular that a black-market system was in operation – from which, of course, Hollingshead claims not to have benefited. Even so, the financial details that he provides reveal the tremendous impact that Bernhardt's presence had upon attendance figures and make it even less surprising that she should have left the Comédie soon after her London triumph. Not that Bernhardt was the first star, by any means, to have chafed against the restrictions imposed by the national company. Both Rachel and Plessy had done so, making their London appearances all the more financially pressing and, with luck, rewarding. Having spotted a market opportunity, Hollingshead brought Bernhardt over in 1882 and by the following year he could boast that he had organised ten seasons of French plays.

Back in the 1840s the St James had found success as the London home of French drama partly because of Mitchell's deliberate policy of inviting performers of many kinds, a pattern followed later by other managements, who imported individuals and companies from the whole spectrum of Parisian theatres: *vaudevilles* from the Variétés, farces from the Palais-Royal, controversial modern melodramas from the Gymnase. By the 1860s, when inferior French companies looked for a London season, Hollingshead was able to remind them that 'English people and especially Londoners, are almost as familiar with the best performances in Paris as the Parisians themselves'.[36]

The English could certainly be critical – even, or perhaps especially, when they visited the Comédie-Française at the theatre in the rue de Richelieu. The acknowledged prestige of an ancient house did little to alleviate mixed feelings, in which respect and alienation were combined.[37] When Hollingshead found himself being taken around 'The First Theatre in Europe', he was initially struck by 'the stage-entrance and the porter's lodge very lofty, clean and quiet; very unlike the dismal and dirty dens

which architects have planned for the stage-entrances of most London theatres', as well as by 'a broad, richly-carpeted staircase', 'walls adorned with
portraits of past literary and artistic celebrities' and a large Green Room
which 'was like a room in the palace of Versailles, loaded with portraits of
those who had done honour to the theatre from the old days of its foundation'. This magnificence contrasted strongly with the front of house where
'our seats were narrow and cramped, the floor was dirty and uncarpeted,
and the dust in the spaces at the back of the seats staring us in the face
might have been taken out with a small shovel'. Most of all Hollingshead
was distressed by the quality of the drama on offer, specifically by Dumas
fils's *L'Etrangère*. He concluded:

> The mission of the Théâtre-Français, if it has a mission, is certainly not to take away
> from the Gymnase or the Vaudeville a commonplace drama of shallow conventional
> intrigue, which would do no credit to any theatre. The Théâtre-Français does not
> draw eight or ten thousand pounds sterling per annum from the pockets of the
> French taxpayers to produce such a tawdry piece of French dramatic workmanship
> as this play. By producing 'L'Etrangère' it has probably put money into the pockets
> of its *sociétaires*, for the piece is undoubtedly popular; but the Français is subsidised
> to fly in the face of popularity, if popularity is only to be gained at the expense
> of art.

Too many people in England regarded the Théâtre-Français with 'a blind
and superstitious reverence – the offspring of hearsay and ignorance',
whereas Hollingshead, the individualist businessman, was 'accustomed to
be governed by what I see, and not by what other people tell me'.[38]

In a number of fictions by Henry James (they include *The Ambassadors*,
1903) the mandatory evening at the Théâtre-Français brings out a similar
ambivalence: an embarrassed sense of lacking the appropriate sophistication
is coupled with disappointment and a wish to mock some dusty preten-
sions. Obliged, at a performance of Augier's *L'Aventurière*, to put up with
'*doublures*' (understudies), the two Americans in James's novella *The Siege of
London* (1883) feel the play to be 'antiquated',[39] yet, as their visit to Europe
continues, they find themselves re-enacting, or 'doubling', a version of its
plot. Augier's *L'Aventurière* – possibly the very first play that James had
seen at the Théâtre-Français,[40] which he would invoke again in *The Tragic
Muse* of 1890 – may be one of those dated French plays (it could almost
equally well be *Le Demi-Monde* by Dumas *fils*) about 'the justice to be
meted out to unscrupulous women who attempt to thrust themselves into
honorable families' (29). Nevertheless, European society seems still to be
mired in its world. Since the term 'doublure' could also be used to decry an
inadequate performance,[41] so the irony of their situation rebounds upon

James's bemused American spectators who are required to behave better than their theatrical prototypes.

James's own fascination with the Théâtre-Français overcame his uncertainty about some aspects of its repertoire. He had, after all, been swept up by the glamour of the place long before he had experienced a performance there, long before he had even set foot in Paris. Even as a boy his father's respect for French culture had made him 'aware of the Comédie'. James's writing on the French theatre is haunted by ghosts, by lost worlds, missed opportunities and the passage of time. Looking back at his youth, he rues that on the occasion of his first visit to Europe, 'Rachel was alive, but dying; the memory of Mademoiselle Mars, at her latest, was still in the air; Mademoiselle George, a massive, a monstrous antique, had withal returned for a season to the stage; but we missed her, as we missed Déjazet and Frédérick Lemaître and Mélingue and Samson; to say nothing of others of the age before the flood.'[42]

James was far from alone in treasuring, despite the creaking repertoire and the sometimes merely vestigial evidence of greatness, Europe's most celebrated national theatre. Until the coming of the Romantic drama (Dumas *père*'s *Henri III* in 1829) the Comédie-Française faltered in the immediately post-Napoleonic years and indeed there were considerable financial difficulties right through the nineteenth century, some of them dependent upon salary negotiations with stars who could earn far more on the boulevards.[43] In reality the national and, as soon as they became practical, the international tours, including the visits to London, carried out independently by the *sociétaires* of the Française were both symptom and cause of the company's precarious finances and its lack of aesthetic direction.[44] But when the company travelled abroad as a complete unit, public mystification of its unique 'tradition' concealed these problems to a quite considerable degree. Following the sensational London season of 1879 (which James ironically found disquieting given the prominence of the commercially motivated Bernhardt) the company returned to the capital in 1893.[45] Later, in 1922, led by Cécile Sorel as a celebrated Célimène, it played *Le Misanthrope* in front of the King and Queen at a charity gala in aid of the Institut Français and the restoration of Reims Cathedral. Returning in the summer of 1924, again led by Sorel, the company filled the New Oxford Theatre for a number of weeks. The spirit of the *entente cordiale* together with Sorel's own fondness for the rich and powerful (she fraternised not only with English royalty but with the Tsar, the King of Egypt, Clemenceau, and Mussolini), meant that Célimène and Marguerite Gautier continued on their international way into the early twentieth century.

Even in the 1870s, whereas Henry James found himself pleasurably wracked by visions of an irrecoverable history, others (including Oscar Wilde) were captivated by what they saw as the still visible potential of the Romantic repertoire. Many never forgot the occasion of their first acquaintance with the French stars. The impact made by Rachel in 1841 and by Bernhardt in 1879 was famously memorable, but sometimes the début would have a personal resonance, as it did for Alice Comyns Carr, for whom Aimée Desclée's London opening in 1873 marked the occasion of her first meeting with her future husband. Joe Comyns Carr was then theatre critic of the *Echo*, though later to become a manager and an intimate of Henry Irving. Personal associations naturally reinforced Alice's memories of 'that remarkable performance of *Froufrou* which set the cosmopolitan world of London aflame in its day'.[46] For a young woman brought up in Italy and currently living in London with strict relatives, a 'wicked French play' held obvious attractions, while her husband would subsequently tell her 'that he marked me down as I came in, and somehow associated me with the personality of Aimée Desclée herself'.[47] Incongruous perhaps, but there are records of supposedly strong men bursting into tears at the pathos of Desclée's acting, the poignancy of her early death adding to a Romantic aura against which the visits of women whose careers lasted far longer – from Bernhardt in the 1870s and 1880s to Feuillère in the 1950s – were inevitably to be set.[48]

It is, though, a cultural story that seems temporarily, perhaps finally, to have come to a halt. When Anglo-French politics take place in a broadly European context, when we have in London subsidised theatres that match in their achievements (if not in the size of their grants) anything offered in Paris, when the 1997 visit of the Comédie-Française to the National Theatre is sponsored by newspapers, the oil industry and a consortium of '75 French companies from the world of luxury'[49] – then the context of appreciation has obviously changed. At the same time, the desire to view French actresses close up, those heady impulses made up of awe, admiration and desire that held English audiences in thrall for so long, may at last have played themselves out.

SEXUAL SPECIFICATIONS

An unpredictable result of Garrick's visits to the continent in the mid-eighteenth century was that he came to play a posthumous, and largely unacknowledged, role in the debates about the psychological nature of acting that would dominate the later nineteenth century. The vexed question of 'identification' was reinforced by the belated publication in 1830 (English translation 1883) of Diderot's *Paradoxe sur le comédien*,[50] which argues that performers must keep their emotional distance from their roles and exercise their own memory if they are to achieve an accurate representation. This theory came to be seen as running directly counter to the developing conviction that the emotional truth of a performance will derive very precisely from immediate personal identification, a belief that tended to reinforce in turn the idea that performers should be sufficiently engaged in what they are doing for them to make no acknowledgement of their audience. In the longer span of history Garrick's involvement with the French was to augment an enquiry into the psychological origins of acting that has dominated discussions of acting ever since.[51]

At this distance Garrick's contribution to Diderot's polemic is hard to estimate and Diderot himself changed his mind about these matters. His own more fluid, 'protean' acting style can be seen as a reaction against the visibly artificial French neo-classical influence that dominated earlier in the eighteenth century as well as his personal repudiation of the formality he had witnessed at the Comédie-Française (McIntyre, 3, 6, 126–7, 384). It is at least clear that, confronted by the acclaimed French performers of the day, especially when they were female, Garrick responded as a representative spectator of his time rather than as a champion of the anti-emotionalist approach later advocated by Diderot. That is to say, he judged performances by their affective power, their impact upon an audience.

Garrick was far from unequivocal about French technique. Even the most celebrated actresses struck him as sometimes needlessly extreme in the ways in which they conveyed emotion. There was, for a start, far too much 'violence', meaning too much untoward emphasis: Dumesnil[52] 'has a face that expresses terror and Despair but she has many faults, too violent at times, very unequal & in ye whole does not seem to me so good an actress as Clarron' [*sic*] (McIntyre, 188). Although he undoubtedly preferred Clairon, Garrick still thought that even she 'might be less violent & tame in ye places of ye highest & finest passages' (McIntyre, 188). There was a pervasive air of artificiality, too. Dumesnil 'has certainly expression in her face, & some other requisites, but she is made up of trick; looks too much upon ye ground & makes use of little startings and twitchings which are visibly artificial & the mere mimickry of the free, simple noble workings of ye Passions' (McIntyre, 337). Even Clairon 'is so conscious and certain of what she can do, that she never (I believe) had the feelings of the instant come upon her unexpectedly' (McIntyre, 355).

'Violence' and extreme self-consciousness are parallel aspects of the same failing: both prohibit the intervention of 'those instantaneous feelings, that Life blood, that keen Sensibility, that burst at once from Genius, and like Electrical fire shoots thro' the Veins, Marrow, Bones and all, of every Spectator'. It is this openness to the unexpected moment, 'the warmth of the Scene' that, of course, constitutes a 'Genius', as opposed to a mere 'good Actor' (McIntyre, 355), and which can ultimately only be measured in terms of an effect of an unpremeditated bonding between actor and audience. All complaints about 'mechanical' acting are basically about closing off this possibility.

An eighteenth-century concern with 'Genius', and the demand for seeming spontaneity, can still be heard in the worries expressed during her 1817 visit to London that Mlle George might not be able to overcome the constraints of the declamatory tradition in which she worked. In the event, George was allowed 'a most commanding air, and an eye full of striking expression and vivacity'. It was reported that she had 'less of the sonorous enunciation, which is the characteristic of the French school, than most of the other artists of the Théâtre-Français' and that 'frequent bursts of applause, and what was perhaps more certain indications of feeling, throbs from many a heaving heart, and tears from many a beautiful eye bore testimony to the force of her delineations'.[53] 'An expressive countenance, a figure not a little inclined to embonpoint, and a commanding air' were said to have made 'a deep impression on the audience'.[54] Most importantly, 'the transitions in her countenance, as well as in her action and her tones, instead of being influenced by the supposed monotony of the French stage, are more quick, more extreme, and more unceasing, than any thing to which we are accustomed on our own'.[55]

Repeated tributes to George's 'commanding air' are reminders that this was still, in effect, the age of Siddons: the power of an actress is measured by her control over the emotional impact she makes through her physical and vocal attributes. For this to be achieved it was still necessary that she break away from traditional French declamation to something more 'natural'. William Hazlitt, who seems to have been present at the 1817 recitations, later remembered George as 'exceedingly beautiful, and exceedingly fat'. Much taken by the oddness of her physique ('the regularity of antique statue, with the roundness and softness of infancy') he was also struck by the contrary characteristics of her delivery: 'her voice had also great sweetness and compass. It either sunk into the softest accents of tremulous plaintiveness, or rose in thunder.' Even for Hazlitt, who was very appreciative of energising opposites, 'effect' was what counted; although, in the case of George, this could be 'surprising; and one was not always reconciled to it at first'.[56]

Like Mlle Mars, Mlle George's career was to be revived by appearances in the new Romantic drama, though when she came back to London in 1827 for a season in which she performed her most famous role in Voltaire's *Semiramis*, a critic typically described her as 'a very fat, elderly lady, of a somewhat dignified presence', and fell back on the old excuse that it was 'hard for an Englishman to judge at all impartially of French acting'. This, inevitably enough, was because 'the monotonous sing-song of the verse disgusts ears not familiarised with it; the enormous length of the speeches, which by bad actors are so drawled over, and by good actors are so hurried over, is perfectly painful to one trained to admire the sharp set-to of question and answer, the gladiatorial dialogue, and busy action of our national stage'.[57] George never returned.

It is an all-too-familiar fate for the female performer to be held responsible for any sign of her own ageing process in a way that is not expected of men. It follows that she has to be replaced by a younger, more sexually appealing, presence. This ungenerous story is always coloured by changing expectations of audiences and by ideas of the body, of sexual conduct and of self-control. Comparisons between actresses are to do with specifications of voice (sometimes almost of pure sound), of what we now call 'body language' (grace, pertinence, redundancy), of rhythm, control and release.

Until quite late in the nineteenth century the French stars provoked discussion of the artistic ability to convey spontaneity, real or contrived, rather than of their personal motivation. The primary requirement for the actress who crossed the Channel from Paris to London was that through sheer force of her presence she should not only overcome prejudice but actually reinvigorate the conventions within which she worked. The quality of the representation depended more upon the deployment of histrionic skills than its origin in the life of the performer – even in the case of Rachel, whose Jewishness was rapidly mythologised. Indeed, it was an essential element of the awe that spectators felt when confronted by Rachel that she should appear to be actually unaware of theatrical tradition and that this should be an index of her Romantic 'egoism':

She does not come on the stage to recite a lesson, but to speak as the spirit prompts her; she does not *act*, she *feels*: with her adoption of the Roman or Grecian dress, she adopts the Roman or Grecian character; she is no longer Rachel, but Camille or Hermione. This is the great secret of her influence over the masses; she stands before them, but is not of them; they have neither time nor inclination to criticise her dress, her manner, or her look; they are spell-bound by the reality with which she invests each of her personations. She has a power, unknown to other actresses, of riveting the attention of her audience, and this power consists in her entire ignorance of, and contempt for, the conventional traditions of the stage.

Rachel, in short, 'imitates no one, not even herself'; she 'keeps perpetually alive the curiosity and interest of the spectator by some new reading of a passage, some peculiar look or gesture, suggested by the inspiration of the moment, and forgotten by her as soon as that moment is past'.[58]

Even Rachel could disappoint. Seeing her in Corneille's *Horace*, Macready was not alone in finding that she 'has no tenderness, nor has she grandeur. She did not dilate with passion; the appeal to the gods was not that grand swell of passion that lifts her up above the things (too little for its communion) of earth to the only powers capable of sympathising with her.'[59] In which respect Rachel contrasted directly with her contemporaries, Mlle Mars and Madame Plessy, whose beauty, talent and preferred genre (comedy rather than tragedy) were rather different in their sexual implications. There was an erotics of performance at work which ensured that spectators expected to be cajoled and overwhelmed and, although the language of libidinous appreciation may be less overt than it is today, it was hardly ambiguous. And so, in the course of the nineteenth century we move from a theatre of mutual seduction towards a theatre of bourgeois charm and, following on from that, to one of 'nerves', of hysteria.

Developing links between late nineteenth-century diagnoses of hysteria, dramatic characterisation and changing acting styles have been much discussed recently, often in the context of Freudian theory.[60] But hysteria can also be understood as pathologising, or at least modifying, an established transaction between spectator and stage in which, by playing to her audience, the actress is rewarded by the most intense scrutiny of her bodily and auditory signs. The obsessive concern with diction and delivery, of which French actresses were always the beneficiaries, already betrayed some deep curiosity about what was really being heard.

Listening to an actress frequently allows an audience to hypothesise about – almost literally to 'see' – her inner being.[61] Early on in the century, the Romantic actress embodied that classic French theatrical type, *la grande coquette*, whose speech is both attractive and threatening because it simultaneously demonstrates and demolishes the myth that the female voice announces presence. Its deceptive invitation hints at access to female interiority but suspends the promise of certainty, of fulfilment and of fidelity: those ideal qualities whose illusory nature much Romantic drama characteristically (and perversely) exemplifies with the death of the heroine.

By the time of Aimée Desclée the inner condition is thought to suffuse the whole body with its symptomatic whimpers and shudders. The feminine is seen as problematised in a new way and the conventions of acting shift accordingly.

Comparisons between Bernhardt and Rachel were, of course, *de rigueur*, but comparisons between Bernhardt and Desclée were also much to the point and related more obviously to questions of gender expectations. Even in 1899 Clement Scott still couldn't decide between them: 'Often and often I have said to myself, which is the greatest actress I have ever seen? Is it the divine Sarah? Is it Aimée Desclée? The one dies young, the Keats of dramatic art. The other happily still lives, still working, still striving, still ambitious, never resting in endeavour, the Alfred Tennyson of the French stage' (Scott, 2, 441). Frederick Leighton, whose playgoing went back many years, told Joe Comyns Carr that the effect produced by Rachel left Sarah Bernhardt's art 'almost in the region of the commonplace'.[62] He confessed to having fallen prey to similar foreshortening nostalgia on another occasion: 'I remember thinking, when I first saw Sarah Bernhardt in *Froufrou*, that her portraiture fell far short of that of Desclée, the original creator of the role. And so, in fact, it did. The countless subtleties, by means of which the earlier performer had established the identity of the frivolous heroine of one of the most masterly of modern French plays, were all lacking in the work of her successor.' But Leighton then pulled himself up by acknowledging that 'in the great scene in the third act, where the tensity of the situation sounds a deeper note of drama, I felt disposed to forget that any other Froufrou had ever existed'. In the end Bernhardt had won him over.

These comparisons not only embraced (and to some extent concealed) questions of gender, they kept the repertoire going. After all, while individuals prosper or decline, plays are merely put on hold, sometimes for many years. It has been said, and quite accurately, that 'the late nineteenth century saw the emergence of a relatively new phenomenon, acting styles named for playwrights instead of actors and directors, as critics began to speak, for example of "Ibsen actors", even in productions not directed by Ibsen'.[63] Nevertheless, those new acting styles, while based on authorship, developed out of old ways which survived along with plays that belonged together not so much by virtue of their having been written by the same person as by the fact that they respected the same set of conventions. English audiences, who were familiar with this repertoire in all its guises, noted, approvingly or otherwise, the various modifications that it underwent. Bernhardt begins as either the new Rachel or the new Desclée; needing to establish herself through these cultural alignments, she is simultaneously innovatory and a repository of the past: her individual strength incorporating and transforming a specifically female inheritance, of which the 'hysteric' as originally represented by Desclée was one, but only one, important element.

So, for instance, Desclée's most famous vehicle, *Froufrou*, was revived continually in both English and French long after her death. Ellen Terry played in an adaptation in Glasgow in 1879; the Polish actress, Modjeska, made it part of her season at the Princess's in 1881; Jane Hading starred in a French production in London in 1885 and Janet Achurch, the Ibsenite's favourite, collaborated with her husband Charles Carrington for an English adaptation in 1886. There were other English productions at the Globe in 1888, at the St James in 1870, 1872 and 1890. In the summer of 1897 Bernhardt and Réjane played in separate London productions simultaneously; Bernhardt went on bringing the play to London until 1903.

For all its longevity, *Froufrou* was a model of those ultimately maudlin dramas that would be subversively reworked not only by Henrik Ibsen but by Oscar Wilde, both of whom took the figure of the repressed woman of spirit and gave her a sympathetic hearing. Interestingly, some thought in retrospect that Desclée, had she survived, would have made the perfect Nora Helmer.[64] In 1894 Wilde began work on a scenario in which a husband and wife would, in the course of conversation, have actually discussed Meilhac's famous warhorse. Wilde's play, in contrast, was to have 'no morbid self-sacrifice. No renunciation. A sheer flame of love between a man and a woman';[65] eventually this idea was written up by Frank Harris as *Mr and Mrs Daventry* and staged in 1900.

It has been said of the hysterics studied by Charcot, with their unladylike expressions of sexuality, that 'their excess of femininity tilted them paradoxically into male modes of behaviour'.[66] Bernhardt's 'male' behaviour, both on and off the stage, born perhaps of her own observation of hysteria, introduced a crucial element of reflexiveness, so that her representations appealed to audiences of many kinds who could appreciate her skills in controlled self-presentation. Here was sexual, even gender, indeterminacy on a global scale. By the turn of the century the female voice had been amplified by reproduction as well as strengthened through the demands put upon it by innovative playwrights such as Ibsen, Strindberg and Wedekind.[67] These processes were accompanied by the slowly waning power of the plays that the 'new drama' set out to replace.

Froufrou, *La Dame aux camélias*, *La Parisienne* and the rest were by no means immediately or entirely forgotten, either by practitioners or by spectators. Inevitably though, the more she sought to express her legitimacy by

A DRIAN ETCHING OF MLLE. CÉCILE SOREL, AS CÉLIMÈNE—NOW AT THE NEW OXFORD.

Figure 1. Drian, 'Mlle Cécile Sorel as Célimène' (*The Sketch*, 28 May 1924)

dressing herself up with supreme elegance, outstripping the extravagances of the past, the more powerfully the Romantic actress alluded to a history under threat. The qualified responses to Cécile Sorel in the 1920s are salutary. 'Mlle Sorel's gowns are very gorgeous, but they do not harmonise with the diction and the sentiments of a play now aged threescore years and ten' wrote the *Times* in 1924 about *La Dame aux camélias*.[68] As Célimène, Sorel's monumental costume displaced attention from both the moral conundrum of Molière's play and any lingering spontaneity in her performance: 'Not every actress could "carry off" that amazing costume, so rich and so fantastic, with its outrageous *décolletage*, its enormous panniers, its headdress of tall plumes: it never embarrasses Mlle Sorel, who, indeed, we are inclined to suspect, invented it . . . You are in the presence of the most elaborately artificial among women.'[69] Sorel, with inherited roles from both Bernhardt and Réjane, might easily have become, for English audiences, the very last of a great line, magnificently embalmed in her ballgown. It is all the more remarkable then that thanks to Edwige Feuillère, who rediscovered the living force of erotic transgression in a drama of Catholic conversion, the cult of the French Romantic actress, with her distinctive repertoire of sexual archetypes, should have been revived in the years immediately following the Second World War.

THE CAST

No performance ever takes place in a vacuum but, to adopt a term employed by Richard Schechner, is always 'nested' in circumstance.[70] When the French actresses came to London the circumstantial layers were not only economic and highly gendered, they were political (the state of diplomacy or outright war between two nations) and historical (the memories of other plays, other people, other parts). Yet these outer conditions of spectatorship never smothered the vivacity of the live performance. It is, after all, a rule of theatre that it should expose the very terms that allow it to exist. The viewing process went into reverse, the radiance of the performer encouraging self-consciousness in the onlooker. For about 150 years, by registering the Otherness of French actresses, the English made lasting discoveries about theatre, politics, sex.

Of course, there were, over the decades, many other French actresses who made their mark in London besides the eight about whom I have chosen to write: Rose Chéri, a contemporary of Desclée; Jane Hading, who succeeded her as a notable Froufrou; the impressively versatile Madame Judith; the flamboyant Cécile Sorel, who appeared in London only twice; Marie Bell, an important Phèdre, if orthodox in comparison with Feuillère. All were powerful performers but they lacked the primacy of my main characters, those French visitors whose English careers, when laid end to end, form a unique historical narrative.[71]

Each one had a moment, or moments, when she outshone all others by reflecting the age. The career of Mlle Mars, favourite of Napoleon and later of Victor Hugo, marks a shift through revolutionary premonition (Beaumarchais) to imperial *gloire* to Hugolian Romantic adventure; Rachel embodies the still turbulent threat of insurrection; Mlle Plessy preserves Mars's comedy but only through a mode of *embourgeoisement*; Déjazet, Réjane, Desclée, and even Bernhardt, display the vulgarity and glamour of the Second Empire with a vitality equal to anything on the London stage; finally Edwige Feuillère brings with her an intellectual sophistication lacking in post-war England.

I have accordingly suited my method to the moment. The first essay traces the volatile reputation created among her English spectators by the Romantic actress, Mlle Mars, who specialised in the role of the theatrical *coquette*. It concentrates upon the admiration for Mars expressed by William Hazlitt, drawing comparisons with his contemporary and critical rival, the great French novelist Stendhal. Because their interest is clearly sexual I draw upon Freud himself and upon post-Freudian theory to help explain the potency of the seductive, flirtatious type that Mars established.

The second and third essays take up the story with studies of Rachel Félix, who brought Romantic passion to the neo-classical repertoire and, in contrast, of a notable exponent of French comedy directly in the tradition of Mars: Madame Plessy, whose calculated charms represented for Charles Dickens the best and the worst of French acting and who eventually came, for Henry James, to symbolise the passing of time itself. If Plessy in comedy was an inviting presence, Rachel in tragedy was austere, alienating, implacable, more Medusa than Circe. Again it took the novelists – Disraeli, Charlotte Brontë and George Eliot – to do her justice.

The present is frequently difficult to represent on stage except through self-consciously contemporary reconstructions of past events, real or imaginary. Later chapters explore the role of theatrical eroticism in the representation of varying historical situations. Virginie Déjazet specialised in *rôles travestis* and in her dandyish poses English audiences recognised the lasting appeal of the *ancien régime*, a theatricalised version of French history that coupled Romantic ambivalence towards the past with the impudent flaunting of sexual ambiguity. Dickens compared one of Déjazet's shows to 'a little picture by Watteau – animated and talking'.[72] I consider explanations for that historical nostalgia along with theories of cross-dressing.

Aimée Desclée, a younger contender who died prematurely, renewed the image of the heroine as victim at the same time as she pioneered intense physical realism and the productions in which she starred signal important developments in *mise-en-scène*. Her short but vivid career (contemporaneous with the Paris Commune, in which notions of gender sustained violent assaults), provides the missing link between Romantic acting and the ultra-modern 'hysterical' style of Sarah Bernhardt. Because theatrical representations of the Commune had to get past the Paris censor and there were no plays on the topic to bring to London, the fragile Desclée conveyed to the English an even greater sense of national crisis. This she did in *Froufrou* and through her interpretations of the bourgeois adulteresses created by that tireless misogynist Dumas *fils*.

A contemporary of Sarah Bernhardt, Gabrielle Réjane, was in England almost equally admired, exerting her own powerful attraction upon 'decadents' such as Aubrey Beardsley and Arthur Symons. This was largely through her ability to match an idea of popular resilience dating from Napoleonic times with a suggestive sexual wit. It was Réjane who first created on stage the modern working-class heroine of the Goncourts' *Germinie Lacerteux*, but her most celebrated and long-lived role was that of Madame Sans-Gêne, the washerwoman in Sardou's comic melodrama of Napoleonic times. With her witty *canaillerie* Réjane contributed to a cult of Paris and its citizens that was felt throughout the English *fin de siècle*.

Inevitably it is Sarah Bernhardt, about whom there are more books than any other actress, who comes next. The reputation, in England alone, was so laden with incident and so enduring that it becomes essential to close in on just one aspect of her historical significance. An extended treatment of her relationship with Oscar Wilde, whom she first met in 1879, highlights some legendary revivals of Victor Hugo and shows how a modern author and a modern actress sought to recapture the Romantic flame for their own ends. Both exploited the new possibilities of publicity and travel – Wilde toured America at much the same time as Bernhardt and caused a not dissimilar sensation – although, since Wilde's professional career in the theatre was effectively truncated in 1895, he didn't have to endure (or enjoy), as Bernhardt did, a middle age lived out in the public eye.

In the early twentieth century new forms of entertainment such as musical comedy and the cinema threatened to overshadow the traditional repertoire, but the reign of the French Romantic actress was not yet over. Some, like Cécile Sorel, turned to film and even to the variety stage. My final portrait is of Edwige Feuillère, a star of the 1950s who, for the critic of the *Sunday Times*, Harold Hobson, was simply 'the greatest actress in the world'. For historical and cultural reasons many other English admirers – the actress Vivien Leigh prominent among them – thought of Feuillère as the Romantic spirit incarnate. Radiating an equinoctial poise she marked the brilliant culmination of a dying line.

CHAPTER I

Mademoiselle Mars, the English and romantic love

FLIRTATION

When Mlle George made her second and last London appearance in 1827 even those spectators who were respectful of her style found that they could justify her seemingly interminable delivery only by acknowledging a cultural difference whereby, for instance, in contrast with the tendency of an English actor to 'burst like a thunderclap, and relapse almost immediately into his former quiet', the French actor, who is 'all self-satisfaction and activity (we had almost said fidget), sees no reason for controlling a single sensation, and is consequently in perpetual motion in obedience to every passing thought or accidental excitement'.[1]

Although this English need to explain French tragic acting within an indisputably alien context has an extremely long history it makes an obvious contemporary comparison with the unqualified enthusiasm that greeted Harriet Smithson when she visited Paris alongside Charles Kemble in the same year. Smithson's spasmodic portrayals of distracted and abused women (Ophelia, Desdemona) would galvanise Delacroix and Berlioz into creativity, and they would consolidate the Romantic convictions, held on both sides of the Channel, that it was the tragic drama of the English Renaissance, rather than its French neo-classical equivalent, that showed the way forward. It would take a very remarkable performer indeed to convince the English that their prejudices were misguided or, for that matter, to persuade the young French Romantics that they might have underestimated their own tradition. That would be the achievement of Rachel Félix in the 1840s.

In the interim, it was a *doyenne* of comedy, Mlle Mars, a visitor to London in 1828 and 1832, who stood the best chance of compensating for Smithson. Tourists in Paris, William Charles Macready and Walter Scott among them, had long been aware of her reputation and had sometimes made special efforts to see her perform. Mars was said to be the most English of continental actresses and, although she had established herself

Figure 2. Mlle Mars as Elmire in *Tartuffe c.* 1815

in classic roles, she reacted to Smithson by cultivating her friendship and, it was said, by studying her methods. Even Mars would, in English eyes, often fall short of greatness, a disappointment that owed something to her national repertoire but quite as much to changes in audience expectation that were to outlast her career, making her look in retrospect like the theatrical embodiment of a lost way of life.

Mars specialised in social gaiety and erotic *nuance*. Born Anne-Françoise-Hippolyte Boutet in 1779, she came from a theatrical family and started her theatrical career young, playing *ingénues*. Encouraged by the established Mademoiselle Contat, she joined the Comédie-Française in 1799 and changed her name. In the 1800s she began varying her roles by graduating from the page Chérubin, played *en travesti*, to the *soubrette* Suzanne in *Le Mariage de Figaro* (1810) and by introducing into her repertoire mature, sophisticated characters such as Silvia in Marivaux's *Le Jeu de l'amour et du hasard* (1808) and Araminte in his *Les Fausses Confidences* (1809), together with major roles in Molière: Elmire in *Tartuffe* (1812) and the notorious *grande coquette*, Célimène, in *Le Misanthrope* (1812). A favourite of Napoleon, Mars managed, by judicious politics, to survive the Emperor's demise and to become a favourite of Louis-Philippe. To leading roles in comedy she then added a variety of heroines as conceived by contemporary writers, including, most famously, in 1822 the part of a blind woman in Scribe's *Valérie*. Eventually she would help pioneer the new Romantic drama of Dumas *père* and Victor Hugo.[2]

By the time that Mars came to play a selection of those roles in the course of the two London seasons the French career was already well established, illustrious even. Nevertheless, some English critics, a significant number in fact, including for instance this anonymous writer in the *New Monthly Magazine* in 1828, felt an overall disappointment with almost everything she did:

The performances, respecting which curiosity has been strongly excited, are quite perfect, but no more. They are complete in themselves, unexceptionable, and faultless; but they are not of so high an order as we had been led to imagine them. They do not realise the idea which we have cherished of the finest comedy, although they are more sustained and consistent than the efforts of any actress within our memory. They want entirely the charm of motion, the triumphant air, the grace beyond the reach of art, which we attribute to the Millamants of our own stage in the days of Cibber. Mars, for the most part, stands quite still, with her hands clasped before her, and exhibits no more vivacity than is consistent with perfect repose. It is true, that her countenance, always intelligent, is occasionally eloquent; that the action of her hands, when she raises them, is beautiful;

and that her speaking is the most delightful that can be imagined – sweet in tone, and combining distinctness with continuity in a degree we never recognised in any other performer, except Mrs. Jordan, who was a creature of a far nobler class.[3]

Not only is Mars compared unfavourably with certain English actresses, her style, while admittedly appropriate to French comedy, looks pale and over-delicate when set against the requirements of the English repertoire from Shakespeare to Congreve. Her most distinctive talent is her ability to apply her perfect diction to what remained an imperfect medium: 'the French language so altered that one could almost believe it capable of being wreathed into genuine verse!' Consequently, 'she charmed, if she did not electrify the house', leaving behind 'a more pleasing impression of French manners and tastes than has ever yet been received by the theatrical public of England'.

'Manners and tastes', though undoubtedly of interest, are hardly the stuff of theatrical legend. Mars achieved her peak in only one play from her London repertoire, on the face of it the least likely. In Scribe's *Valérie* she played a beautiful young woman, blind since a girl, who is revisited by a childhood sweetheart, unrecognised at first, who has, it turns out, spent his life seeking, and ultimately discovering, a cure for her condition. It may seem extraordinary that in this short and sentimental drama, entirely forgotten by theatrical history, Mars should have won near unanimous approval. Yet, for one member of the audience in 1828, the climax of the play, when Valérie regained her sight, was nothing less than 'the greatest triumph the dramatic art ever achieved'. At the close Valérie returned to the stage 'exclaiming in a voice that electrified the house, – "Laissez-moi, laissez-moi; je vois! Je vois!" . . . "Oui, c'est la le jour – c'est la lumière – c'est la vie! Oh mon Dieu – je te rends grace – je sors de ma prison – J'EXISTE!"' ['Let me be, let me be; I can see! I can see! . . . Yes, the day is there – light – life. Oh merciful God – I thank you – I'm out of my prison. I'M ALIVE.'] 'Admirable woman!' exclaims this writer 'such as heaven sends us once a century to show what human creatures can be and do'.[4] That sounds madly extravagant, yet the same spectator claimed to see signs of an equal involvement all around him as 'each one turned to his neighbour to read in his face the rapture that possessed himself; and not a few seasoned hearts were surprised by an emotion of which they had ceased to dream themselves susceptible'. 'Rarest touches of pathos' brought 'innocent and ecstatic delight' and 'touches equally effective and equally exquisite'.

On her second visit to London, in 1832, Mars's Valérie was greeted with applause even on her entrance and when, at the conclusion, she was led forward by the manager it was rapturous; a response all the more remarkable given the size of the theatre and the relative quietness of her acting style.[5] But Mars attracted an unusually literate audience, many of whom were said to have enough French to grasp her meaning, so that the perfection of her delivery was fully appreciated, at least as far as the fairly limited demands of *Valérie* were concerned. In any case, for the role of a blind person, stillness and audibility were natural advantages and compared very positively with those bad English habits, those actresses who would have 'given screams, and hysteric sobs, and hands crossed on bosom, and staring eye-balls'.[6]

According to another witness, *Valérie* succeeded because it was:

> a pretty dramatic composition perfectly Parisian, and of which we have no counterpart on our English stage. Almost all our comedies are either satirical or farcical. This is neither; it is sentimental – not melodramatically, but pleasantly, and with but a slight and piquant touch of the pathetic. It is a chapter out of the endless Book of Love, written lightly, briefly, delicately, and feelingly.[7]

The distinctiveness of the performance is further brought out by comparison with the response Mars gained in more animated parts. She did have one other relative success ('the most perfect French performance we have perhaps witnessed in this country', according to one spectator[8]): Suzanne in *Le Mariage de Figaro*, in which she delighted her audience 'by her ease, her grace, her naïveté, the exquisite polish of her utterance and the womanly tones of her voice'. At the moment when Chérubin avoids being caught with his mistress by leaping from a window, Mars as Suzanne struck a pose which 'was the very perfection of ease and verisimilitude of nature: her abrupt shuddering scream upon his taking the leap, and when she sees him safely landed and off, her triumphant wave of the arm, completely delighted us', making her attitude look 'as fine as a study by Sir Thomas Lawrence'.[9] In this instance Mars's very physical indication of Suzanne's emotional involvement enlivened what was otherwise 'coquetry so chaste, occasionally so delicious . . . never before seen on this side of the Channel'.

'Coquetry so chaste' may look like a contradictory formula yet, as this unusually perceptive critique recognised, when it was accompanied with glimpses of underlying passion, the combination provided the key to an important element in Mars's theatrical style. The same quality of sexual *nuance* is perhaps most closely associated with the plays of Marivaux, though these never attracted much enthusiasm among the English. Despite many English adaptations stretching back to the seventeenth century, even Molière was controversial, and had been so for some time. When, for instance, the popular novelist and adventurous socialite, Lady Morgan, first visited post-Napoleonic Paris in 1817 and headed for the Théâtre-Français, she found little compensation in Molière's comedies for the undoubted pomposity of Racine. Despite the presence of Mars as Elmire, *Tartuffe* 'almost put me to sleep'.[10] In the 1820s it was to become a common English complaint that the part offered the actress 'no great opportunity for the display of her powers, beyond the exhibition of graceful manners'.[11] Lady Morgan already shared in this feeling. For the scene in which Elmire attempts to prove the treacheries of Tartuffe by having her husband hide under a table while the hypocrite attempts to seduce her, Lady Morgan had high hopes. These were not satisfied:

I expected much; even after I had been disappointed through four successive acts. But, affecting as it is in perusal, it was in action, false, cold and ineffective. Mademoiselle Mars, as Elmire, received the declaration of Tartuffe, and reached the most interesting and piquant point of the denouement, with the most freezing inanition. Her beautiful eyes, generally so rapid and so shifting in their brilliant glances, were here fixed and at rest and when she occasionally coughed, or raised up the cloth of the table, under which Orgon lies concealed, it seemed as if she took her cue from the prompter, and performed this little by-play entirely by his dictation.[12]

It may be that Lady Morgan simply missed the point here, failing to appreciate the frozen tension that the actress brought to Elmire's dilemma. Certainly, when Mars played the same scene in London, a few critics were rather more impressed. It was 'nature in all its details: when she twitches the cloth to signify to her husband that she requires his assistance, her agitation, sometimes subdued, and sometimes irrepressible – the hurried emotion of her words – her agony almost breaking out into sobs, were so many evidences of the intensity of her study of the human heart'.[13]

Eventually, having irritated her French friends with her continual complaints that French acting was entirely 'unnatural', even Lady Morgan did come to learn that 'by comparing the representation with the real life and manners of French society, that nature adopts diversified modes of expression for the same feelings, in different countries; and that what would be true to nature, on an English stage, as applied to genteel comedy, would be very false to it, on a French one'. Finally, she would concede that 'the error of judgement, however lies principally in a confusion of terms, where nature is substituted for life; for genuine comedy takes the relations of civilised and modern society for its subject: and the actor embodies them in the manners and forms of the country, for which they are written, and to which he represents'.[14] In other words, Lady Morgan eventually absorbed the lesson that visions of the natural are invariably partisan. Indeed, the fascination of Elmire, such as it was, remained culturally determined and to do with the character's insistence, regarded as typically French, on the absolute priority of courtesy, even at a time of considerable moral risk.

Neither exquisite conduct nor a sense of danger were displayed by Mars's other great role in Molière, Célimène, the *grande coquette* of *Le Misanthrope*, and her rendering of this part won even less enthusiasm. In fact, English dislike of Célimène was validated by strong precedents from abroad, in particular by Augustus William Schlegel in his celebrated *Course of Lectures on Dramatic Art and Literature*, an influence on ideas of the drama at least since the first English translation in 1814. Although Schlegel's main concern had been with tragedy, he had also made some passing observations about French comedy and had taken a firm line on Célimène. How is it possible for Alceste 'to be enamoured of a coquette, who has nothing amiable in her character, and who entertains us merely by her scandal?', Schlegel had asked.

We might well say of this Célimène, without exaggeration, that there is not one good point in her whole composition. In a character like that of Alceste, love is not a fleeting sensual impulse, but a serious feeling arising from a want of a sincere mental union. His dislike of flattering falsehood and malicious scandal, which always characterises the conversation of Célimène, breaks forth so incessantly, that, we feel, the first moment he heard her open her lips ought to have driven him for ever from her society.[15]

Reviewing Mars in the role in 1832 the London *Times* effectively concurred, noting that *Le Misanthrope* had never been popular: 'there is scarcely a personage in the whole play who is not perfectly contemptible, and hardly an incident that varies the excessive dullness of the representation'. Nevertheless, 'all that could be done for the character of Célimène was performed by Mademoiselle Mars. Her declamation, which is extremely skilful and perfect, gave full effect to the fine verses with which the part abounds.'[16] 'Of the parts in which we have now seen her, the greatest is the least favourable', wrote *The Spectator* in the same year. Yet

Célimène is a witty, clever, cunning coquette; thoroughly artificial, and covering any feelings she may have under a veil of perfect *nonchalance*. Even when she is unmasked, and her disabused lover pronounces the decisive 'Allez – je vous refuse!' her hidden emotions manifest themselves only by a small, indescribable change of countenance, the slight toss of the hand and movement of head which accompany her exit. Volumes were uttered by Mademoiselle Mars in these almost imperceptible indications of feeling; but they were the only traits of nature which she could possibly exhibit during the whole piece.[17]

Even when Mars as Célimène was at her most entrancing, her most verbally inventive, she remained relatively static. In that respect the sheer conventionality of what she did by way of interpreting Molière and Marivaux, and their now dated version of coquetry, meant that she would fare badly in any comparison not only with younger performers working in a different theatrical genre, but with her own playing of any of those other roles in which she was asked to represent not complexity and depth so much as emotional wholeness – body and voice unthreateningly united – a role such as Scribe's quintessential Valérie. The contrast between the two aspects of Mars becomes apparent: nothing could be further from the repellent Célimène than the inspirational Valérie. One character made audiences uneasy, the other made them weep.

Le Misanthrope is a drama of verbal dexterity, its eroticism cerebral and sometimes cruel. Though the *Spectator* critic, for one, was at least prepared to allow that Mars's acting had an undeniable element of spontaneity that could, on occasion, transform her old-fashioned material ('The agreeable badinage, the naïve remark of innocence or coquetry, the sly innuendo, and sallies of a humour sometimes playful, sometimes malign, are the flowers of a wit that enlivened perchance the days of Louis Quatorze'[18]), Célimène remained problematic, not least because she was a reminder that erotic conventions are historically relative.[19] And yet the actress 'issues her borrowed wealth as from the mint of native wit; and the intelligence of her face seems even to announce the moment of conception'. As a consequence, 'the naïve remark of innocence or coquetry' is matched paradoxically by 'the intelligence of her face', giving a curiously ambiguous impression not always easy to imagine at this historical distance.

Yet innocence, coquetry and intelligence can, in practice, coexist, and sometimes very powerfully, as the contemporary psychoanalytic writer, Adam Phillips, has recognised in his recent writings on the dynamics of flirtation. For Phillips, flirtation is a form of experimentation, of exercising curiosity and irreverence. 'Disfiguring the difference between innocence and experience, intent and opportunity, flirtation does not make a virtue of instability, but a pleasure', he writes. 'It eroticises the contingency of your lives by turning doubt – or ambiguity – into suspense. It prevents waiting from becoming a useless passion'. The reason for this is entirely Oedipal since flirting begins very early on when the incest taboo provokes teasing attempts to intervene in the relationship between parent and child. 'Flirtation', says Phillips, 'is the game of taking chances, of plotting illicit possibilities'.[20]

It follows that, for Phillips, flirting is a form of self-narration that denies closure since 'in flirtation you never know whether the beginning of the story – the story of the relationship – will be the end; flirtation, that is to say, exploits the idea of surprise. From a sadistic point of view it is as though the known and wished-for end is being refused, deferred or even denied.'[21] Which is precisely the case with the final scene of *Le Misanthrope*, which ends with Alceste and Célimène further apart than ever, something comedy should not really tolerate, while Alceste's self-imposed banishment may or may not be permanent. Célimène's unapologetic commitment to flirtation avoids tragic disappointment, keeps the narrative going, by way of a formal sophistication that the nineteenth century, publicly and increasingly committed to the ideal of permanence in love, found hard to admit.[22]

Mars's success in *Valérie* (together with the relative lack of interest in plays by Molière, let alone Marivaux), is evidence therefore not simply of changing tastes in theatrical genres but of a more basic, if still unresolved, shift in the social structures to which those genres were supposed to relate. Seventeenth- and eighteenth-century French comedy, with its carnival array of *soubrettes*, of *jeunes premières* and, in particular, of *coquettes*, was increasingly upstaged by the extreme emotion and the pathetic interplay of victim and redeemer that characterised both sentimental tradition and Romantic innovation. Put that another way: in the theatre the endless pleasure of deferral that flirtation allowed was frequently brought to a queasy halt by social suspicion and the implacable intervention of sacrifice and devotion.

Resistance to flirtation accompanies the elevation of an idealised view of love whereby the development of relationships advances smoothly through what orthodox psychoanalysis might see as the untroubled substitution of lover for parent. Not surprisingly (though not in *Valérie*, which opens with grief and ends with joy) the process is frequently flawed – as many writers of the Romantic age would invariably discover for themselves. For all her charms Mars came, from very early on, to stand for an unstable mixture of devotion and coquetry, for both the permanence of love and the pleasurable delay of love.

CONSUMMATION

For some English members of her audience Frenchness was a disadvantage that she could never overcome. The reliance upon crude nationalism in newspaper and journal, the competitive boasting and sneering use of stereotype are tedious to encounter even now, and popular rhetoric undoubtedly tended to inhibit critical response at the time. But then again, mediocre writing about the theatre usually is constricted by prejudice and presupposition, whereas good criticism is open to surprise, appreciation of the unexpected making it seem spontaneous, like good acting. The very finest critics, the ones we still read and remember, go even further and convey their own unpredictable responses to theatre through the physical act of writing itself. Which is why their reviews can vary in pace, can be rapid, excited, impatient, awe-struck and breathless: by academic standards, wildly over the top. At such times, the dramatic moment is not described so much as relived, exposing the susceptibilities of the spectator along with the uniqueness of the performance. Mars had the mixed benefit of two such critics and they vied with one another in their attempts to do her justice. One was French, Marie-Henri Beyle, better known as the novelist Stendhal, the other was English, William Hazlitt.

When Stendhal, then in his twenties, saw Mlle Mars for the first few times in 1804 and 1805 it was like a series of *coups de foudre*: 'an angel',[23] he breathed, 'that divine actress' (138), 'ever more perfect' (162). Of her performance in one insignificant play, he wrote, 'she evokes the idea of love at its most sublime' (188–9). In another, *Folies Amoureuses* by Regnard, she reminded him of his lusty youth in Italy; she was 'one of the liveliest pleasures that love can bestow' (204). In 1810, when she played Suzanne in *Le Mariage de Figaro*, Stendhal confessed that he was 'charmed to the point of falling in love'. 'Mlle Mars', he told his journal, 'has awakened the heart that I thought was dead' (551). At another time, having just experienced her in Marivaux's *Les Fausses Confidences*, he noted how 'my heart was full; a little later, I dissolved into tears' (557). In 1817, seeing her at the Français, he would record that she was, 'still a divine object, who has touched me in the tenderest part of my soul'[24] Admiration for Mars would feed into the treatise *Racine et Shakespeare* (1823), with its accompanying argument that a certain lightness in delivery, typified by her style, was essential if the theatre were to appeal to a modern audience.[25] The initial success of *Valérie* Stendhal would attribute largely to the presence of his favourite actress.[26]

A touchstone not just for other actresses but for all other women, Mars made Stendhal feel emotionally equipped for life. Indeed, his instantaneous reaction to Mars is consistent with his celebrated definition of love in the half-philosophical, half-autobiographical treatise, *De l'amour*, a process of 'crystallisation' that transforms the whole of the surrounding world into a vista of shining beauty.[27] And Mars does in fact have a tiny cameo role in *De l'amour* when her delivery of a line from Marivaux's *Les Fausses Confidences* 'Hé bien! Oui, je vous aime!' is cited as creating the kind of sublime moment that lovers subsist upon, even if it cannot be maintained for very long.[28]

For Stendhal, to experience Mars in the theatre was to be reborn, much as it was for William Hazlitt, though for a shorter time. Not only did the two men know and esteem one another (meeting in Paris in 1824),[29] they were aware of what they had in common, which included reverence for the power of romantic love and respect for the skills of performing artists, among whom Mars was supreme. But if Stendhal was simply smitten by Mars, Hazlitt was invariably moved, and, characteristically, much more prepared to admit that theatrical experience is rarely all at one level, that concentration waxes and wanes, that individual performances move in and out of focus. Consequently he tries to capture the uniqueness of the moment through comparison, apparent digression and, if necessary, self-contradiction, an unbounded mixture of praise, doubt, censure. Tom Paulin captures these moves quite brilliantly when he writes of Hazlitt's 'conversational' mode of criticism that it

allows the provisional, contradictory nature of critical judgement to fissure in front of our eyes, like the sudden star-pattern that happens when a stone hits a pane of glass. Criticism can leap like a spark between opposite poles, it can be on both sides of the street at the same time, it can dance contradictions. Dramatic and intense, it must aim never to be fixed or finished.[30]

When he first experienced Mars in Paris in 1824, though, Hazlitt was initially so bowled over that he began by writing about her as if she were pure perfection and his language – including his performative use of syntax, which is cumulative yet precise – seems to suggest as much. Not only did Mars redeem English suspicions of French acting, said Hazlitt with some irony, she matched English intellectual understanding of dramatic texts:

What Englishman does not read Molière with pleasure? Is it not a treat then to see him well acted? There is nothing to recall our national antipathies, and we are glad to part with such unpleasant guests.[31]

The play in question was, somewhat surprisingly, *Le Misanthrope*. As Célimène Mars immediately matched all Hazlitt's expectations, and a single virtuoso sentence shows just how that felt at the time. Each dash is like an intake of breath as the writer–spectator struggles to keep up with his own appreciation of every little particular:

Her few first simple sentences – her '*Mon Ami*' at her lover's first ridiculous suggestion, the mingled surprise, displeasure and tenderness in the tone – her little peering eyes, full of languor and archness of meaning – the peaked nose and thin compressed lips, opening into an intelligent, cordial smile – her self-possession – her slightest gesture – the ease and rapidity of her utterance, every word of which is perfectly distinct – the playful, wondering, good-nature with which she humours the Misanthrope's eccentricities throughout, and the finer tone of sense and feeling in which she rejects his final proposal, must stamp her a favourite with the English as well as with the French audiences. (148)

Away from home in France, Hazlitt speaks for England, but in a highly individual way:

She is all life and spirit. Would we be thought entirely without them? She has a thorough understanding and relish of her author's text. So, we think, have we. She has character, expression, decision – they are the very things we pique ourselves upon. Ease, grace, propriety – we aspire to them, if we have them not. She is free from the *simagrées*, the unmeaning, petulance and petty affectation that we approach the French with, and has none of the awkwardness, insipidity, or vulgarity that we are so ready to quarrel with at home. (148)

'It would be strange if the English did not admire her as much as they profess to do', Hazlitt concluded (148). This may not have been strictly true, but did provide a basis of seeming emotional objectivity from which to explore cultural difference. And here the French, after many concessions, invariably come off the worse from a quiver full of barbed compliments. The glory of the French theatre belongs to the past, the achievement of the present merely its recreation. Seated in the Théâtre-Français, watching Mars, Hazlitt forgets that he is in a theatre and imagines himself transported back to the age of Louis XIV:

Blest period! – the triumph of folly and of France, when, instead of poring over systems of philosophy, the world lived in a round of impertinence – when to talk nonsense was wit, to listen to it politeness – when men thought of nothing but themselves, and turned their heads with dress instead of the affairs of Europe – when the smile of greatness was felicity, the smile of beauty Elysium – and when men drank the brimming nectar of self-applause, instead of waiting for the opinion of the *reading public*! Who would not fling himself back to this period of idle enchantment? But, as we cannot, the best substitute for it is to see a comedy of Molière's acted at the Théâtre-Français. The thing is there imitated to the life. (150)

Even so, the retrospection effect only really works properly with French comedy since 'heroes in comedy, pedants in tragedy, they are greatest on small occasions' (150). Qualifications creep in. The concentration of a French audience may be absolute but this makes them 'like flies caught in treacle. Their wings are clogged, and it is all over with their friskings and vagaries. Their bodies and their minds *set* at once' (152).

Astonishingly, within a matter of months the balance of Hazlitt's opinion had shifted fundamentally: 'I liked Mademoiselle Mars exceeding well, till I saw Madame Pasta whom I liked so much better',[32] he announces at the start of an essay 'Madame Pasta and Mademoiselle Mars' in the *New Monthly Magazine* of January 1825, in which he compares the French actress, almost entirely to her disadvantage, with the celebrated Italian opera singer.[33] When Mars speaks, 'She extends first one hand and then the other, in a way that you can foresee every time she does so, or in which a machine might be elaborately constructed to develop different successive movements'. 'Habit' takes over so that it's like watching a 'consummate rehearsal' for a performance that never takes place. When Mars smiles, 'a slight and evanescent expression of pleasure passes across the surface of her face; twinkles in her eyelids, dimples her chin, compresses her lips, and plays on each feature'. In contrast, when Pasta smiles, 'a beam of joy seems to have struck upon her heart, and to irradiate her countenance. Her whole face is bathed and melted in expression, instead of glancing from particular points.' And when Pasta speaks, 'it is in music' (325).

The fact that one performer deals in speech, the other in song, is ultimately of less importance than their widely differing approaches to the art of acting. Pasta: 'does not act the character – she is it, looks it, breathes it'. Mars, in contrast, exploits a tradition in which wit, digression, extravagance and love of detail are all prized. Pasta practises an art of reaction, of concentration upon the situation in hand, whereas Mars appears to be acting marginalia: reciting her own notes rather than Molière's lines. No longer inward with the text her performance is now imposed upon it. This self-conscious, over-prepared or 'mechanical' performance suggests something 'withheld'. Hazlitt's complaints about Mars's lack of spontaneity are validated by his own testiness, venom even. With sentences that now accelerate with irritation, stumble over reluctant concessions and delight in ugly metaphors, he plays out his own treachery:

When Mademoiselle Mars comes on stage, something in the manner of a fantoccini figure slid along on a wooden frame, and making directly for the point at which her official operations commence – when her face is puckered into a hundred little expressions like the wrinkles on the skin of a bowl of cream, set in a window to cool, her eyes peering out with an ironical meaning, her nose pointing it, and her lips confirming it with a dry pressure – we admire indeed, we are delighted, we may envy, but we do not sympathise or very well know what to make of it. (329–30)

And this new antipathy to the actress bolsters a heartfelt argument for naturalism, for spontaneity against premeditation, for flowing movement against rigid gesture, against, in short, everything falsely theatrical – and undeniably French.

There is a cultural phenomenon at work here with which later theatre historians are very familiar. It depends upon an authoritative announcement that a new style of acting has made all others seem redundant, usually on the grounds that the new is self-evidently more 'natural' than the old. Since the early nineteenth century such moments have been part of the long shift from acting conceived as a conventionalised, technical and rhetorically persuasive art to one that is psychologically attuned, relying upon identification and sympathy. Though the claim is often made, 'natural' obviously does not in such contexts bear an exact relation to an essential human psychology (if it did, we would never have the experience of finding previous styles old fashioned) but rather to a new set of conventions, of changes in the agreed ideas as to what constitutes normal social behaviour, including the realm of the erotic.

At the same time Hazlitt's passion, his rush to repudiate the old, suggests something deeper, more insistent, than a mere change in theatrical tastes. In this process of endless discarding psychoanalysis would surely identify the workings of love itself. 'When the original object of a wishful impulse has been lost as a result of repression, it is frequently represented by an endless series of substitute objects, none of which, however gives full satisfaction', writes Freud in his most celebrated essay on the subject. 'This may explain the inconsistency in object-choice, the "craving for stimulation", which is so often a feature of the love of adults.'[34] Because it's a substitution in the first place, a surrogate for the primal maternal presence, love, for Freud, is always a search for irretrievably lost, endlessly disappointed.

Of course, it may well be the case that Mars really did fall off in her middle years, lose touch with her own instincts and training and the seeming effortlessness that had first marked her out.[35] It might easily follow that a performer who specialised in the erotic would have to be punished by exclusion, reminded of her fate by being replaced by someone more reliably young. That is hardly enough to explain the intensity of Hazlitt's rejection or the speed with which it took place. The chilling first sentence – 'I liked Mademoiselle Mars exceeding well, till I saw Madame Pasta whom I liked so much better' – rejects the older actress as a jaded *roué* might cast off a faded mistress who compares badly with her youthful rivals or, more pertinently perhaps, as Hazlitt himself was to blame Sarah Walters, his landlord's daughter, for her flirtatious refusal to commit herself to him in his bitter work of sexual confession, *Liber Amoris or The New Pygmalion* (1823). When Hazlitt complains that Mars's forte is 'that sort of expression which is hardly itself for the two moments together, that shifts from point to point, that seems to have no place to rest on, no impulse to urge it forward' it is not just her Frenchness but her unreliable sexuality that he wishes to repudiate. It is as if Stendhal's 'crystallisation' no longer worked, that the actress could no longer be guaranteed to irradiate her surroundings. According to Hazlitt then, Mars's inspirational gaiety is not to be counted upon – for all manner of reasons, but mainly because, paradoxically, the natural has become the artificial. In such circumstances flirting can seem like the opposite of opportunity, more like a self-conscious and self-protective performance in which the other person is held at bay.

Stendhal was equally convinced of the sublimity of Pasta (he included a fine essay upon her in his book on Rossini), but he refused to accept Hazlitt's lordly dismissal of Mars. Within a matter of weeks he had published a chivalrous reply to his English friend, that 'man of talent', in the *London Magazine* in which he insisted that the actress still gave him greater aesthetic satisfaction than many Romantic writers. His defence drew, ingeniously enough, upon the actress's private life and her place in French culture rather than upon her acting style. Since Napoleon, says Stendhal, it has been expected of respectable French couples that they should always be seen together in public but Mars, on or off the stage, reminds them of other possibilities. Hazlitt therefore

has not understood Mademoiselle Mars. Many Englishmen fancy they understand the French language and French manners, who have not the slightest idea of either. Mademoiselle Mars, with her sublime talent, the finest eyes of all Paris, and her 50,000 francs a year, has also the most *piquant*, the liveliest, and the most cutting wit.[36]

The tribute proceeds with an account of a recent sexual intrigue in which Mars has come off worst, leaving her in despair, but once more the talk of Paris and still the envious butt of other women. The reason for the pre-eminence of Mars, as Hazlitt has completely failed to understand, is that she embodies a spirit of amorous adventure in an age of encroaching *embourgeoisement*. Constraints upon public behaviour inherited from the Napoleonic era, says Stendhal, have made the sexual glamour of actresses seem all the more fascinating.

Thus, thanks to Napoleon, a Frenchman passes the 20 hours of the 24 with a woman whose only recommendation to him is her money. You see that the necessary result of this state of things is an abominable dullness and ennui; thence also the immense success of the 14 theatres of Paris which are filled every evening. Judge then of the dreadful envy which poor women, condemned never to quit for a moment their yawning husbands, must feel for Mademoiselle Mars, who, in fortune, education, and *esprit*, yields to none of them, and has, moreover, a sublime talent, whatever the *New Monthly Magazine* may say.[37]

Although these two male critics, Hazlitt and Stendhal, may have been divided between themselves over the endurance of Mars's erotic presence, and divided *within* themselves about the place of flirtation in the pursuit of love, they remained united in their conviction that the theatrical representation of erotic feeling is a significant element in social life. Nor were they alone. It was because Mars still signified sexual independence that she gained so much attention in middle age. Ambivalence, hostility even, is evidence of cultural unease and debate, sometimes hidden but ever-present nonetheless, which hinges on a clash between the erotic as a mode of testing and experimentation in which people vie with one another for control, in a word 'flirting', and romantic love in which the lovers spontaneously coalesce and profess undying devotion. This was also a debate about the place of the intellect and of curiosity in sexual relations against the claims of emotional wholeheartedness and sincerity or, in cultural terms, a conflict between independence and monogamy. As the social historian, Theodore Zeldin, explains,

Ways of putting vague sexual attraction to useful purpose were investigated in the seventeenth and eighteenth centuries, particularly among the French, who developed flirtation and coquetry as arts of sociability, avoiding exclusive entanglements. At that time, in old-fashioned ways, a lover (*amant*) could still mean an admirer, and not necessarily a sexual partner; to 'make love' originally meant to court, rather than to engage in intercourse. Flirtation gave a new direction to courtly love, it was sex without sex, a prolongation of the preliminaries to sex which need never be consummated; but instead of idealising the loved one, it tried to understand him or her, and to probe how they could be mutually agreeable and stimulating.[38]

The provisional nature of flirting placed it in dangerous opposition to goals of marriage and procreation. And yet, over time, with changes in concepts of gender and an increasing stress on individualism, the practice came to be realigned with sexual independence and 'the first step in the creation of a relationship whose purpose is joint and mutual exploration'. Consequently, by seeming to avoid sincerity and sexual commitment, flirting simultaneously undermined and enhanced the possibilities of harmony between men and women.[39] In a climate of professed monogamy the fascinating performances of Mars were the delicious epitome of this dilemma, tipping the scales against the coquette while raising questions about national differences.

In early nineteenth-century England, flirting and its close relation coquetry are sometimes seen as ambiguous qualities not easy to decipher. An 1830 essay on 'Coquetry', which carries as epitaph a quote from Stendhal's *De l'amour*, puts it like this: 'If coquetry excite the female to that adornment of person and of mind which will best exalt her beauty, and increase her attraction in the eyes of man, it operates no less serviceably in enabling its possessor to keep importunity at arm's length, and in protecting her from the first assaults of her own affections.' Indeed, 'there are thousands of girls, who, if they had not been coquets [*sic*] and flirts, would have been the dupes of designing scoundrels, or the repentant victims of ill-assorted and unsuitable matches.'[40]

Even on this topic there was no final agreement. Much as there was debate over the function of coquetry in social life, so was there disagreement about the national culture to which the habit most naturally belongs. Was flirting more French than English? (Lady Morgan, perhaps surprisingly, would have said that it was English.[41]) Was it attack or defence? Deceptive foreplay or surrogate act? The general uncertainty simply proves how difficult and how fundamentally serious the issue had become, and was to remain throughout the nineteenth century. The problem of whether flirtation is compatible with friendship, let alone with love, already underlay, for example, Jane Austen's sympathetic if somewhat askance vignette of her heroine in conversation with Frank Churchill during the Box Hill picnic in *Emma* (1816):

To amuse her, and be agreeable in her eyes, seemed all that he cared for – and Emma, glad to be enlivened, not sorry to be flattered, was gay and easy too, and gave him all the friendly encouragement, the admission to be gallant, which she had ever given in the first and most animating period of their acquaintance; but which now, in her own estimation, meant nothing, though in the judgement of most people looking on it must have had such an appearance as no English word but flirtation could very well describe. 'Mr Frank Churchill and Miss Woodhouse flirted together excessively.' They were laying themselves open to that very phrase . . . Not that Emma was gay and thoughtless from any real felicity; it was rather because she felt less happy than she had expected. She laughed because she was disappointed; and though she liked him for his attentions, and thought them all, whether in friendship, admiration, or playfulness, extremely judicious, they were not winning back her heart. She still intended him for her friend.[42]

Emma, like all true flirts, though still susceptible to admiration, and still unsettled in her life, wants everything – friendship as well as love – and on her own terms. Her prurient observers cannot know precisely what is going on in her head; as a result they miss the essential point and

resort to a simple-minded and misguided conclusion based on appearance alone. Events will prove them wrong. The stimulus of flirtation
extends beyond participants to reveal spectators – that is what makes it so
dramatic.

SEPARATION

In a purely theatrical context, flirting is a resource that allows a play to
question its own moral boundaries by inviting the audience to become
implicated in the games that its characters play with one another. To turn
the invitation down, as English audiences seem to have done in the case
of *Le Misanthrope*, was to resist possibility, to opt instead for singularity
and the hint of regression which, however unconsciously, soothes the often
fateful progress of love. This explains the appeal to the English of Mars in
Valérie. But in France, in the late 1820s and early 1830s, the drama went off
in a very different direction with Mlle Mars, to general surprise and with
some personal reluctance, in the vanguard. As the Duchesse de Guise in
Dumas *père*'s *Henri III et sa cour* in 1829 and (possibly inspired by Harriet
Smithson) as Desdemona in Vigny's adaptation of *Othello* in the following
year, and then, overwhelmingly, as Dona Sol in Victor Hugo's *Hernani* also
in 1830, she remade herself as a definitively modern, that is to say a fully
Romantic, actress.[43]

French Romantic drama officially begins with *Hernani*, its legendary
first night attended by Théophile Gautier, sporting an emblematic red
waistcoat, accompanied by his young friends, cheering Hugo's play against
the booing forces of the conservatism. The famous occasion was noted in
England, but in a surprisingly low-key, dispassionate way:

The new tragedy, which promises, from the nature of its incidence and the favour
of its reception, to give a new turn to French tragedy, was performed for the first
time, at the Théâtre-Français, in the course of last week. In the account of it . . . it
will be seen that the story is full of fine situations the most favourable to stage effect,
and that they are too numerous to admit of much of that weary and monotonous
declamation which has hitherto formed the chief ingredient of French tragedy,
and been by French critics considered its indispensable requisite and its greatest
ornament. We translate from the French, but the French adopting from us, are
gradually getting rid of their fettering unities, and enlivening their pieces with that
bustle of action and incident which the translations of Shakespeare have made
them acquainted with, and which have long been considered absolutely necessary
to the gratification of English taste. The name of the author was announced amidst
a burst of applause, which completely drowned the feeble attempts that were made
at opposition.[44]

In France though, Romanticism was, for a time, unstoppable. Already, when Lady Morgan returned to Paris in 1829, she was astonished to find neo-classical drama so deeply out of fashion. A young man ('there was something of an *exalté* in his air, in his open shirt-collar, black head, and wild and melancholy look')[45] insisted that she must only go to the Français when 'our divine tragic muse' is playing in a *reprise* of Dumas *père*'s *Henri III*:

'What tragic muse?' I asked: 'Mademoiselle George, or Duchenois?'
   'Oh! No, *cela est passé comme le déluge* – I mean Mademoiselle Mars, the pearl; of pearls, the Melpomene of age!'

'Mademoiselle Mars the tragic muse! – the Melpomene!' exclaims Lady Morgan, amazed to hear the great comic actress referred to in this way.[46]

   At the same time as Mars becomes a tragic actress in the Romantic mode, playing roles that were emotionally all or nothing, possessed, 'abandoned', not at all flirtatious, so English critics begin to assume the status of Victorian judges, with Hugo a test case for dramatic probity. This development can be traced in the changing attitudes towards the French playwright adopted by the critic and theorist, G. H. Lewes, who was initially prepared to welcome Hugo for his energy and novelty alone, and to defend his *Marion de Lorme* (in which the heroine rescues her lover from prison by submitting to his gaoler) on the grounds that the loss of chastity was not the woman's fault but rather the inevitable result of the situation in which she found herself. 'We are very certain that people have very confused notions about female virtue, as it is the error of all moralists to trim their boat with an eye to the rocks of convention, against which alone they dread to split', wrote Lewes, anxious to establish his own moral credentials. 'Were we not too apt to take words for deeds, we should never have made the blunder of supposing chastity could reside elsewhere than in the soul, or that impurity could arise from inwards, from what was done *to us*, rather than proceeding from inwards *from us*. To suppose a woman less chaste because she has been violated, is as reasonable as to suppose a man murdered on the highway for his gold, is a *particeps criminis* – and yet this logic has been used (for pathetic purposes) by poets and novelists without number.'[47]

   This tolerance was not to last. Lack of enthusiasm for Hugo's conspicuous supporters (Lewes certainly knew all about Gautier's red waistcoat)[48] helped fuel new reservations. These were voiced as early as 1844, and they concentrated upon what Lewes called Hugo's 'paradoxes', by which he meant the playwright's fondness for finding moral good in unlikely places, and his celebrated mixture of the sublime and the grotesque. Neither complied with Lewes's growing desire for aesthetic order:

The paradoxes of Victor Hugo, however they may startle and amuse, can never last: they are like ice-palaces built for Russian fêtes, – brilliant, but uninhabitable and melting at the first approach of summer . . . Does he wish to delineate parental love? – he selects a Triboulet and a Lucrèce Borgia. Does he wish to paint man's love? – he selects a monk, a monster and a valet; a Claude Frollo, a Quasimodo, a Ruy Blas.[49]

The same complaint even encompasses the typical condition of Hugo's heroines: 'Woman's love? – he has no fitter types than two notorious prostitutes, Marion de Lorme and Tisbé'. By no means narrow in his tastes or illiberal in his attitudes, Lewes was now looking for human norms, rather than for what he considered to be social extremes, and for the theatrical structures that would permit analysis, that obeyed what he called 'rule' or 'law' in art: 'the precept dictated by universal good sense, by universal feeling, by universal precedent'.[50]

There is a more literary equivalent of Lewes's distrust of Hugolian drama in the intense dislike towards Stendhal's *De l'amour* voiced by the woman who was by then his partner, George Eliot. Reviewing the book when it was reprinted in 1856, she found it 'repulsive' for reasons that had as much to do with form as with content. It was 'a collection of notes, written down in various moods, from the cynical to the sentimental'. Stendhal only redeemed himself by 'his pithy arguments in favour of giving women a thorough education'. Even this might not be an entirely mixed blessing: 'Since, however, in spite of all discouragement, from the days of Faust until now, the number of silly men who rush into print has been constantly on the increase, we see no reason to think that silly women would follow a different law.'[51]

Neither prudes nor snobs, Lewes and Eliot were, by their own designation, 'realists', which meant, in this instance, that they were worried by the ways in which exaggerated or 'deformed' feelings were sometimes allowed to go unexamined as a result of lazy or unprincipled authorship. Of course, in the event, life and art would always destabilise this aesthetic by throwing up discordant movements, unexpected areas of experience that would demand prolonged and careful observation in order to re-establish the supposed norm. The emergence of new styles of acting would provide Lewes with one such challenge.

Because Mlle Mars retired in 1841, and died in 1847, few of the critics who came to dominate the English scene in later years ever had a chance to see her. She survived, despite the original ambivalence, despite the ignorance or dislike of Hugo and Dumas *père*, as a sensual myth of 'bewitching elocution',[52] a commonplace journalistic phrase for the sublimely sirenic sounds that Hazlitt and Stendhal, among many others, believed that they had heard in their youth. The actress, playwright and later friend of Henry James, Fanny Kemble, always regretted that she experienced Mars

only in two parts, when, in the autumn of her beauty and powers, she played a short engagement in London. The grace, the charm, the loveliness, which she retained far into middle age, were, even in their decline, enough to justify all that her admirers said of early incomparable fascination. Her figure had grown large and her face become round, and lost their firm outline and proportion; but the exquisite taste of her dress and graceful dignity of her deportment and sweet radiance of her exquisite countenance, were still indescribably charming; and the voice, unrivalled in its fresh melodious brilliancy, and the pure and perfect enunciation, were unimpaired, and sounded like the clear liquid utterance of a young girl of sixteen. Her Célimène and her Elmire I never had the good fortune to see . . .[53]

Yet, seeing Mars as Elmire in Paris in 1835, many years after she had first encountered her, the writer Mrs Trollope still marvelled at her 'strange witchery', at the uncanny harmony of voice and gesture:

That the ear should be gratified, and the feelings awakened, by the skilful intonations of a voice the sweetest perhaps that ever blest a mortal, is quite intelligible; but that the eye should follow with such unwearied delight every look and movement of a woman, not only old . . . but one known to be so from one end of Europe to the other, is certainly a singular phenomenon . . . There is still a charm, a grace in every movement of Mademoiselle Mars, however trifling and however slight, which instantly captivates the eye, and forbids it to wander to any other object – even though the object be young and lovely.[54]

Throughout the nineteenth century there would be continual harking back to an imagined Romantic past when the female voice was teasingly integrated with the female body, a physical presence in an established set of conventions.[55] 'La voix de Célimène', the sound of sexual independence, was deferred, suspended, disembodied. As they strove to hear for themselves a sound that they had only heard about, so audiences would apprehend it first in Madame Plessy and later, presumptuously transformed, in Sarah Bernhardt. But if, for the English in particular, Mademoiselle Mars stood for an unforgettable mode of the feminine, simultaneously inviting and elusive, the undoubted presence of Rachel Félix, subject of the next chapter, would demonstrate an implacable female identity – located in what, for the French as well as the English, was a traditionally masculine space: neo-classical tragedy.

CHAPTER 2

Rachel's 'terrible beauty': an actress among the novelists

And all that faith creates, or love desires,
Terrible, strange, sublime and beauteous shapes.
                                    Shelley, *Prometheus Unbound*[1]

In the minds of critics, English and French ideas of tragedy have always been treated as rivals. During the Romantic period the fortunes of the Racinian style were at a particularly low ebb. 'The genius of Shakespeare is dramatic', declared Hazlitt; 'that of Racine is didactic'.[2] A playwright who relied on moral instruction had demonstrably failed to achieve the object of the drama, which is 'to make us sympathise with the sufferer, or feel as we should in his circumstances, not to tell the indifferent spectator what the indifferent spectator could just as well tell him'. For Hazlitt, the dramatist should lay bare 'the heart of the sufferer with all its bleeding wounds and palpitating fibres . . . Tragedy is human nature tried in the crucible of affliction, not exhibited in the vague theorems of speculation' (346). The English Romantic argument is there summarised with peremptory authority; the case of Racine against Shakespeare is no sooner opened than it is shut.

In France, the process was different. The title of Stendhal's famous treatise of 1823 announces an argument for Shakespeare's supremacy by linking the two playwrights with a conjunction but reversing their chronological order. *Racine et Shakespeare* means Racine *then* Shakespeare, Shakespeare as a model for reform. The English, their historical impatience with French tragedy re-endorsed by Romanticism, had no need for monitory discriminations of that kind. If they persisted with the comparison, they did so because it offered a convenient starting-point for explorations of the 'sympathy' and 'nature' to be found above all in Shakespeare.

All the more startling, then, were the appearances in London between 1841 and 1855 of an actress who had already caused the French to revalue their tradition. That Rachel Félix was the greatest actress of her time was beyond dispute; what made her unique was her regeneration of the

46

Figure 3. Rachel as Phèdre

ancient classics of the French stage: Corneille's *Horace* (London début, 1841), Racine's *Andromaque* and *Bajazet* (also 1841) and, overwhelmingly, his *Phèdre* (1846).[3] So profound was the impact of Rachel that she obliged even the English to revise the time-honoured antithesis and allow for the possibility of Shakespeare in Racine, or occasionally, Racine *despite* Shakespeare; the unsuspected presence of 'sympathy' and 'nature' within a supposedly didactic and moribund form.

Rachel came to stand for the entirely unforeseen, her seismic power witnessed not only by the disruption of critical tropes but, more remarkably, by the inspirational hold that she gained on the imagination of the Victorian novelist. More than most performers she became, even in her own lifetime, a creature of myth, her substantive presence long since dissolved in the mists of reminiscence and recreation. Indeed, if the nineteenth century needed fiction to do justice to the revelation of Rachel, then it might seem that the theatrical experience she offered now lies beyond any kind of verification. Yet there is a way of comprehending her volatile significance, and it requires that we concentrate upon those moments when a fictional portrait can be shown precisely to interact with the critical record. While the manipulations of the novelist may uncover the subjectivity of the commentator (provisional view-points exposing concealed interpretation), the *actualité* of his or her testimony nevertheless works to constrain and channel the possibilities of fictional appropriation.

This interventionist approach is particularly inviting in the case of Rachel because the ability to evoke her genius was generally credited to one critic above all others: G. H. Lewes. Well qualified to write about the drama, Lewes, as a young man, wrote several plays himself and briefly worked as an actor.[4] Personal experience gave a worldly tone to his writing yet did nothing to diminish the intellectual content. As a theoretician Lewes combined Romantic memories (always of Kean, whom he had seen in 1825 when he was eight) with polymathic knowledge of European literature and contemporary science. He represented the full force of Victorian intellectual enquiry, bringing to the theatre an unusually wide range of critical speculation.

All sightings of Rachel must start with Lewes's tributes, among them the following:

Rachel was the panther of the stage; with a panther's terrible beauty and undulating grace she moved and stood, glared and sprang. There always seemed something not human about her. She seemed made of different clay from her fellows – beautiful but not lovable . . . Her range, like Kean's, was very limited . . . Scorn, triumph, rage, lust and merciless malignity she could represent in symbols of irresistible power; but she had little tenderness, no womanly caressing softness, no gaiety, no heartiness. She was so graceful and so powerful that her air of dignity was incomparable; but somehow you always felt in her presence an indefinable suggestion of latent wickedness . . . A beautiful devil . . . [her] thrilling voice, flexible, penetrating, and grave, responded with the precision of a keyed instrument. Her thin, nervous frame vibrated with emotion. Her face, which would have been common, had it not been aflame with genius, was capable of intense expression. Her gestures were so fluent and graceful that merely to see her would have been a rare delight . . . Like Kean, she had a power of concentrating into a single phrase a world of intense feeling.[5]

Those celebrated passages come from the extremely influential essay that Lewes eventually included in his book *On Actors and the Art of Acting* (1875), but had first published in his series *Retrospects of Actors* in the *Pall Mall Gazette* (1865). And even in 1865, seven years after Rachel's death, the essay was little more than a compilation of phrases that Lewes had been using ever since he first wrote about her in the 1840s. Moreover, although they later became indelibly associated with Lewes, he had been by no means the only critic to employ them.

The unusual force of Lewes's evocation lay in the skill with which he fore-grounded and tightened commonplace epithets other critics were prepared to squander. Even the tragic oxymoron 'terrible beauty' was established by others as early as Rachel's first London season in 1841, though frequently deployed in the more relaxed form of a loose antithesis.[6] In many other respects, Lewes, whenever he wrote about Rachel, simply confirmed general verdicts: on her gestures, 'so fluent and graceful', on her delivery, 'a power of concentrating into a single phrase a world of intense feeling', and on her physique, 'her thin nervous frame vibrated with emotion'. As for her limitations – 'little tenderness, no womanly caressing softness, no gaiety, no heartiness' – these too were widely perceived from the start.[7]

But while he frequently concurred with others, Lewes did have his own obsessive concerns, and these easily led him to repeat himself. When he wrote about Rachel in the *Atlas* in 1846, he had been thinking about the drama for some years, and came equipped with certain demands and pre-suppositions that enabled him immediately to establish the key terms of his analysis, such as her 'panther-like nature,' and to make what was to become his staple comparison with Kean. In addition, he insisted that Rachel's intensity was not just a matter of her delivery but derived from the plain fact of her presence. This was sensed above all in the way that she appeared to be oblivious of her audience: 'Speaking or listening she is wholly absorbed in her character. The effect of this is incalculable. You never take your eyes off from her; because she is so much in earnest, you are so interested.'[8]

This belief that audience response reciprocates a performer's absorption in a part lies at the heart of Lewes's dramatic theory. He was also exceptional among critics in his appreciation of Racine as the creator of strong characters. In his respect for Rachel the two convictions validate one another. English audiences, said Lewes in 1846, were not entirely wrong when they concluded that it was only because of Rachel that they had been moved by Racine. 'Had not Rachel been able to see and to render what the poet had written, their eyes would never have been opened.'[9] On the other hand, had not Racine created such passionate individuals there would have been nothing for Rachel to match with her own temperament: 'As a painter of the passions – subtle, deep and vehement – he has no superior, except Shakespeare.'

THE JEWISH HEROINE: 'HER FACE WHICH WOULD HAVE BEEN COMMON . . .'

There was one comment about Rachel that Lewes did modify slightly in later years. It related to her race. Though Lewes himself acted Shylock as a sympathetic and wronged character in 1849, his thoughts on Rachel often include a crude and casual anti-Semitism. In the 1860s he was still capable of writing that 'Rachel made a common Jewish physiognomy lovely by mere force of expression'.[10] His earliest criticism is even more blatant:

It will ever remain a curious problem how this little Jewess, this *enfant du peuple*, should, from the first moment of her appearance on the stage, have adopted – or let us rather say exhibited – the imperial grace and majesty which no one but herself can reach . . . If you wish to form an idea what Rachel would be without her exquisite intelligence, look at her brother Raphael Félix, who so closely resembles her. Is he not a vulgar Jew Boy? Can anything wipe out the original stain of his birth? Yet Rachel herself physically is no better; and were it not for the 'o-er-in-forming spirit', she would be as vulgar.[11]

In other words, the same unique qualities that enabled Rachel to bring out the aristocratic passion in Racine were evident in her ability to transform her own origins. Of course, Lewes was only free to put forward that kind of idea because he was confident that his readers would share his preconceptions – the national trait challenged by Benjamin Disraeli in his 'Young England' novels of the 1840s, to one of which, *Tancred* (1847), Rachel makes a brief but eloquent contribution.

The plot of *Tancred*, though thoroughly snarled, traces the adventures of a young English nobleman who is convinced that his country is in need of spiritual revival. Searching for a religious basis for his mission, Tancred embarks on a trip to the Holy Land, accompanied by one 'Baroni', apparently of Italian origin, who has been assigned by Tancred's protector, Sidonia, a Jewish financier. At one point they are captured by brigands, and Tancred has Baroni while away the time by telling him the history of his family, and how his father, old Baroni, first met Sidonia.[12] It turns out that the family had, in the distant unspecified past, earned their living as travelling entertainers. One child had been a singer, another a dancer and a third, Josephine, an actress. Sidonia had seen one of their shows – as young Baroni recounts:

She advanced . . . as Andromache. It seemed to Sidonia that he had never listened to a voice more rich and passionate, to an elocution more complete; he gazed with admiration on her lightning glance and all the tumult of her noble brow. As she finished, he applauded her with vehemence. He was standing near to her father leaning against the wall.
   'Your daughter is a great actress,' he said to Baroni.
   'I sometimes think so,' said the father . . . 'I let her do this to please herself.'

Sidonia is so impressed that he becomes a patron to the family, providing each child with an education appropriate to its talents. Josephine is sent to Paris and, by the time of the novel, so the narrator tells us, has become

the glory of the French stage; without any question the most admirable tragic actress since Clairon, and inferior not even to her. The spirit of French tragedy has risen from the imperial couch on which it had long slumbered, since her appearance, at the same time classical and impassioned, at once charmed and commanded the most refined audience in Europe.

Josephine has most of the standard ingredients of the Rachel type: her art is instinctive, irrepressible, quite overwhelming to the unprepared spectator. She is both classical and 'impassioned'; though sympathetic, she nevertheless 'commands' her audience. Her background, too, resembles that of the great *tragédienne*, who came from a family of wandering theatricals (though a considerably less united one than the Baronis).

   Only one aspect of Rachel is conspicuously absent from the character of Josephine, and Disraeli withholds this until young Baroni, at the very end of the story of his family, reveals the Sephardic origins of their name: 'Baroni; that is, the son of Aaron; the name of old clothesmen in London, and of caliphs at Bagdad.' Josephine, then, is a Jewess. In Lewes's critiques of Rachel, Jewishness is an inheritance which she brilliantly transforms;

in Disraeli's novel, Jewishness is a partial and delayed explanation of Josephine's genius, corroborating Sidonia's belief that 'All is race; there is no other truth'.[13]

But *Tancred* is more than an affirmation of racial prowess. Its ultimate message is racial synthesis: the belief that Judaism anticipates its completion in Christianity. Echoes of Rachel are useful here too. Like Rachel, Josephine initially demonstrates her ability in Racine's *Andromaque*, though significantly Disraeli gives her the name part, that of the Trojan outcast, rather than the Greek heroine Hermione, which was the preferred role of the historical actress. Nevertheless, like Rachel, Josephine is a Jewish actress who will recreate the Greek heroines of a Christian dramatist. She will become, in Arnoldian terms, Hebrew and Hellene incarnate.[14]

Rachel serves Disraeli as a talisman, an entirely recognisable point of reference that encapsulates the themes of the novel as a whole. Yet although she is linked typologically with the main plot, the fact that she appears in an anecdote that reaches from the tenuous past to the narrative present – a story within a story – doubly distances her from its findings. Lewes himself, in a review of *Coningsby* (1844), and another application of racial heritage to creative talent, commented that Disraeli's writing suffered from 'that love of ornament, which is characteristic of his race', and that as a result, 'his eloquence like his imagination, like his poetry, like his philosophy, like his statesmanship, is the Prospectus, not the Work!'[15] The racial premise is distasteful as ever, but the critical point holds true of *Tancred* as well as *Coningsby*. Josephine is a retrospective anticipation of a Jewish triumph in the present that the wildly disorganised and episodic novel never manages to ratify for the future. *Tancred* degenerates into romantic adventures and rambling dissertations on 'the Great Asian Mystery'; and ends, in notorious bathos, when the hero's parents descend upon Jerusalem to rescue their errant son.

THE FEMALE IMAGINATION: 'AN INDEFINABLE SUGGESTION OF LATENT WICKEDNESS'

While Disraeli may not have been specifically thinking of Lewes when he conceived of Josephine – there were others who said similar things about Rachel – it does seem likely that Charlotte Brontë had him in mind when she wrote *Villette* (1853). Halfway through the novel, in chapter 23, the heroine, Lucy Snowe, sees a performance by a celebrated actress known as 'Vashti' in the company of a man who exerts a power over her that she is unable or unwilling to admit even to herself. The mixed desire and hostility that the man arouses in the woman becomes exposed by the turmoil that she undergoes at the vision on stage. Vashti, inspired by Rachel, whom Brontë saw in London in 1851, is evoked in transfiguring prose:

Suffering had struck that stage empress; and she stood before her audience neither yielding to, nor enduring, not in finite measure, resenting it; she stood locked in struggle, rigid in resistance. She stood, not dressed, but draped in pale antique folds, long and regular like sculpture. A background and entourage and flooring of deepest crimson threw her out, white like alabaster – like silver: rather be it said, like Death.[16]

To Lucy Snowe, the actress is nothing less than diabolical: 'something neither of woman neither of man: in each of her eyes sat a devil'. She is a terrifying yet exhilarating image of a woman for whom mind and body, imagination and experience, are one. 'To her what hurts becomes immediately embodied'.[17]

Seated in the theatre, Lucy finds herself possessed by an exhibition of violent sexual feelings that she cannot release within her own life. Whether she recognises her own emotions in Vashti's performance, or whether she projects them upon it, we cannot know, so finely merged are the voices of character and narrator in the first-person mode. Lucy's male companion remains entirely unmoved – more concerned with the actress's moral reputation than with her performance – and the play ends prematurely with the threat of fire in the auditorium, although this later turns out to have been something of a false alarm.

Since Vashti serves Brontë primarily as a mirror for Lucy Snowe, there is no call to take chapter 23 as a documentary record of Rachel – though on closer examination, Vashti can be seen to illuminate the dilemma of Brontë herself, who had long been locked in conflict with male authority, one of its chief representatives being G. H. Lewes. Among the very first to acknowledge Brontë's gifts, Lewes had reviewed each of her novels as it appeared, and corresponded with her at some length, but underlying these communications there had always been considerable tension, barely concealed by the surface respect that they professed for one another. This was probably to do with Lewes's habit of treating Brontë as *protégée* and pupil, roles that she found impossible to accept, but given her generally correct manner and provincial location, difficult to reject outright. Their exchanges had grown into sparring matches, in which each dared the other on.

Even in his comments upon *Jane Eyre* (1847), Lewes had mixed praise with caution. Despite the fact that the novel was 'soul speaking to soul', despite Brontë's 'passion; and knowledge of life', it would, he believed, be unwise for her to venture again beyond her own experience.[18] Brontë immediately countered, 'Is not the real experience of each individual very limited? . . . Imagination is a strong, restless faculty which claims to be heard and exercised'.[19]

In 1850 they had again crossed swords when Lewes, in his review of *Shirley*, disparaged the book's 'over-masculine vigour' and proclaimed that 'the grand function of woman . . . is, and ever must be. Maternity.'[20] Brontë's response was appropriately acid: 'I can be on guard against my enemies, but God deliver me from my friends!'[21]

Begun in 1851, not completed until November 1852, *Villette*, Brontë's next novel, was difficult to write, but the strain of composition was relieved in the summer of 1851, which is when she visited London and twice saw Rachel. There is no record of her having met Lewes at this time, though Rachel's season was of great interest to the two of them. For Lewes, it was the test of reacquaintance; for Brontë, a long-awaited first encounter: 'I wonder whether she will fulfil reasonable expectation.'[22] In the event, Rachel satisfied them both. Lewes, now contributing theatrical columns under the name of 'Vivian' to the *Leader*, the journal he had helped found in 1850, characteristically recapitulated his old reviews:

Her appearance as she entered, wasting away with fire that consumed her, standing on a verge of the grave, – her face pallid, – her eyes hot, – her arms and hands emaciated, filled us with a ghastly horror.[23]

Brontë returned to Yorkshire and created Vashti, whose regenerate strength places her in the line of performing heroines familiar from Mme de Staël's *Corinne* and George Sand's *Consuelo*.[24] Brontë knew *Consuelo* – in fact she had discussed the novel with Lewes, who was also sensitive to the awesome aspect of actresses. In 1851 he had continued to maintain that Rachel, in *Phèdre* in particular,

looked bewitchingly beautiful, and yet with something unearthly, unhealthy, fever-ish, bewildering. For her sake you could do anything, you could commit any folly, almost a crime – but you could not love her!25

As Brontë was composing *Villette*, she must also have remembered not only the Romantic heroines, Lewes's criticisms of Rachel and the strictures he has passed upon her novels, but his own two inadequate attempts at the genre: *Ranthorpe* (written in 1842, published in 1847) and *Rose, Blanche and Violet* (1848). Brontë had read these novels soon after they appeared, passing comments upon them quite as harsh and rather more justified than those Lewes had directed at *Jane Eyre* and *Shirley*. She objected both to the intrusiveness of the novelist's own opinions ('G. H. Lewes . . . decidedly the most original character in the book') and to the opinions themselves. Above all she disliked the way Lewes imposed intellectual categories and ethical distinctions upon the characters he created. On reading *Rose, Blanche and Violet* she wrote to her publisher, W. S. Williams, that Lewes 'might even stigmatise imagination as a figment and delicacy as an affectation', and envisaged herself reprimanding Lewes with the words: 'You are deserving of all attention when you lay down the law on principles, but you are to be resisted when you dogmatise on feelings'.[26] What she had in mind, presumably, were passages like this from *Ranthorpe*, in which a character describes an actress as

the portrait of a very unprincipled woman, sacrificing everything to her intense egotism; but no demon. A demon, in our conception the incarnation of malignity, is not so odious as the incarnation of egotism. Malignity is respectable in comparison: there is force and energy in it; here is a defiance, and a power which extorts sympathy from us . . . The cruelty of egotism is not less than that of a pure malignity; but the motive is more contemptible. Satan is grand, terrible, sublime; Iago is utterly despicable. Moloch is lovable in comparison with Blifil.[27]

Lewes's laborious method of writing fiction relies heavily upon such lengthy philosophical disquisitions, which are intended to help the reader with plausible explanations for behaviour. His technique is thus the very opposite of Brontë's, where the discursive language and hallucinatory images both invite and resist the reader's intellectual involvement. In the case of the actress in *Ranthorpe*, Lewes's spokesman divides her female instincts into 'egotism', a Comtian impulse which can be diagnosed and contained, and malignity, a quality of Romantic heroism deserving of sympathy but in the present instance easily discounted. Such confident analyses of the female artist are defied in *Villette* when Brontë has Vashti vaunt her malignity ('Fallen, insurgent, banished, she remembers the heaven where she rebelled') so that Lucy Snowe can glimpse an expressive potential which she might otherwise repress within herself as 'egotism'. But then the actress in *Ranthorpe*, unlike Rachel, is neither grand, nor terrible, nor sublime.

In Lewes's *Rose, Blanche and Violet* Rachel is actually named. The scene is a reception in Belgravia, where a group of socialites discuss, in terms that lightly parody the author's own reviews, 'a little Jewess they call Rachel, quite a girl, picked up from the streets, but an empress on the stage', for whom 'acting is not acting it is suffering'.

'Is this Rachel – I think you call her – handsome?' asked Lord Boodle, tapping his lips with his cane.

'Yes and no – the beauty of the mind.'

'The only beauty worthy of the name,' said Miss Harridale, sententiously. It was the only style of beauty to which she could lay claim.

'She is beautiful enough,' continued Cecil, 'for the part she plays – you never feel any contradiction between the poet's idea and her representation of it. You should see her in *Phèdre*.'[28]

These same clichés recur in *Villette*, but imbued with a new energy. Before experiencing Vashti, Lucy Snowe has also 'heard this woman termed "plain"', but her routine perception, condensed into 'Suffering had struck that stage empress', turns out to be the prelude to her unexpected self-revelation. By re-creating Rachel as Vashti, Brontë was invading Lewes's special territory and, in the bedevilment of his critical categories, asserting the validity of her own creative conflicts. 'There is something divine in the thought that genius preserves from degradation', she commented about *Rose, Blanche and Violet*, 'were it but true'.[29]

Lucy Snowe is typical of all Brontë heroines in that she is torn between a yearning for release and an urgent need for restraint, yet in her imagination she risks 'degradation' by reaching beyond circumstance towards assertion. It is in this way that the novelist refuses to be confined to what she and her character are supposed to have experienced. Brontë had good reason to answer Lewes's reports of Rachel with Vashti. Though praising Brontë's novels for their power, Lewes had attempted to bind her to his own rules. This restriction repeated the pattern of his reviews of Rachel, which paid tribute to the actress's effect while frequently complaining that she was unable to represent the natural qualities of her sex. With Vashti, it was as if Brontë was challenging Lewes's repressive systems and the patriarchal defence they concealed. Vashti is Brontë's alternative version of Rachel, a fictional portrait of the living actress who embodied the truth that the representation of female desire, however diabolic it might appear, could be vehement proof of the reality of female identity. But whether Rachel might also presage freedom through passionate expression lies not only beyond chapter 23 but outside the boundaries of the novel as a whole. *Villette* ends in enigma. Vashti, we have been told, 'went years ago to her rest', and in the last chapter, when Lucy

Snowe awaits the return of her lover, cryptic shifts of tense, from present to past, leave her true condition unknown, for the prying reader rightly unknowable.

Villette was published late in January 1853 and twice reviewed by Lewes.[30] In June, Rachel again appeared in London, and Lewes again wrote about her for *The Leader*. On two of his visits to the St James, he was accompanied by a young woman, Marian Evans, who had never previously seen the actress perform, but who had high expectations raised in part by her reading of novels. She had found the portrait of the Baroni family in Disraeli's *Tancred* the only point of interest in an otherwise 'thin' book, and had greatly admired *Villette*, believing that Lewes had failed to do it justice.[31]

Lewes had mixed feelings about some of Rachel's performances that summer: 'Rachel has greatly fallen off from her own standard', though in some roles she did inspire him to his customary pitch of fervour, and he was able as usual to rhapsodise over the 'wild unearthly grandeur of that "little rod" of Moses'.[32] Marian Evans, in contrast, was seriously disappointed. Rachel, she complained, did not live up to Vashti. Yet she was moved when Lewes took her backstage and they saw 'the green room and all the dingy dusty paraphernalia that make up theatrical splendour'.[33] Twenty years later she recalled this disenchantment when, as George Eliot, she wrote her last novel, *Daniel Deronda* (1876), her invocation of the actress rooted in an early disillusionment that Lewes's devotion to Rachel could never quite remedy.

In *Daniel Deronda* Rachel becomes a sign for deluded expectations, her memory a kind of retrospective mirage. The important episode occurs in the sixth chapter of volume 1, which involves a private theatrical entertainment devised by the heroine, Gwendolen Harleth, as a means of drawing attention to her own talents.[34] Gwendolen has already been wondering 'whether she should become an actress like Rachel, since she was more beautiful than that thin Jewess', so it is clear where she sets her sights. She poses in a favourite Greek dress and pesters her mother:

'Do I look as well as Rachel, mamma? . . .' 'You have better arms than Rachel,' said Mrs. Davilow; 'your arms would do for anything, Gwen. But your voice is not so tragic as hers: it is not so deep.'

'I can make it deeper, if I like,' said Gwendolen, provisionally; then she added, with decision, 'I think a higher voice is more tragic; it is more feminine; and the more feminine a woman is, the more tragic it seems when she does desperate actions.'

In the event, it begins to look as if Gwendolen will lose her opportunity to rival Rachel: her amateur friends are unable to declaim French verse, and her mother won't have 'any Greek wickedness'. She does, though, manage to wear her Greek dress when they decide to stage the transformation scene from *The Winter's Tale*, with Gwendolen as Hermione and the amiable Rex Gascoigne as Leontes. What follows recaptures the opposition of Racine to Shakespeare. Even more precisely, it re-enacts the difference between a Romantic Racinian actress who intensified tragic convention and a Shakespearean actress who naturalised tragic experience.

Racine is signalled by the name of Rachel, and the unnamed actress who inspired Eliot's choice of *The Winter's Tale* would surely have been her long-standing friend Helen Faucit, whose performance of Hermione with Macready's Leontes in 1837 was part of theatrical history. When Eliot had first met Faucit in the spring of 1853, just before she saw Rachel and consolidated her relationship with Lewes, she had been greatly struck by Faucit's personality:

[The] most poetic woman I have seen for a long while. Her conversation is not remarkable in any way but there is an ineffable charm of a fine character which makes itself felt in her fact, voice and manner.[35]

On and off the stage, Faucit's 'ineffable charm' continued to provide both Eliot and Lewes with a subject of almost scientific interest. In 1864 they went to Glasgow to see her act and to discuss the tragic drama that Eliot was then considering, the project that eventually became *The Spanish Gypsy*. It was conversation with Faucit that became the basis of the lecture delivered by the Jewish musician Herr Klesmer on the subject of artistic dedication in volume 2, chapter 23, though the medium is transposed from theatre to music, presumably on the grounds that music occupies a higher rung in the hierarchy of the arts. Not that Lewes and Eliot were uncritical admirers of Faucit – they were so unimpressed by her performance in *As You Like It* in 1865 that Lewes, by now supplying reviews and the *Retrospects of Actors* series to the *Pall Mall Gazette*, wrote a disapproving piece and Eliot came to the forlorn conclusion that 'it was a great mistake ever to see one of Shakespeare's plays acted'.[36]

In theatrical lore Faucit had long been compared with Rachel. And the two actresses had in reality met in Paris in 1841 and talked about their art, disclosing differences that an English newspaper would recall as late as 1864:

There was one gesture of Helen Faucit's which Rachel would practise for hours – the graceful turn of the head over the shoulder when leaving the stage, which, however, is acknowledged by connoisseurs to be unique; and, when unable to acquire the same ease and grace, Rachel would declare that 'it must have been acquired during a state of somnambulism, for no waking will could command the same grace and power of motion'.[37]

Faucit's effect, as Eliot was aware, depended upon a flowing grace that signified sincerity. As her husband, Theodore Martin, insisted, on no account should this be mistaken for the 'statuesque':

No attitude was ever studied or consciously assumed by the actress, or what is understood by the phrase 'statuesque'. Her movements, no doubt suggested infinite studies for the sculptor, but they were transitory movements dictated by the feeling of the moment or the requirements of the situation, and never long enough arrested for the most dexterous artist to draw them.[38]

Faucit's most devoted admirers said that at her best she reached a sublime level of art simply by following her natural instincts, her organic unity conveyed in the flow of her gestures rather than by a fixed attitude. It is this kind of graceful motion that we might expect Gwendolen Harleth to strive for when, as Hermione, she assays one of Faucit's most memorable parts. Certainly the narrator has promised that we shall see Gwendolen in an 'unforeseen phase of emotion'. Yet in the event, and against all the odds, it turns out to be not Faucit but Rachel whom Gwendolen briefly but vividly resembles. At the very moment of transformation there is an unexpected incident. A panel door opposite the stage suddenly flies open, disclosing the concealed picture – 'an upturned dead face, from which an obscure figure seemed to be fleeing'[39] – which had so disturbed Gwendolen in an earlier chapter:

Everyone was startled, but all eyes in the act of turning towards the opened panel were recalled by a piercing cry from Gwendolen, who stood without change of attitude, but with a change of expression that was terrifying in its terror. She looked like a statue into which a soul of Fear had entered: her pallid lips were parted; her eyes usually narrowed under their long lashes, were dilated and fixed.

But Gwendolen's spontaneous impersonation of the marmoreal gaze of Rachel doesn't last either. The reader has been warned that how the incident came about was 'at first a mystery', but the chapter ends with only half an explanation. While we are given details of what caused the panel to open,

Gwendolen's response is less conclusively accounted for. She is torn between mortification at 'the betrayal into a passion of fear' and complacency at what Klesmer charitably informs her was a powerful theatrical effect.

Evidently Eliot had chosen the climax of *The Winter's Tale* precisely because it was a traditional locus for theatrical ambiguity. Behind the episode lies the convention that the mutuality of art and nature revealed by Shakespeare can be demonstrated in performance when the intensity of the moment makes the actress playing Hermione forget her art and express her own nature. Faucit had made her own special offering to this tradition when she had played opposite Macready, and although her account was not published until 1891,[40] she would surely have recalled the experience in the fervent conversations she held with her novelist friend in 1874.[41]

Characteristically, *Daniel Deronda* probes theatrical legend by replaying history with substitute actors: Rex Gascoigne and Gwendolen Harleth as Macready and Faucit. As it has been previously arranged that Rex will, at the moment of Hermione's descent, 'kneel and kiss the hem of her garment', there is no risk of his repeating Macready's improvised effect – 'Now he was prostrate at her feet, then enfolding her in his arms'. Like Faucit (in a tradition going back at least to Mrs Siddons), Gwendolen does have the benefit of a pillar on which to lean, but whereas for Faucit this served a practical purpose ('By imperceptibly altering the poise of the body, the weight of it being on the forward foot, I could drop into the easiest position from which to move'), Gwendolen has other advantages in mind:

Hermione, her arm resting on a pillar, was elevated by about six inches, which she counted on as a means of showing her pretty foot and instep, when at the given signal she should advance and descend.

Nevertheless Faucit, like Gwendolen, had also experienced a spasm of involuntary shock at the miraculous moment. The carefully arranged hair 'came unbound and fell on my shoulders', only to be 'reverently kissed and caressed' by Macready. 'The whole change was so sudden, so overwhelming that I suppose I cried out hysterically', Faucit was to recall, describing a reaction very similar to Gwendolen's 'piercing cry' at the same point. Faucit was fortunate in having Macready whisper 'Don't be frightened, child!' and she remembered 'a tumult of applause that sounded like a storm of hail', followed by a lull that enabled her to find her own 'broken trembling voice' with the line, 'You Gods, look down.' Gwendolen, who has to make do with the assistance of her mother and Rex, remains mute, though she does have 'self-consciousness enough to aim at controlling her signs of terror'. After her period with Macready, Faucit was never again to play Hermione in London, though she did occasionally perform the part in the provinces. Always, she says, 'The sympathies of my audience for the suffering Hermione were reflected back upon me so warmly as to make me feel that they entered into my conception of her beautiful nature', yet always, in the statue scene, she became quite unaware of being observed: 'my imagination was too full of what I felt was then in Hermione's heart, to leave me eyes for any but Leontes'.

Gwendolen fails where Faucit had triumphed, which certainly proves that she has no future as a sympathetic actress; the role is in any case premature, as she has yet to experience suffering comparable to Hermione's. Moreover, her untimely rendering of the part tacitly subverts the pious reputation of Faucit herself, who had learned to project an image of redemptive womanhood that *Daniel Deronda* comes to view with considerable hesitation. But if Gwendolen fails to sustain Faucit's achievement as Hermione – the statue who becomes a woman – then neither will she again recapture the effect of Rachel – the terrifying woman who came, in performance, to look like a statue.

So self-conscious is *Daniel Deronda* as a work of fiction that it continually questions the images of which it makes use. In its later sections, a need to dissociate from the tragic manner experienced by Rachel becomes much more pressing. Deronda himself is our guide in this. Confronted by his mother, the Princess, a retired diva who, though she has denied her Jewishness, has a thoroughly Rachelesque style, Deronda cannot tolerate the way in which she makes all her experience the basis for 'sincere acting . . . and all the more when it was tragic as well as real'. The Princess, for whom 'each nucleus of pain and pleasure had a deep atmosphere of the excitement or spiritual intoxication which at once exalts or deadens', has the actor's 'double-consciousness'. She survives by acting out the love that others feel for her, and so, she says, avoids the 'subjection' of love, an outburst accompanied by tragic display:

She raised her arms till they were bare to the elbow, her brow was contracted in one deep fold, her eyes were closed, her voice was smothered: in her dusky flame-coloured garment, she looked like a dream visitant from some region of departed souls.[42]

Thus Eliot estranges herself from her major predecessor by critically exposing the Rachelesque attitudes that Brontë had summoned up for Vashti. In a similar way, she inverts the racial inspiration of Disraeli's *Tancred* by having Deronda's revulsion at his mother's tragic pretence serve to deepen his commitment to his people's cause. And the correctness of Deronda's response would seem to be confirmed when Mirah, the woman that he will marry, whose background is sketched in an interpolation resembling the

Baroni story, proves her potential as a wife and her dignity as a Jewess by abandoning her career as a performer, despite her undoubted talent.

The rival options of performer or wife being unavailable to her, Gwendolen is left to confront alone the doubtful possibilities of an independent female life. Her final stasis reflects the novel's inability to reconcile its two guiding principles. While conventional theatrical types have been used to convey the crippling influence of pre-established identities, the narration, with less than convincing optimism, has frequently argued that the past can be thrown off according to the development of private experience.[43] Yet theatrical images are the product of a confrontation between performer and spectator, and belong to a social nexus; which is why in *Daniel Deronda* Eliot chose to make theatrical history one of her starting-points, her means of enquiry, not least into her own experience.

Chapter 6 might even be read as her version (playful or retaliatory) of Lewes's nostalgia, especially his reverence for Rachel. Gwendolen's strategic use of the pillar, her consciousness of personal effect, breaks the rule of total involvement that Lewes had derived from his study of the French *tragédienne* – yet, in the event, not only is Gwendolen effective despite herself, at the moment of crisis even she loses self-consciousness. Although she may be thought naive when she offers her physical attributes as evidence of her Rachelesque potential (as Lewes had always insisted, Rachel's genius lay in her ability to transform her body), nevertheless her rebuke to her mother – 'The more feminine a woman is, the more tragic it seems' – is an unwitting critique of the proposition debated by Lewes and Brontë in the early 1850s that the less 'feminine' a woman might appear, then the more tragic she might be. For Gwendolen Harleth, there will be no refuge in the 'inhuman' and the 'diabolic'. It may not be insignificant that memories of Rachel, Lewes's forte, should here be the prerogative of Gwendolen's foolish and conventional mother. Was George Eliot's failure to appreciate Rachel, whom she first saw in the company of Lewes in 1853, eventually vindicated when, writing in the 1870s a novel that is set in the 1860s, she could cite the actress and the mystique of the tragedy queen as a Romantic anachronism?

CONCLUSION: 'THERE ALWAYS SEEMED SOMETHING NOT HUMAN ABOUT HER'

Lewes's work as a dramatic critic falls into four phases: the early reviews in the *Atlas* in 1846, 'Vivian''s contributions to the *Leader* in the early 1850s, the *Retrospects of Actors* series in the *Pall Mall Gazette* in the 1860s, and the compilation of *On Actors and the Art of Acting*, which coincided with the rekindling of his interest through the London appearances of Salvini. In his last essay on the theatre, 'First Impressions of Salvini 1875',[44] he came to the conclusion that 'Tragic pathos to be grand should be *impersonal*'. Lingering Romantic notions of tragedy, which required that the spectator be exposed to extreme individual suffering, were about to undergo a subtle change, already foreshadowed in the repudiation of Hugo. In Lewes's late formulation, 'impersonality' is a means through which sympathy is engendered by the absence of self-pity in the tragic protagonist: 'Grief, however intense, however wild in its expression, when borne with a sense of its being part of our general heritage, excites the deepest sympathy'. Out of such precepts, austere enough for George Eliot herself, a modernist aesthetic would eventually emerge, taking 'impersonality' as its cornerstone.

For the most part, though, Lewes's critical terminology remained stable throughout his career. Like all Victorian critics, he had no qualms about repeating himself: to pay the same tributes to a performer time after time simply proved their lasting power. Creativity was not yet threatened by consistency – it was Sarah Bernhardt, late in the century, who was to bring on that fear. And perhaps it is this homogenising tendency in dramatic criticism that most convincingly proves the superiority of novels when it comes to rendering the evanescence of theatrical experience.

Disraeli's Jewish heroine, Brontë's insubordinate female, Eliot's decayed ideal: in each case Rachel threatens to pre-empt the narrative in which she intervenes, but in each case she fails, and her appearance turns out to have been an unreliable foreshadowing of closure. Novels can reconstitute the effect of a performance; they are formally unable to recuperate the uncertainties of its moment. Yet if they are to liberate history, and if their events are to seem less than wholly predetermined, they may still strive for the immediacy of drama. The theatrical episode then becomes a display of achievements that each novel must aim to replace with its own more deeply provisional sense of what lies ahead.

What Lewes recorded in his portrait of Rachel was his own lingering Romantic susceptibility to 'terrible beauty', the enlarging spectacle that individual suffering affords the spectator, a world of grief unexpectedly concentrated in Racine's single figures. What the Victorian novel provided was an antidote, an appropriate form for an enquiry into the increasingly antiquated grounds that underlay his attempts to preserve the inimitable. Was there or might there be such a woman as Lewes wrote of, the novelists asked? Invariably they answered no.

CHAPTER 3

Memories of Plessy: Henry James restages the past

In chapter 7 of Henry James's *The Tragic Muse* (1890) an aspirant English actress called Miriam Rooth is taken by an English diplomat, a keen *amateur* of the French stage called Peter Sherringham, together with Peter's friends, Nick Dormer, a would-be painter, and Gabriel Nash, a wandering English Aesthete, to meet Madame Carré, a distinguished French actress. They assemble in her drawing-room which is packed with 'votive offerings . . . the presents, the portraits, the wreaths, the diadems, the letters, framed and glazed, the trophies and tributes and relics collected by Madame Carré during half a century of renown'; these are the mementoes that convert it 'into a theatrical museum'.[1]

Though now retired from the Comédie-Française, Carré still offers lessons and Sherringham's idea is that she will evaluate Miriam's potential. So she does, briskly apportioning judgements when Miriam displays different aspects of her still undeveloped talents. Carré's manner is autocratic as befits her status, her discriminations apparently respected, and yet, through the responses of both Sherringham and Nash, and even of Miriam, James creates a scenario in which it is the teacher herself who is also under scrutiny, the *doyenne* who is being measured by what she was, by what her professional life means today, now that it is over.

This historical placing is immediately apparent in Nash's reply when first she greets them: '*Ah, la voix de Célimène!*' he exclaims (94). The voice of the youthful *grande coquette* in Molière's *Le Misanthrope* no doubt, but issuing from a bizarre source since 'Célimène wore a big red flower on the summit of her dense wig, had a very grand air, a toss of the head and sundry little majesties of manner; in addition to which she was strange, almost grotesque, and to some people would have been even terrifying, capable of reappearing, with her hard eyes, as a queer vision in the darkness' (94).

Figure 4. Madame Plessy as Emma in *La Fille D'Honneur c.* 1835

We know, because Peter Sherringham knows, that Carré had indeed played Célimène, had been tutored in the role (though the mentor goes unnamed) by the 'great *comédienne*, the light of the French stage in the early years of the century' (92). We know, too, that Carré had gone on to play many other celebrated roles, including Clorinde in Emile Augier's *L'Aventurière*. Later in this chapter Carré and Miriam will together recite the scene from Act III of the *L'Aventurière* in which Clorinde, the adventuress, by profession an actress, is confronted by Célie, the *ingénue*, fiancée of the son of the ancient widower Clorinde plans to seduce into marriage. Should she succeed in her deception, Clorinde, who operates in collaboration with her drunken braggart of a brother, will gain not only money but social respectability. James gives us just one line from the play – Clorinde's '*Vous ne me fuyez pas, mon enfant, aujourd'hui*' – and, to draw attention to the game he is playing, reverses the obvious casting so that young Miriam recites old Clorinde's speeches to old Carré's young Célie.

Though set in sixteenth-century Italy, *L'Aventurière* was thought at its première in 1848, and even much later, to be distinctly contemporary in what it had to say about female behaviour and James must surely have hoped that at least a few of his readers would have been able to recall the subsequent lines, including the powerful words in which Clorinde justifies her treachery:

> Oui, ma vie est coupable, oui, mon coeur a failli . . .
> Mais vous ne savez pas de quels coups assailli!
> Comment le sauriez-vous, âme chaste et tranquille,
> A qui la vie est douce et la vertu facile,
> Enfant qui pour gardiens de votre tendre honneur
> Avez une famille et surtout le bonheur! . . .
> Comment le sauriez-vous ce qu'en de froides veilles,
> Le pauvreté murmure à de jeunes oreilles?
> Vous ne comprenez pas, n'ayant jamais eu faim,
> Qu'on renonce à l'honneur pour un morceau de pain.[2]

Even if Miriam's tones fail to match the passion of Augier's lines – 'a long, strong, colourless voice came quavering from her young throat' (102) – Sherringham nevertheless responds instinctively to her physical appearance, finding in her an extraordinary resemblance not to Carré, but to another French actress of the past:

She frowned portentously; her low forehead overhung her eyes; the eyes themselves, in shadow, stared, splendid and cold, and her hands clinched themselves at her sides. She looked austere and terrible . . . (102)

That vignette evokes, quite unmistakably, one of the most potent images of Rachel Félix,[3] the great *tragédienne* of the mid-century who set the standards of hard work that Carré still respects. "'I don't care a straw for your handsome girls'", Carré will say, "'but bring me the one who is ready to drudge the tenth part of the way Rachel drudged, and I'll forgive her her beauty'" (106).

It is an essential part of James's quasi-historical scheme that he should have us believe that Carré was once the contemporary of Rachel, and that she should share the *tragédienne's* professional values. In this respect alone, Carré's fictional career matches that of one real-life French actress, and one only: Madame Plessy, who lived from 1819 to 1897,[4] who had been comedy's answer to Rachel's triumph in tragedy, whose performance as Célimène had been coached by the renowned Romantic actress, Mlle Mars, the 'light of the French stage in the early years of the century'.

Starting young, Plessy made her début at the Comédie-Française in 1834 as Emma in *La fille d'Honneur* by Alexandre Duval, ascending to the roles previously the property of Mars: Elmire in *Tartuffe* as well as Célimène. Her repertoire also included Suzanne in *Le Mariage de Figaro* together with roles in the newer *pièces bien faites* of Scribe and in the Romantic drama of Augier, in particular his *L'Aventurière*, which she had famously revived in 1860 and played into the 1870s. According to Pougin's *Dictionnaire historique et pittoresque du théâtre* of 1885 she was incomparable in these parts; she made them her own.[5]

Throughout her career Plessy paid many visits to London and took a regular part in the French seasons at the St James that had begun in 1842. Three years later, in 1845, immediately following the visit of Macready and his company to Paris, she reciprocated by appearing at the St James as part of John Mitchell's 'French Play' season. It was then that she caused something of a stir by marrying the writer Auguste Arnould and, instead of returning to Paris, departing for a long and remunerative engagement in St Petersburg, despite an attempt made by Mitchell to keep her in London by matching roubles with pounds. From the point of view of the Comédie-Française the move to Russia was intolerably disrespectful (she was actually taken to court for breach of contract in 1846) but Plessy was still a sufficiently valuable property to be accepted back as a *pensionnaire* in 1855, and she stayed with the company until her retirement, when she took up teaching.[6] At the *maison de Molière*, she specialised not only in the house dramatist but, later, in eighteenth-century comedy, in particular Araminte in *Les Fausses Confidences*, a predilection that James's *Tragic Muse* acknowledges obliquely by having old Carré interrupt a conversation with 'charming overdone stage-horror and the young hands of the heroines of Marivaux' (271).[7]

It may well have been Plessy in *L'Aventurière* that James saw on his very first visit to the Comédie-Française in 1870.[8] In any case, she soon assumed symbolic status in his personal gallery of performers, living embodiment of history, of French theatre and all that came to stand for in his enthralled perception of a European lineage in which ancient performers counted for as much as the dramatic characters they impersonated through the influence 'of a personal set of idiosyncrasies, the voice, the look, the step, the very *physique* of a performer'.[9] Even so, running alongside James's 'veneration' for what he said the French called Plessy's 'authority', her 'spirit and style and grace', was his allowance that 'there is something always rather hard and metallic in her style' (50), and his awareness of what others had long seen as the limitations of tradition, the widespread accusation that Plessy, in particular, was 'too mincing and too artificial' (89).

Indeed, in some quarters, Plessy who was short in stature with a small mouth that she accentuated by much pursing of her lips or '*minauderie*' (smirking) was controversial. Some found her respectability unattractive, disliked her air of antiquity, and considered her theatrical inheritance to be flawed.[10] Though aware of these charges, James could not, at first, bring himself to concede their justice since, to him, 'Madame Plessy's *minauderies*, her grand airs and her arch-refinements have never been anything but the odorous swayings and queenly tossings of some splendid garden. Madame Plessy's. Never had an actress grander manners. When Madame Plessy represents a duchess you have no allowances to make.' Even if her 'limitations are on the side of the pathetic', even if 'she is brilliant, she is cold; and I cannot imagine her touching the source of tears' (89), James still preferred to maintain that the broader cultural significance of his favourite actress outweighed any expressive deficiencies she might also possess.

In *The Tragic Muse*, then, James has Carré listen for a repeat of herself in Miriam, much as her real life model, Madame Plessy, had echoed, though imperfectly, Mlle Mars. Yet the lesson of the novel overall will be that even if the past can occasionally be ventriloquised, usually inadequately, it can never be fully re-embodied. An initial description of Carré's drawing-room has already warned us of

the confession of something missed, something hushed, which seemed to rise from it all and make it melancholy, like a reference to clappings which, in the nature of things, could now only be present as a silence: so that if the place was full of history, it was the form without the fact, or at the most a redundancy of the one to a pinch of the other – the history of a mask, of a squeak, a series of movements in the air. (91)

And, much later, Sherringham will find himself meditating that 'Miriam Rooth's face seemed to him to-day a finer instrument than old Madame Carré's', and will conclude that 'It was doubtless that the girl's was fresh and strong, with a future in it, while poor Madame Carré's was worn and weary, with only a past' (151). The passing of time, James insinuates, is measured cruelly by the pastness of performance, by ageing bodies and, equally cruelly, by changing tastes, new demands. At the same time James allows for new possibilities. The career of Miriam Rooth lies in the future; she will have to make her own way, as she is beginning to do when the novel ends, with plays far removed from those of Carré's world. Miriam will never reincarnate Carré, let alone Plessy, let alone Rachel; she may though become herself, whatever we (or James) may think of that.

In 1876, at the time of Plessy's retirement, James insisted that the 'conditions of artistic production are directly hostile to the formation of actresses as consummate as and as complete'. 'One may not expect to see her like, any more than one may expect to see a new manufacture of old lace and old brocade', he admitted. 'She carried off with her something that the younger generation of actresses will consistently lack – a certain largeness of style and robustness of art' (89–90). What James did not care to say, or perhaps in 1876 had yet to realise, was that, while they might lack 'a certain largeness of style and robustness of art', a younger generation of actresses would actively strive to leave Plessy's *coquetterie* behind. More than a decade later, in *The Tragic Muse*, he was obliged to concede the point.

A *roman à clef* only in the sense that its characters are composites, hypothetical lives made up from available material and from personal encounters, *The Tragic Muse* records an extended period of change,[11] showing how such processes came about, and how they felt at the time. That is why its surface is carefully scattered with verbal and visual memorabilia (many of them relating to Plessy) which hark back to moments that might be personal, shared, or even institutional. Readers must bring what they know, and what they can remember. As its author was very much aware, most theatre survives not only as a kind of mental residue, but in objects which act like mnemonics, whose very fragility speaks the ephemeral truth of the art they commemorate: 'the form without the fact'.

SOCIAL GESTURES

Henry James's memories of Plessy, so deeply embedded in his consciousness that she came to stand for the passing of time itself, were his personal take on a career that, more than most, had flourished and suffered with the emergence of new ideas, and on a style of acting that was revived, eroded, and finally displaced in the course of the nineteenth century as a whole. We can think of it as the slow demise of *la grande coquette*, the type perfected by Mars for Romantic tastes, as well as a chapter in the endless sequence of transformations of the 'natural' that make up theatrical history. Plessy's audiences certainly changed their minds. In 1855 Charles Dickens, in Paris with Wilkie Collins at the time of Louis-Napoleon's first Paris exhibition, saw and admired her in *La Joconde*, a play by his friend François Joseph Regnier, and he wrote enthusiastically to the author, 'If I could see an English actress with but one hundredth part of the nature and art of Madame Plessy, I should believe our English theatre to be a fair way toward its regeneration'.[12] He ended, coupling politeness with genuine resignation: 'I have no hope ever of beholding such a phenomenon'. Twenty-five years later, in 1880, he was sighing, 'the Lord deliver us from Plessy's mechanical ingenuousness'.[13]

This prolonged turnaround is not to be attributed solely to personal preferences. Dickens undoubtedly had mixed feelings about some aspects of French theatre, but he delighted in others: in French melodrama, for instance, holding that Frédérick Lemaître was the supreme actor of the age. He had admiring friendships with Regnier and with Charles Fechter, the French actor who was credited with bringing a new kind of relaxed naturalism to the English stage. Whenever Dickens visited Paris, and he did so constantly throughout the 1850s and 1860s, play-going was always part of the anticipated pleasure.[14] In London he knew John Mitchell and paid appropriate attention to the many French actresses who came to the St James.[15]

But, as his jokes at the expense of the unities in *Nicholas Nickleby*, and his antipathy to Rachel – 'odious'[16] – make very clear, Dickens did have profound difficulties with neo-classicism. This instinctive dislike of the stuffier French styles was at one with his conviction that acting, at its best, was always a mode of authenticity. 'But is it not always true, in comedy and in tragedy, that the more real the man the more genuine the actor?',[17] he wrote when he witnessed the intensity of grief displayed by Regnier at the funeral of the Frenchman's own fourteen-year-old daughter. For Dickens an inbuilt capacity to feel and to express was inseparable from moral integrity. The best acting always brings out truths about the actor so that, even when impersonating a villain, the 'genuine' performer will seize the opportunity to show just what wickedness can do, providing evidence of his moral imagination through the clarity and discretion of his rendering. Dickens, the great scourge of moral hypocrisy in life, would not have been greatly impressed by Diderot's theatrical 'paradox', which argues for a necessarily critical space between actors and their roles: for Dickens, dramatic modes that were conventional and unyielding made the essential sincerity, the 'naturalness', of acting almost impossible to achieve.

Whereas Dickens's position on the emotional importance of acting was at least unambiguous, and unlikely to respect either the force of staid tradition or the value of personal subtlety alone, for some of his mid-Victorian contemporaries there was the possibility of a more measured approach. G. H. Lewes borrowed Talma's term, '*optique de théâtre*', to describe the appropriateness of style to character which creates an effect of the 'natural' through the application of symbolic devices.[18] In Lewes's eyes, both Rachel and Plessy benefited from this aesthetic. Just as he allowed Rachel to be the supreme tragic actress because she represented her roles with an intensely physical literalness, so he recognised that Plessy, because she was 'the most musical, the most measured, the most incisive speaker (whether of verse or prose) now on stage', was equally natural in her comic roles.[19] According to the '*optique de théâtre*', naturalness in acting is a matter of proportion of measure, of balance; and Lewes took matters of diction very seriously, to the extent that he could write that, although she was capable of expressing 'the quintessence of feminine wile' (190) and was 'as a woman, without much charm', Plessy remained always 'well worth studying, not only because of the refined naturalness of her manner, but also on account of the exquisite skill of her elocution' (194). For Lewes, reliably perfect delivery was enough to counter any suspicions of the 'mechanical ingenuousness' that Dickens eventually came to loathe.

English interest in French acting has invariably to be related to current battles within the English theatre where foreigners were often brought in as counters for debate. This was certainly the case in the 1840s when English perceptions of Plessy were heavily coloured by the comparison between different schools of acting. The French might be stuck with a rigidly formalised theatrical tradition, but at least that was serious, and, in any case, they did seem to be anxious to develop, in directions that owed much to the ways of the English, above all to Shakespeare.

Plessy became caught up in this cross-channel exchange early on. When William Charles Macready and his company, which included Helen Faucit, visited Paris in late 1844 and early 1845 Plessy was on hand to help with the hospitality, perhaps because of her previous experience in England. If, in comparison with the theatrical events of 1828–9, when Macready and Harriet Smithson had inflamed the Romantic aspirations of Berlioz and Delacroix, the Paris season 1844–5 seems anti-climactic, we should bear in mind that the primary aim of the later trip was consolidation of what was by then an established cultural phenomenon. If Mitchell actually hoped to set up an English theatre in the French capital on the basis of native interest, this was because the palpable contrasts between the two theatrical traditions were still ripe for exploitation.[20]

Where Smithson had been revolutionary and explosive, Faucit offered a graceful, 'feminine' softness and, by French standards, an unusual ability to transform herself to suit a variety of different roles. Later she remembered 'how strange they seemed to think it, that the same actress should play Juliet, Ophelia, Desdemona, and Lady Macbeth – impressing each, as they were indulgent enough to say, with characteristics so distinct and so marked, as to make them forget the actress in the women she represented'.[21] Macready may, in respect for local custom, have closed the curtain at the very moment when Othello murdered Desdemona,[22] but still the French who, according to some reports, considered it indecorous even to applaud, were enraptured, or at any rate intrigued, by the artistic difference of English acting. And this reaction meant that English members of the Paris audience were fascinated in turn to discover their inscrutable neighbours engaged with an alien style.

So near, and yet so far – united, yet severed by an impassable gulf, we sat. Nations, like individuals, know each other but in part; they cannot penetrate the labyrinth of each other's thoughts.[23]

All too true. On 16 January 1845 there was a gala evening held at the Tuileries in front of the French Royal family, the diplomatic corps and an audience of 500–600. The entertainment was made up of *Hamlet*, performed by Macready and his company, and *The Day after the Wedding*, a farcical variation on *The Taming of the Shrew* by Marie-Thérèse De Camp, in which Plessy played Lady Elizabeth Freelove in English 'with accustomed grace'.[24] The following evening Plessy repeated the same performance while Macready gave the death scene from *Henry IV* and Helen Faucit portions of Juliet. Yet, both on and off the stage, the seasons were shrouded in diplomacy, of several kinds. Away from the theatre there was considerable tension in political circles as a result of clashes between English and French agents in the distant protectorate of Tahiti.[25] On stage, Faucit, who was allowed by Macready to play Ophelia to his Hamlet for the very first time, appears to have been infatuated with her leading man, which may have brought a special intensity to her performances, but caused personal irritation and embarrassment. A few French observers, including Théophile Gautier, believed, for some reason, that Plessy's gestures were a cheeky parody of Macready's mannerisms, while Macready in turn found her 'sometimes graceful, but not quite concentrated enough in the passion'.[26] At the final grand gala the French Emperor presented Macready, a stalwart Republican, with an encrusted dagger in an exquisitely chiselled gold case, its hilt apparently 'enriched with diamonds, and other precious stones'.[27] The actor subsequently discovered the whole thing to be paste.

When, later that spring, Plessy reciprocated by playing in London she again performed Lady Elizabeth Freelove and, again, there was curiosity about the piquant effect of French delivery on English words. Plessy's pointed emphases, every syllable in place, made a 'pretty mincing of our northern consonants'.[28] To speak in English was only to reveal yourself as ineradicably French. And, despite a generally polite response, the London papers (who, as we have seen in a previous chapter, had had similar difficulties with her mentor, Mlle Mars, some twenty years earlier)[29] sometimes found it hard to be wholeheartedly enthusiastic about the actress even in her more familiar native roles. Still bothered by her mannerisms, they note that sometimes her very quietness seemed to rule out the passion that they valued most in a performance.[30] Crabb Robinson, who actually found Plessy 'pleasing' and liked the way in which she enunciated verse, told his diary that, as for acting, he 'saw nothing but ladylike talk – genteel comedy when good excited no enthusiasms'.[31]

The same pattern was to be repeated when Plessy visited London at other times in the mid-century: the appreciation, even when warm, remained qualified. Her Suzanne in *Le Mariage de Figaro* may have been 'spirituelle',[32] but more often she was simply 'redolent of the *parfum de bonne Société*';[33] sometimes there was express relief at 'an entire absence of her usual mannerisms'[34] or, not much better, the kind of double-edged tribute which noted that 'there is charm and piquancy in her utterance that would make the dullest nonsense sound like bewitching eloquence'.[35] Plessy's obvious belief in her own power to deflect moral opprobrium, while entertaining her audience with the studied deployment of verbal subtleties and physical signals, was often felt to be unattractive and undramatic. There were growing complaints about her mannerisms, the way in which she ignored the dynamics of a situation in favour of 'pursing up her lips and elegantly posing her drapery'. No wonder that 'the continual puckering up of the lips in order to round a sentence nicely, and the everlasting smile, make the art rather an elocutionary than a dramatic effort'.[36]

When a role depended almost entirely on stylish dissembling, then English distaste became much more intense. This was above all true of Célimène, the role for which Plessy had been coached by Mars, the role which set her apart from all her rivals.[37] Though Rachel had, it is true, performed Célimène in London in 1847, even she had never dared to follow the venture through in Paris where memories of Mars and the present rivalry of Plessy were more serious threats. The antipathetic response to her London experiment must have also contributed to Rachel's decision not to repeat it in her native city:

In a certain sense the performance was perfect – there was not a single fault to find – but we doubt that sympathy between the artist and the person represented which can give a joyous naturalness to a part. With the agony and passion of Phèdre still in our minds, we find our imagination unsatisfied by the neat and polished Célimène.

So Lewes pronounced on Rachel in the *Atlas*.[38] Other critics were equally grudging about the play itself. 'The comedy has not a plot which is calculated to interest an English audience; it terminates most unsatisfactorily, and there is a heartlessness about the character of Célimène which produces a very disagreeable impression' – though in the early days Plessy's comic delicacy saw her through: 'threw a gloss over the less pleasant portion of the character, and was throughout warmly applauded'.[39] Later, as her poise became more confident so it became less welcome: the *grande coquette* was now under scrutiny on all sides.

If Célimène is the great instance of the *coquette* who may (or may not) redeem herself though her expressive self-control and her evident superiority to her courtly surroundings, Elmire, Plessy's role in *Tartuffe*, by merely mimicking *coquetterie*, raises rather different questions. When she issues her challenge to the lecherous *dévot* who has invaded her home – '*Faites-le moi descendre*' – does Elmire risk exposing her own sensual nature to temptation? Alternatively, is she entirely confident in her inherent virtue? In which case, might she not then be said to behave with a dishonest streak comparable to that of the hypocrite himself? Plessy herself claimed that if there was no risk then there was no scene, but still insisted that the point of her performance was to show how Elmire's virtue would always protect her.[40] But the actress's proven ability as *une grande coquette* meant that for some, not all, she would never be quite as effective as Elmire, the housewife who risks her honour for her husband, than as Célimène, the court beauty who cruelly mocks her male suitors with her evident sensuality.[41]

With all nineteenth-century versions of *la grande coquette* the issues remained much the same as they had been in the case of Mlle Mars. Does flirtation imply a deep female trait that permeates the whole being or is it rather a means of preserving autonomy, exerting control, possibly for moral ends? Can sexual attractiveness be used safely as a trap, as a deceitful weapon against harassment? Or is *coquetterie* in a young woman simply a sign of a misguided upbringing?

English and French views on these matters could be very different. George Eliot was happy simply to describe Hetty Sorrel plotting to seduce Adam Bede 'as if she had been an elegantly clad coquette alone in her boudoir', because it was her intention as narrator simply to expose social pretension and suggest common ground: 'it is noteworthy how closely her mental processes may resemble those of a lady in society and crinoline, who applies her refined intellect to the problem of committing indiscretions without compromising herself'.[42] And when T. W. Robertson adapted *L'Aventurière* for English audiences as *Home* in 1869,[43] he provided no real equivalent for the lines of self-justification that Clorinde, the sexual adventuress, speaks in Augier's original, the lines that Henry James had Miriam recite in *The Tragic Muse*. Instead, there is a final confessional which the adventuress (no longer a professional actress, but a harmless musician) calls her 'punishment' and in which she lays most blame upon her sinister male accomplice:

I am not all to blame. I never knew a mother's love or guidance . . . I am but a woman, and I had been schooled into the belief that all the world was bad. This home, your father's kindness, your sister's gentleness, and this young lady's goodness, have taught me better. I have one talent, music! And that will enable me to live away from this bad, silly man, whom I have now renounce for ever. Forgive me for the evil I might have worked you. If ever you should hear of me, you will know that my repentance is sincere.[44]

Robertson opts for domestic pathos where, in the original, Augier had rescued Clorinde with self-justification as well as contrition, allowing her a moral condition that was problematic and complex. Correspondingly, in contrast with the popular English stress on hearth and home, Plessy's stylish courtly ways made her seem not only insensitive, heartless, but increasingly irrelevant. First Molière, next Marivaux and then a string of other parts in *la grande coquette* mode: all connected her with the past. This is surely why her mannerisms, which had always been suspect, eventually became for some English observers, Dickens among them, quite intolerable.

But even the French had problems with the latter-day Plessy:

These days she hears herself speaking, and she speaks as much like a woman in a dream as a woman in a swoon. Listening to her it is impossible to understand how she has gathered so many admirers around her, for she is really not a living person at all. Every movement is measured; every blink of the eye is calculated.[45]

That appeared in *La Revue des Deux Mondes* as early as 1856. When Francisque Sarcey tried to sum up her career twenty years later he found himself reviewing his own past responses. Here was an actress, still in the shadow of Mars, whose strengths lay not so much in the representation of great passion (certainly not tragic passion as she had demonstrated with a disastrous Agrippina in Racine's *Britannicus*) so much as *nuance*. Sarcey had seen her for the first time when he was still a student and had been greatly disappointed: 'She seemed to me simpering and coquettish – too affected and refined'.[46] Later, he had come to appreciate her more, though he was unenthusiastic about her Clorinde, for all that it marked a break with her established roles. When it came to Molière, Sarcey maintained, rather against the grain, that she made a better Elmire than she did a Célimène. But this was largely because her performances in Marivaux coloured his view of her in plays by the earlier playwright. For Sarcey, Plessy's unique skill lay in representing characters from the milieu of the eighteenth-century *haute bourgeoisie* where it was mandatory to imitate aristocratic manners. It followed that her representation of Elmire, a wife, a mother and a householder, whom Sarcey saw as a kind of prototype *bourgeois* woman, would necessarily be more engaging than her attempt to become Célimène, the heartless creature produced by the even more distant life style of a seventeenth-century court.

Sarcey writes as a man of his own generation for whom Plessy's *grandes coquettes* became more explicable, if not always more interesting, when they could be referred back, in a reverse replay taking in Mlle Mars, to the *ancien régime*. As with some other French performers, the self-consciously aristocratic style, though it might attract some elements in a post-Revolutionary audience, would always alienate others. Theatre being an art of the present, as well as an object of antiquarian study, the appeal of her old-fashioned *minauderie* had to be disowned before it could be appreciated – and that, at least, was true on both sides of the Channel.

BERNHARDT BREAKS OUT

At first Henry James tried to stay faithful to his earlier vision. Plessy's retirement in May 1876, the 'brilliant solemnity' of her benefit, showed her once again to be, 'the last depository of certain traditions which can never, in the nature of things, be renewed. She was the perfect great lady of high comedy, as high comedy was possible before the invention of slang.' When, at the end of the evening, 'she took Mesdemoiselles Sarah Bernhardt and Croizette by the hands, and, with admirable grace, presented them to the public as her substitutes', James thought it 'more than likely that she had measured the irony of her gesture; for from the moment it takes two actresses to make up a Madame Plessy, the cause is obviously lost. Clever as these young ladies are they will not fill the void. Their art is small art; Madame Plessy's was great art.'[47]

But faith in the enduring charm of lost causes was hardly enough to withstand the calculated force for change that came about when an individual will and talent combined with a brilliantly astute recognition of a new constituency. In the summer of 1879, having as a member of the Comédie-Française troupe conquered London, having routed her rival, Sophie Croizette, Sarah Bernhardt saw her chance. She left the company and embarked on the independent career that was to last some forty years and to take her around the world in a repertoire of plays, each one selected to show her talents to their greatest advantage and to hold the attention of a modern audience. Ironically this meant reviving plays associated with past performers, but in a new guise.

Bernhardt had made her name in the plays of Victor Hugo – including *Hernani* – in the rehearsals for which Mlle Mars, the first Dona Sol, had famously quarrelled with the poet over the supposedly indecorous line, '*Vous êtes mon lion! superbe et généreux!*'[48] In contrast with Mars, Hugo's erotic *frisson* now suited Bernhardt very well indeed. In addition, she revived Desclée's *Froufrou*, Doche's *La Dame aux camélias* and brandished her modernised Phèdre, a role that, forty years on, was still replete with memories of Rachel. But just as she co-opted some aspects of the past, so Bernhardt implicitly disavowed others: first and foremost among them, the roles of Plessy.

The precise occasion, many said it was a pretext, for Bernhardt's final break from the Comédie was a bad review of her performance as Clorinde in *L'Aventurière* by the critic Auguste Vitu[49] in which he wrote that she made use of 'impetuosities, excessive in all ways'. These were not only vocal but involved 'certain movements of the body accompanied by the fists on the hips' which would have been more appropriate to Zola. In other words, they were blatantly sexual. Bernhardt blamed the whole fiasco on a lack of rehearsal and walked out.[50] She was replaced by Croizette who had been trained in the part by Plessy herself, and who played it in a sober brown velvet dress quite different from the bright yellow satin creation favoured by Bernhardt and thought by some to be unsuitable for a fallen woman on the brink of repentance.[51]

Never was the antithesis between two actresses more marked than that between Madame Plessy and Sarah Bernhardt. The former, *grande dame* to her finger-tips, incomparable as an elocutionist, the embodiment of careful, painstaking study of every most minute effect, and exquisite in the refinement of her manner; the latter, impulse, instinct and imagination personified . . . But Mdlle Bernhardt was, it is now evident, under the influence of her nerves; she played excitedly – shall I say recklessly?[52]

Bernhardt never played Clorinde again. She renounced Plessy's *grande coquette* for good. Or rather, she shifted the motivational emphasis from the *coquette* to the *nerveuse* while retaining the sexual flamboyance of the established type. To act the flattering *coquette* had been to play with false faces and, in order to maintain the essential gap between what is suggested, physically and verbally, and what is actually on offer, it was essential that both actress and character had absolute physical control. This devious inauthenticity – a slippage between the bodily sign and emotional or intellectual initiative behind it – protected the *coquette*, made her morally interesting, but at a certain dramatic cost. Unlike the tragic heroine, the *coquette* was never 'abandoned', never lost consciousness, was never at one with herself, whereas the *nerveuse* (or the 'hysteric' as she was coming to be known and would soon be described by Freud) was at the mercy of an inner compulsion that pushed to the surface. The hysteric may have had a body that was out of control, but it could not help but be expressive; it manifested what has been called 'a condition of bodily writing'.[53]

To put that another way: *nerveuses*, unlike *coquettes*, do not act roles; they perform themselves, a distinction that was becoming increasingly important in the developing naturalism of late nineteenth-century theatre. An inability to sustain the part of a *coquette* is what kills the heroine in Meilhac and Halévy's seminal *Froufrou*, and yet in Ibsen's *A Doll's House* her perception of the falseness of coquetry provides Nora Helmer with the precondition of her liberation. That Sarah Bernhardt could triumph in the one, but never even attempt the other, had much to do with her adherence to the lingering Romantic cult that linked sex with death. That there was also, at the same time, a universal readiness to renounce or redefine the *coquette* and to welcome the new type is shown by Bernhardt's ability to make the *nerveuse* commercial, popular, and international and to make theatrical erotics democratic, available to all audiences, including those made up in an unusually large part by women.[54]

Perhaps, though, some members of her audience recalled that Bernhardt's breakthrough, her subversion of Plessy, had been foreshadowed by another remarkable actress, now dead, but still mourned. The performances of Aimée Desclée (subject of a later chapter) had reflected, even more accurately than those of Bernhardt were to do, the mood surrounding the Franco-Prussian war and the Commune, when the sexual relationships represented in the plays of Dumas *fils*, the arch misogynist, were taken to be symptomatic of national trauma.

By an apt coincidence, Desclée's London début in 1873 overlapped Plessy's last season in the capital. In theatrical terms alone this was an auspicious spring in that, before the young actress could perform her repertoire, her management had to fight the long-standing ruling of the Lord Chamberlain which banned the more *risqué* works of Augier, Hugo, and Dumas *fils*.[55] And, even if it was reported in London that Plessy had recommended to the Comédie-Française that it should engage Desclée,[56] and some thought that she might attempt Célimène, it was generally agreed that Desclée's innovative presence was of a very different order from that of the *grande coquette*. Desclée 'était une femme de 1871',[57] her mode was strangely realistic, and yet she was no simple flirt, but something more complex. As the critic of *The Spectator* put it: 'Madame Arnould Plessy and Mademoiselle Aimée Desclée are the leading representatives of their respective wholly distinct orders of dramatic art'.

On the one hand, Plessy:

There is no vehement gesture, not a word is spoken above the natural tone of a highly-bred woman's voice; but what subtle expression there is in the slight shiftings of the hands, in the action of the wrist and forearm, quite peculiar to Madame Plessy, in the perfectly enunciated sentences, wherein no point is ever omitted, or ever forced, in the delicate intonation which marks her relation to each person in the scene, in every motion where movement is necessary; in the easy, dignified attitude when she sits still and listens, as none but she, even among French actors can listen, without the slightest indication that she knows what is coming next, or ever so faint recognition of the presence of 'the House'.

On the other hand, Desclée:

intense passion, the noiseless entrance, the gentle approach, the hopeless questioning, the quick inspiration of relief, hope, faith, joy, resolve; the wild clinging embrace of perfect reconciliation, the 'at last!' that is in every line of the face, in every quivering nerve . . .[58]

Significantly enough, although Plessy won dry respect for her performances in her long-established roles, she was applauded most wholeheartedly for her unusual appearance in a play by Dumas *fils*, *Les Idées de Madame Aubray*, in which she played a mother who is obliged to consent to her only son's marriage to a fallen woman:

> Suppressed anguish, heart-broken despair, and a distorted nervous system has seldom been displayed with more truth, less exaggeration, and more consummate force. She is crying inwardly. The eyes are red and wet but there are no tears; the whole frame is agitated with suppressed convulsion; the fingers twist and wring the lace pocket-handkerchief, which assists the exhibition of a strong woman with a great sorrow hardly under control.[59]

'A distorted nervous system', the very phrase heralds the future. Even Plessy benefited briefly, and perhaps inadvertently, from the criteria that were to surpass her.

'You can't be a great actress without quivering nerves', Henry James would have Gabriel Nash proclaim, ironically but accurately, about Miriam Rooth in *The Tragic Muse* (439). Dedicated to the old, always alert to the new, James would soon go on to describe Ibsen's fictional character, Hedda Gabler, as 'furiously nervous'.[60]

All of which left Plessy's reputation suspended in the past, like one of Madame Carré's 'votive objects'. Frederick Wedmore's precise summing up of Plessy's career at the time of her retirement in 1876 suggests that, in the hierarchy of actors, her position, while indubitably her own, was second-rank, eventually leading nowhere: 'the concentrated but subdued passions of Desclée was as far from her as the poetical reverie of Sarah Bernhardt'.[61] Which may be just, though it lacks James's philosophical anguish in the face of his lost cause. '*Quelle connaissance de la scène . . . et de la vie*', the novelist had once heard one of the 'old gentlemen' who haunted the orchestra of the Théatre-Français murmur about Plessy. That was in 1872 when James was still under thirty; the 'old gentlemen' were 'classic play-goers' who looked 'as if they took snuff from boxes adorned with portraits of the fashionable beauty of 1820'.[62] Four years later, in a specific comparison with Plessy, James was to describe Bernhardt and Croizette as 'children of a later and eminently contemporary type, according to which the actress undertakes not to interest but to fascinate. They are charming – "awfully" charming; strange, eccentric, imaginative.'[63] Learning how to appreciate Plessy was one of the *rites de passage* of James's youth; the ability to recognise Bernhardt's novelty provided uncomfortable evidence that his maturity would take place in the context of the world's modernity, which would necessarily have to include the fascinating spectacle of the strange, eccentric, imaginative *nerveuse* who had replaced the classic *coquette*. It became Plessy's fate to demonstrate that not only is theatrical nostalgia always compensation for loss, but that private memories, however protected, are little match for the forces of historical change. Even in her lifetime the actress had become evidence of the past, no more, no less: her face, a 'mask'; her voice, 'a squeak'; her body, 'a record of movements on the air'.

CHAPTER 4

Déjazet/déja vu

'Soldiers and women. That's how the world is. Any other role is temporary. Any other role is a gesture.'
                                        Jeanette Winterson, *The Passion*[1]

On the evening of 6 May 1842 the French actress Virginie Déjazet opened her first London season at the St James Theatre with *Vert-Vert*, a play that had been an enormous success when she had first performed it at the Palais-Royal in Paris ten years earlier.[2] According to most reports it was equally well received when it eventually reached London. Most, but not quite all: for one of Fanny Kemble's letters, written at the time, tells us that Professor William Whewell, a well-known public figure who was there with his wife, walked out of the theatre in the middle of the first piece – 'I suppose from sheer disgust'.[3]

What had the Whewells seen and why did they leave? Why, throughout the nineteenth century, was this amusing French actress able to provoke such strong feelings among the English – usually of admiration, sometimes of distaste? After all, *Vert-Vert* is neither an obscene nor even an erotic play, certainly not in any modern sense. Adapted from a popular poem by the eighteenth-century writer Jean-Baptiste Louis Cresset about a parrot that escapes from a convent, samples the delights of the outside world and then returns to shock the nuns with vulgar language, it concerns a boy who has been brought up by a religious order of women so that he will develop feminine tendencies and not, like his father, die in a duel. On a visit to his mother he escapes with the convent gardener and has a series of adventures, including a meeting with a young actress who discovers that he is romantically naïve, and a stay at an inn with a pair of dragoons who have been separated from their wives, now housed in the convent. 'Vert-Vert' tricks the men into giving him their supper but rapidly becomes their companion, quickly educated into the ways of the military: alcohol, oaths and tobacco. Soon he is helping his new friends to infiltrate the convent

82

and become reconciled with their wives. At the end, all innocence lost, he determines to leave the convent for good and to join a regiment, taking the gardener with him. Déjazet, in 'powdered wig, green coat, and scarlet inexpressibles', played the boy.[4]

Not only does Fanny Kemble record the public outrage of the Whewells, she registers her own private shock at Déjazet's performance, most of all at the equanimity of the surrounding audience:

> The house was filled with our highest aristocracy, the stalls with women of rank and character, and the performance was, I think, one of the most impudent that I ever witnessed . . . She is a marvellous actress, and without exception the most brazen-faced woman I ever beheld, and that is saying a great deal.[5]

Later on, when she discussed the performance with the dowager Queen Adelaide (widow of William IV) and their mutual friend, Mlle d'Este, Kemble felt uneasy even at describing what she had seen:

> Upon her pressing me, however, to state my opinion upon the subject, I reiterated what I had said in a previous conversation with Mademoiselle d'Este upon the matter, objecting to the extreme immorality of the pieces, and expressing my astonishment at seeing decent Englishwomen crowd to them night after night, since they certainly would not tolerate such representations on the English stage.

Mlle d'Este replied that had the play been in English, the response might have been very different. Kemble, in turn, who had excellent French, consoled herself with the thought that Déjazet, 'the clever, cynical, witty, impudent Frenchwoman', would have taken pleasure in seeing 'these *dames trois fois respectables* swallow her performances *sans sourciller*'.[6]

At a later date, when Kemble again wrote about Déjazet in *Vert-Vert*, she was still stressing her amazement at the apparently uncomprehending audience:

> If you can conceive this part, acted to the life by a woman, who moves with more complete *disinvoltura* in her men's clothes than most men do, you may imagine something of the personal exhibition at which we assisted. As for me, my eyes and mouth opened wider and wider, not so much at the French actress, as at the well-born, well-bred English audience, who women as well as men, were in a perfect ecstasy of amusement and admiration. I certainly never saw more admirable acting, neither did I ever see such uncompromising personal exposure and such perfect effrontery of demeanour.

Even the most obvious point of comparison seemed otiose, since

> I do not think even ballet-dancers more indecent than Mademoiselle Déjazet, for their revelation of their limbs and shapes are partial and momentary, while

Figure 5. Virginie Déjazet by Nadar *c.* 1865

hers were abiding and entire through the whole of her performance, which she
acted in tight-fitting knee-breeches and silk stockings; nor did I ever see such an
unflinching representation of unmitigated audacity of carriage, look and manner,
male or female, on or off the stage.

Déjazet, says Kemble, always wears men's clothes on stage, and is rarely
seen without a cigar in her mouth. Witty in conversation, famous for her
'pungent repartees', she is nevertheless plain and 'has a disagreeable harsh
shrill voice in speaking; her figure is thin, but straight, and well made, and
her carriage and movements as graceful as they are free and unembarrassed;
her singing voice is sweet, and her singing charming, and her spirit and
talent as an actress incomparable'.

'If I had not seen it', Kemble concluded, 'I should not have believed
that so impudent a performance would have been tolerated here: tolerated
it not only was, but applauded with enthusiasm; and Mademoiselle Déjazet
carries the town before her, being the least decent actress of the most
indecent pieces I ever saw.'[7]

It was probably because of her own cosmopolitan education that Kemble
was so untypically critical in her responses to the actress. Marginal to both
cultures – English and French – she was well placed to observe the contrast
between them. She was unusual, too, in making such frank references to
the 'indecency' that Déjazet's performance could imply. Long after the
London première of *Vert-Vert* most English newspapers and critics were
still insisting upon Déjazet's 'tact' and 'perfect good taste', even if, as the
Atlas put it in 1844, 'Déjazet's assurance would probably, in the hands of
an English actress, degenerate into vulgar audacity'.[8]

The repeated insistence among English journalists that despite her
undoubted 'impudence' and 'audacity', Déjazet's stage demeanour was, by
and large, acceptable suggests that her audiences may have been well aware
of the unspecified risks she courted, yet usually kept at bay. Like other
Victorian performers considered dangerous in their day, Déjazet crossed
boundaries that have subsequently shifted beyond recognition.[9] Kemble's
glimpses of her on the London stage – and of the Whewells' disapproval –
bring formative differences back into focus.

Déjazet continued to feature in comparisons between English and French
theatre, not only because her typical performances marked a borderline
between what was permitted in London and what was freely available in
Paris, but because the rivalry between the two theatres had, by the mid-
century, a financial as well as a cultural significance. Following on from the
Dramatic Copyright Act of 1833, which had produced some improvement

in the economic situation of dramatists, the Theatre Regulation Act of 1843 resulted in greater opportunities for popular styles of performances, increased competition for roles, growing interest in theatrical matters and in cash rewards. The market for French plays translated into English was certainly growing, but so too was English resentment at lost or reduced revenue. In 1852 a further Copyright Act, 'so ill-drafted that it destroyed what it sought to promote', intensified competition between English and foreign dramatists still further by allowing indiscriminate adaptation of works from abroad, the great majority coming from France.[10]

This resulted in some strained or even contradictory attitudes. When, in 1852, Charles Mathews, actor, manager and husband of Madame Vestris, who had very often relied upon adaptations of pieces initiated by Déjazet,[11] defended his new policy of taking fewer French plays than before, it was on the intellectual grounds that not all French plays were suitable for English audiences. His example, which demonstrated culpable Gallic ignorance of English history, was a play about Mrs Siddons, who 'represented by the piquant Déjazet, puts on the disguise of a village idiot, and runs about the muddy lanes barefoot, accompanied by a mysterious stranger, who turns out to be "Sheridan"'.[12]

Yet when Mathews' own acting style was compared to Déjazet by his own sometime colleague J. R. Planché, a ferocious adaptor of French material, it was to disparaging effect. Mathews, said Planché, actually went out of his way to avoid passages of pathos and emotion. Consequently, whereas 'an English nobleman was wont to speak of Mdlle. Déjazet, the celebrated French actress (in a complimentary sense), as "the incarnation of impudence", Charles Mathews might have been called "the incarnation of *whim*"'.[13] Mathews' restraint was typically English, Déjazet's 'impudence' characteristically French – yet neither was quite adequate in itself, and each was hard to conceive of without the other.

Caught up in a web of manners, morals and money, the sparkling *vaudevilles* of Virginie Déjazet were to remain a test-case for Anglo-French theatrical relations. In France, though, despite her financial vicissitudes, her status went unquestioned to the very end, as Henry James made clear when he reported back to readers of the *New York Tribune* on Christmas Day 1875:

Mademoiselle Déjazet has just died, and 150,000 people have followed her to the grave. She was seventy-eight years of age, and she had acted almost uninterruptedly from her fifth to her seventy-seventh year. It was in its way a stupendous career. When she was a child she played the parts of old women, and as a septuagenarian she represented giddy lads and lasses. She has had the funeral of a crowned head; there could not be a better example of the ingrained Parisian passion for all things theatrical than this enormous manifestation of homage to the memory of a little old lady who was solely remarkable for the assurance with which she wore trousers and sang free-and-easy songs.[14]

For these grieving Parisians there was obviously a great deal more to Déjazet's 'stupendous career', as James terms it, than the wearing of trousers and the singing of 'free-and-easy songs', or even, for that matter, her long list of glamorous lovers, which had included Charles Fechter, the actor, and Arthur Bertrand, wealthy son of one of Napoleon Bonaparte's last allies. In 1842, when she made that first London appearance as Vert-Vert, Déjazet was already forty-four years old and had been appearing on the stage since she was five. Though she has been noticeably overlooked in the recent flurry of books about cross-dressing,[15] in the nineteenth century she was, along with Madame Vestris, *travesti*'s most celebrated exponent. In addition, she single-handedly transformed the art of *vaudeville* by 'bringing mournful canvases to life, elevating banal situations, making vigorously casual figures out of paltry characters, and finally transforming even incorrect dialogue into a special language, full of intentions, of feeling, and of variety'.[16]

It was largely thanks to Déjazet that *vaudeville* (the term had originally simply referred to an amusing song) developed into a full-length comedy of intrigue, though often relying on repeated tunes.[17] Even when *opéra comique* came into its own, *vaudeville* survived through the power of its wit and the opportunities it gave for individualistic performance. G. H. Lewes, for one, realised that Déjazet had the ability to make a line 'flash upon you as a brilliant witticism . . . a service which good actors render authors for which they do not often get the credit'.[18] With its essentially optimistic and unsatirical approach, its simple plot-lines, *vaudeville* was a typically self-contained product of the heavily censored theatre of nineteenth-century Paris.

Although that theatre was strictly controlled it was still quite varied, and moves between one theatre and another generally involved changes in repertoire; in Déjazet's case, these shifts reflected developments in what the *vaudeville* form was able to express. In 1806, appearing at the Théâtre des Jeunes Artistes, Déjazet was a dancer; in 1807 she moved to the Vaudeville, in 1817 to the Variétés, then, after a period in the provinces, to the Gymnase, where she created up to eighteen roles in a single season, ranging from Parisian *grisettes* to provincial peasants, many of them devised by the playwright Eugène Scribe. When Scribe went on to the Comédie-Française, Déjazet moved to the Nouveautés where she initiated another forty roles including, in 1830, an impersonation of the Emperor Napoleon in *Bonaparte à l'école de Brienne*. In one of the songs for this show Déjazet, as 'le petit caporal', dreamed of future glory, fully justifying a contemporary description of her role as a 'stage deification': 'Now the crown is ready / Shining on the altar / I'll take shelter there / Now it's on my head / I'm mortal no longer!'[19]

Once it was recognised that Déjazet had a flair for the kind of *travesti* that involved great historical personages, writers began to produce plays with her special talents in mind. In 1831 she moved to the Palais-Royal where she stayed for thirteen years, introducing *Vert-Vert* in 1832. It was at the Palais-Royal, too, that in 1839 she had a great personal success with *Les Premières armes de Richelieu* by Bayard, a former collaborator of Scribe, a play which she also performed during that first London season of 1842.

Richelieu, aged only fifteen, is married to Diane De Noailles, but is forbidden to spend time with her. He then becomes romantically involved with a much older woman and there is the threat of a duel. This, said the *Morning Post* in 1842, was one of Déjazet's very best *rôles travestis*:

It is, indeed, scarcely possible to wear with more gracefulness the various elegant costumes allotted to the *Duc de Richelieu*, and to invest with more fascination the youth who, in order to win the affections of his consort, seduces the wife of his friend. The renowned *roué* of the days of Louis XV would exult could he witness the lustre which his representative sheds over *un nom chéri des dames*.[20]

Like *Vert-Vert* the play is about initiation; the hero, again young, again played by a mature woman, learns what it is to be a man by imitating his elders. A revealing comparison might be made between Déjazet's amusing vehicle and the much weightier *Richelieu* by the English writer Bulwer-Lytton, which was staged at Covent Garden in March 1839. Bulwer's play, extravagantly spectacular, laden with historical detail, won some disapproval because of its author's prominently liberal views.[21] Déjazet, in contrast, escaped criticism in London by being relentlessly lightweight – though that, as we shall see, had its own implicit political significance.

Another Palais-Royal favourite, *La Lisette de Béranger* (1843) by Frédéric Bérat, had less success in London than *Richelieu*. In this sung monologue Déjazet evoked the leading character of Pierre-Jean Béranger's popular ballad *La Bonne Vielle*; Lisette is imagined surviving in a remote village where she tells her neighbours about the life of the poet who created her. In France *La Lisette* became, in effect, Déjazet's signature tune, which she delivered for over thirty years, invariably finishing her shows with it by public demand. In London, where the life and work of Béranger, a profoundly nationalistic poet, was less revered and his Republican sentiments not immediately to the point, the piece was less euphorically received.[22]

In 1844 Déjazet left the Palais-Royal, in 1845 she was back at the Variétés; in 1859, she took her own theatre, a tiny *salle* dating back to 1770, just off the, by then, largely destroyed 'Boulevard du Crime', which she renamed the Théâtre Déjazet. This she ran until 1870 when she was forced to close, overwhelmed by the debts accumulated by her feckless manager son. Losing her own theatre was, she said, like being stripped of her medals: it had been her 'red ribbon'.[23]

Déjazet paid a final visit to London in 1870, and later that year, while the Commune raged in Paris, she made an extended tour of the French provinces and of Italy. Now, burdened with yet more debts and a series of related lawsuits, she consoled herself with the thought that Frédérick Lemaître, that other great survivor from an heroic past, for whom a charity benefit was then being held, was no less unhappy than she was. In 1874 she was herself the recipient of a benefit: an evening given over to excerpts from her great successes in which she was accompanied on stage by Sarah Bernhardt. When she died in December 1875, her funeral was hugely attended, as the bemused Henry James so faithfully reported.

Whenever an act of cross-dressing takes place there are invariably two signifying elements at work, the erotic and the social, and though the balance can vary greatly, they are usually interconnected. Sometimes the point of gender reversal is to excite the eager spectators by exposing a performer's body in some unconventional guise; sometimes the reversal actually works to divert the erotic appeal so that its social function can be more clearly revealed. That is why Beaumarchais, for what is perhaps the most famous of *travesti* roles, asked that Chérubin in *Le Mariage de Figaro* be performed by a woman. Chérubin's polymorphous potential disrupts the sexual order that surrounds him. 'The basis of his character is an undefined and restless desire', claimed his creator. 'He is entering on adolescence all unheeding, and with no understanding of what is happening to him, and he throws himself eagerly into everything that comes along'.[24] Déjazet performed Beaumarchais's Chérubin for at least one benefit and had a vaudeville song, *Le Capitaine Chérubin*, based on the idea that Chérubin had joined the army.[25]

Sarah Bernhardt, who inherited the *espièglerie* (mischievousness) of Déjazet as well as the Romantic force of Rachel, also played Chérubin. In the course of Bernhardt's career the same double aspect of cross-dressing can still be seen: the teasing sexuality of the page-boy, but later, in a play such as Rostand's *L'Aiglon*, the troubling masculinity of a national figure. In her early years at the Comédie-Française Bernhardt played Richelieu in *Les Premières armes de Richelieu*, the play that in 1839 had brought renewed fame to Déjazet.[26] Later Bernhardt would make a significant change to tradition by playing roles originally written for male actors, most famously Hamlet and Lorenzaccio. The *travestis* that Déjazet specialised in, however, had always been designed to be performed by a woman, and they belonged to a well-established French idea of the feminine; indeed they are perhaps best considered, as Pougin put it in his *Dictionnaire du Théâtre* of 1885, as a late incarnation of the traditionally vigorous *soubrette*.[27]

Pougin's explanation for the development of *travesti* actresses is that, having showed themselves 'to be so lively, so vivid, so original when dressed in men's costume, so keen, moreover, to fulfil masculine roles, and lending themselves to it so marvellously and with such natural talent, writers, giving in to their fantasies, felt the urge to produce a mass of *travesti* roles which the actresses then played to perfection'.[28] Typically Pougin stresses sexual difference rather than sexual ambiguity. Indeed, as Laurence Senelick has more recently observed, *travesti*, the term which in the legitimate theatre designates cross-dressing, precedes by several centuries those more transgressive reversals (also much studied of late) which flourished between the 1860s and the First World War, mainly in the music-halls but which also affected much Edwardian entertainment, *Peter Pan* included.[29]

This later form of cross-dressing bore a complex relation to current notions of effeminacy and masculinity, and, though it's hard to document, probably had a particular appeal to lesbian and gay audiences.[30] The Déjazet repertoire, still rooted in the past, was very different. *Vert-Vert*, for example, is a good instance of the sexual role-playing inherent in the earlier 'legitimate' *travesti* because it depends not so much upon transgression as upon knowledge: what women secretly know (a secret broached by the act of cross-dressing itself) is how men live: a kind of assured voyeurism that many (both male and female) could find intriguing and amusing, even if a minority, such as Professor Whewell and his wife, and even Fanny Kemble, felt disturbed by what they saw.

Pougin distinguishes between simple *rôles travestis* and the *rôles à traves-tissements* (sometimes known as *rôles à tiroirs*) in which Déjazet excelled.[31] *Travestissements* (not, as Pougin also insists, to be confused with *transformations*, which are a form of stage magic) are ordinary changes that take place at extraordinary speed. It was, in many ways, a very decorous business. Sometimes, in the wings, *travestissements* would actually make use of 'a sort of makeshift dressing-room, surrounded by a folding screen, which contains all the clothes and objects that the actor needs, and in which they undress and dress again very rapidly, sheltered from indiscreet looks'.[32]

This same delight in speed for its own sake is what comes through most strongly in the celebrated tribute to Déjazet's persona, composed by the poet Théodore de Banville:

Joy, gaiety, ecstasy, humour, a song, forever twenty, the self-conceit of Lauzun, the spirit of Richelieu, the curiosity of Don Juan! Those looks that know everything; those long thin lips that could tell all if they so desired. The eyes are small, impudent, the forehead thoughtful, the chin wicked; the woman is as light as a pen, her imagination quick as a flame. Her mind is like the urchin who jeers at a duller time; her body! she has as little of it as possible. She has no need of it, she has never had any need of it. She flies about like a verse, a winged stanza; you could put her to bed in a cavalier's glove.[33]

An 'imagination quick as a flame': these brilliant disguises were designed to inspire awe and incredulity. Like all cross-dressing, *travestissement* (despite the literal derivation of the word) was not about changing costume so much as displacing signification, a double movement that involved both revelation and realisation. In the case of female to male *travestissement*, what is revealed (if only partially: the tight jackets, tight trousers) is the lightness of the female body and the energy of the female imagination; what is realised is the gravity (and occasional absurdity) of the male role.

Déjazet's characters may have been historically remote, they were always culturally exact. Among the most famous were *Le Vicomte de Létorières* (introduced at the Palais-Royal in 1841, performed in London in 1842), in which the Vicomte rescues his cousin, with whom he is in love, from condemnation to a convent, mingles at the court of Louis XV, battles with his brother over an inheritance, and joins in a drinking bout with one of the official arbitrators; and *Le Marquis de Lauzan* (introduced at the Variétés, performed in London in 1852), another typical *vaudeville*, in which the hero, played by Déjazet, again wins a legal battle, this time by brilliantly mimicking his opponents. Along with other famous drunk acts, *Lauzun* featured a string of obviously masculine props: sword, bottle, cigar and pipe, all happily seized on by illustrators. The symbolism though is over-determined, its significance lying beyond phallic sexuality to what accompanies and regularises phallic power. For a woman to smoke (either on stage and off – one thinks of George Sand) was to usurp, to lay claim to, a male prerogative, a male consolation and the outward expression of male confidence.

So, for example, Baudelaire's poem *La pipe*, to draw a near-contemporary comparison, assumes without question the male claims to autonomy, the

MDLLE DÉJAZET.
FRENCH PLAYS.—SCENE FROM THE "MARQUIS DE LAUZAN,"—(SEE NEXT PAGE.)

Figure 6. 'Déjazet: Scene from the *Marquis de Lauzan*' (*Illustrated London News*, 21 February 1852)

consolations for male trials, that are epitomised in the very act of smoking itself:

> I am the pipe of an author:
> I encircle and cradle his soul
> In the shifting blue net
> That rises out of my fiery mouth
> And I send out a powerful dictate
> Which charms his heart, curing him
> Of his spiritual fatigue.[34]

Correspondingly, the vision of Déjazet alone and smoking on stage offered powerful confirmation of her poise and self-control, both theatrical and sexual.

A famous anecdote elaborates the picture. This involves a performance of *Le Triolet bleu*, a *vaudeville* about three male students (all played by actresses) where much of the comedy came from drinking, fighting and smoking, all carried out with what one of Déjazet's biographers calls 'a thoroughly Germanic calm':

> It was at a performance of *Le Triolet bleu* that Déjazet, for the only time in her life, missed her entrance, and the memory of it is preserved. At first the surprised spectators murmured and then, as the situation continued, uttered violent outbursts: 'She will come!' 'She will not come!' The actress did arrive however, pipe in mouth, and without much sign of fear approached the footlights. The cries and whistles increased. Déjazet, sending puffs of smoke left and right, waited for this storm to subside. After ten minutes the public was tired out and went quiet.
>
> 'Gentlemen,' said Déjazet, 'May I be permitted to explain myself?'
>
> 'Yes, Yes! speak! explain yourself!' screamed the pit, who wanted nothing better than to be able to absolve their favourite.
>
> 'Well, gentlemen, the key to my dressing-room was lost.
>
> Someone had to run to the nearby locksmith, and then to another one, but all that took time, and meanwhile the play was continuing. Could I decently have appeared before you without my costume?'
>
> 'No! Bravo! Very good!' cried the restored public, and throughout the rest of the performance Déjazet received a continual round of applause.[35]

The very gestures of smoking demonstrate self-containment and – in a word frequently used about Déjazet – 'assurance'.[36] It is on record, however, that when she performed her favourite trick of exhaling through her nostrils in London, the audience remained unmoved and unamused. For a woman to smoke on stage was a calculated act of provocation which for its comic effect required a willingly responsive audience, an audience accustomed to and admiring of her independent power, otherwise the gesture might appear either gratuitous or threatening.

Given the high degree of self-presentation involved in her performances it is not really surprising that so many of Déjazet's vehicles should have involved an element of the meta-theatrical. In *Mademoiselle d'Angeville*, again set in the time of Louis XV, she played an actress who persuades a disapproving Jesuit of the importance of theatre by demonstrating three different male roles one after the other; in *Madame Favart* she recreated the life of the famous actress; in other plays – such as *Déjazet au sérail* and *Un Scandale* – she actually played herself. Famous for her brazen performance of men, she performed brave women too.

Though Déjazet's roles may often have been physically ribald, they were also spectral, fleeting incarnations of a mythic past. It was in this respect that her art was political, in the most literal sense of that word, bound up with ideas of state, of government, and ideology. Yet she was rarely subversive in the radical manner we tend to admire these days; in fact her work was often directed at the reinforcement of a political *status quo*, and the enhancement of a deeply conservative regime. She practised nostalgia.

So, for example, when she turned down Dumas *fils*' offer of the role of Marguerite Gautier in *La Dame aux camélias* (a play that was to be banned in England for much of the century) it was on historical rather than moral grounds: 'For me to play the role, you would have to change to a Louis XV setting, give me some verses to sing, and let me marry my lover at the end'.[37] Not only was Déjazet, the performer, closely associated with the eighteenth century, the actress herself apparently believed she had actually lived a previous life at that time. Her biographer describes one such moment of literal *déja vu*:

> She adored this period, as we find in her inclinations, her habits, even her hand-writing. 'I have lived in that time,' she said. 'The first time I went to Versailles, I recognised a staircase that I had definitely been up and down before.' Her nature found its full flowering only under a wig, a taffeta costume and short breeches. To the point that, dressed normally and without much harmony in town, she was marvellously *travestie* in the theatre, without allowing her hairdresser or her dresser the slightest anachronism. This did not involve any research or erudition – only a sure instinct, a memory perhaps of that previous life in which Déjazet believed so fervently.[38]

On the one hand she brought back to life the exquisite styles of Old France and *galanterie*, on the other she was *androgyne par excellence*. Déjazet may have played men because, in performance at least, she could do all the things that French men, especially soldiers, have traditionally done: swearing, fighting, smoking; at the same time she put a particular frame around that rough masculinity: the elegant outline of the dandy. A Déjazet dandy, however, was not at all of the now familiar Baudelairean kind, smooth epitome of modernity, but rather a synoptic type based on figures upon whom the Second Empire could back with pride and possessive affection.

Déjazet, always a Bonapartist at heart, publicly welcomed the election of Louis-Napoleon as President of the Republic, tried to visit him when he was in prison in 1847, and later received him in the Green Room of the St James in London.[39] As a form of absolute monarchy, based on centralisation, his administration had a great need of unifying myths and myths of unity, and consequently national icons figured strongly in her repertoire: Richelieu, for example, who in Déjazet's representations became yet another attractive *roué*, and, most famously, Napoleon I, the emperor himself. A widespread propagandist need to associate the economic and political achievements of his nephew with the military victories of Bonaparte produced what Theodore Zeldin has called an 'expurgated history of the good old days'.[40] It was through her amusing invocations of this supposed history, which also embraced aspects of the *ancien régime*, that Déjazet made her contribution to the political super-structure of the Second Empire and, to some limited degree, sold it to an English audience.

In distinct contrast, Napoleon III's own attempts to find support in England were never very successful, nor was the cross-dressed role of his uncle, though popular in Paris, thought at all appropriate for London, even in mid-century. When Déjazet delivered her farewell speech at Covent Garden in 1842 the more recent history of the relations between the two countries was deliberately left out:

> Howe'er they blame me, I am not so naughty
> As many life stories may have taught you.
> If not perfection, let me make amends –
> I never will forget my English friends.
> Let critics rail, and newspapers indite,
> And strive to make two gallant nations fight –
> It will not do: for now thro' ladies' eyes
> It is that war and desolation flies.
> We'll fight – if needs we must – by tender glances.
> And not with guns, and swords, and horrid lances . . .
> And, when in Paris, I'll report enough;
> I found and left you, right old British stuff.
> That, though, as nations, you may rivals be,
> I found none, but for exiles' charity.
> Farewell, kind patrons, once again adieu,
> May you but think of me, as I of *you*.[41]

None the less, several of her military roles were popular, and even when Déjazet didn't wear military dress, her performative presence reminded her audience of the masculine power of the countless uniforms she had worn at other times. The effectiveness of the celebrated '*pochade*', *Indiana et Charlemagne*, for instance, depends on the blatant use of a uniform to undermine male pretension.[42] The stage is divided into two rooms separated by a partition: on the left the audience sees a young woman, Indiana, played by Déjazet, who has just returned from a *bal* where she has met a dashing young man dressed as a Hussar. In the right-hand room, unknown to her but clearly visible to the audience, is the young man, Charlemagne, still wearing the uniform, though he is, in fact, a humble shirt-maker.

When Charlemagne discovers that he has been served with a notice to quit he throws his plate and a bottle at the door in a tantrum. Indiana complains at the noise, the two recognise each other from earlier in the evening and perform an elated dance, '*un galop*', each on either side of the partition. Soon they are both in Indiana's room agreeing to marry; meanwhile Charlemagne will move his belongings in with his future bride and thus escape his persecuting landlord.

Indiana et Charlemagne became one of the great war-horses of nineteenth-century French theatre because it juxtaposed a lively femininity with a shrinking masculinity and acted out their mutual attraction in comic form. In this instance it was the young shirt-maker who had adopted a uniform to which he was not entitled.

A recent historian of cross-dressing, Marjorie Garber, believes that the wearing of military uniform, whether by men or by women, is always a kind of fancy dress, even when the wearer is clothed in the uniform officially prescribed for their sex. 'The spectacle of women in men's clothes, or at least in men's uniforms, both military and lay', Garber suggests, 'seems to lead back to the question of male cross-dressing and its relationship to structures of hierarchy and power'.[43] That cultural truth undoubtedly applies to many of Déjazet's roles. Tight uniforms – breeches and tunics – obviously expose the outline of the female body – buttocks and breasts – in a way that conventional women's dress disallowed, and yet Déjazet, like Vestris in her 'buckskin' roles, and indeed like many other nineteenth-century actresses, adopted uniforms to exploit the myth of a raffish, romantic military life, quintessentially masculine, in which roles are everything.

When in 1859 she took her own theatre, the Théâtre Déjazet, the actress immediately had a much-needed hit with Sardou's *Les Premières armes de Figaro*, which was based in some degree on her earlier success, *Les Premières armes de Richelieu*. In a parody of *Le barbier de Séville*, Sardou's Figaro replaces Beaumarchais's pre-revolutionary servant-hero with a would-be opera composer, previously a travelling entertainer, whose philosophising aspires only to the level of sexual cynicism. His advice to Suzanne evokes the tradition of male rakes in which Déjazet had always specialised:

Learn to be philosophical, my dear, and in the interests of peace in our future domestic life, remember that man is both angel and demon, and that under this double heading he can love with wings, or he can love with claws.[44]

Sardou followed *Les Premières armes* with *Monsieur Garat*, staged in 1860, set in 1795. In this Déjazet, now over sixty, played a twenty-year-old '*incroyable*', costumed in 'grey coat and pantaloons, grey wig, lace neckerchief, and

Figure 7. Déjazet as Monsieur Garat

top-boots',[45] complete with monocle and cane. Yet another Déjazet dandy, Garat's function is irresistible and unquestioned: to charm the revolutionary mob with his dashing wit and his cynical songs.

With an irony typical of Déjazet's whole career, that backwards look was already prophetic. In the summer of 1870, when Napoleon III declared war on Prussia, she again performed *Richelieu* in Paris and, in a performance of a play called *Gentil-Bernard*, dressed as a dragoon, and perhaps with memories of Rachel's 1848 intervention in mind, she interspersed her performance with some lines from *La Marseillaise*. These apparently went down well, though events necessarily took their course.

In September, after some time spent in Dieppe, Déjazet embarked for England where, in addition to opening the new Opera Comique just off the Strand, she performed for wounded French soldiers and refugees. The Prince of Wales visited her dressing-room and another admirer, Lord Dudley, who knew of her financial difficulties, presented her with 2,000 francs in homage to her art. As the English press could not help but observe, it was especially remarkable that the aged Déjazet, who with her representation of Napoleon Bonaparte had helped prepare the way for Napoleon III, 'should live on and on until the mock nephew of the mock uncle should be once more a prisoner, and his so-called family dispersed'.[46] It was almost as remarkable that she should have been chosen to launch this new theatre, named after a form of theatrical art in whose development she had played little part. Simply to be French was enough. The Opera Comique was bright, shiny and new, well appointed with refreshment bars, smartly decorated with flowers and mirrors, all done out in a colour scheme of white, blue and gold. It opened with a vision from the past: Déjazet in *Monsieur Garat*.

As we have already seen in the preceding chapters, significant performing styles are always both the product and the projection of surrounding politics, but Déjazet is difficult to place since she stood for Romantic nostalgia, her 'impudence' softening and legitimising the operations of a harsh modern state. 'As light as a pen, her imagination quick as a flame': her ubiquity was the measure of her meaning. Déjazet in drag was history in reverse.

CHAPTER 5

The modernity of Aimée Desclée

In the spring of 1873 Squire Bancroft was appearing at the Haymarket Theatre in Wilkie Collins's *Man and Wife*. His part being brief, he sometimes found himself at a loose end, and would fill his time with trips to the neighbouring Princess's, where a visiting company from Paris was playing. What he saw there astonished him then, and remained in his memory ever after. No other actress, not even Sarah Bernhardt, he later swore, could ever match 'the reality of emotion and passion' conveyed by Aimée Desclée.[1]

As Bancroft and his wife had perfected their own (very English) version of 'reality', this testimony should be listened to, though Desclée's talents, hallowed by her death in 1874 at the age of thirty-eight, haunted many other memories. Emile Zola recalled that 'Desclée alone seemed modern to us, breathing our air and expressing precisely the nervous problems of the present époque', and felt that 'she was born to help the naturalist movement'.[2] Henry James said that she was 'the first actress in the world', but wondered if she would have succeeded at the Comédie-Française, where it was possible that 'her great charm – her intensely modern quality, her super-subtle realism – would have appeared an anomaly'. 'At the Française', he observed, 'you must know how to acquit yourself of a *tirade* . . . It would probably have proved Desclée's stumbling-block, though she could utter speeches of six words as no one else surely has ever done'.[3] For the critic Clement Scott, she was 'the tragedian of an age when tragedy was found in the salon and the street, as well as in the crypt and in the dungeon'.[4]

These tributes to Desclée's 'modernity' are remarkable, all the more so given that she had specialised in a kind of theatre that might have already begun to look old-fashioned: the problem plays of Dumas *fils* and *Froufrou*, the pathetic dramas by Meilhac and Halévy. Great actresses, though, acknowledged Desclée's precedent by preserving her repertoire despite its growing anachronism: Sarah Bernhardt's choice of play was often prompted by memories of Desclée: *Froufrou* and *La Princesse Georges* in 1881, *La Femme de Claude* in 1894.

99

Figure 8. Aimée Desclée

Bernhardt's friend and director Félix Duquesnel actually said that Bernhardt fell short of the emotional qualities of Desclée, because her style was 'composite' while Desclée's was much simpler, relying less on *mise-en-scène*. A more fruitful comparison, thought Duquesnel, was between Desclée and Eleonora Duse because, like the Italian actress, Desclée 'took her more powerful effects from her nervous and passionate nature; she filled the spectator with the same emotion that she felt'.[5]

Certainly, it was the case that Duse did well in plays made famous by Desclée. These she performed under protest (preferring Ibsen), all the while anxiously studying her copy of Desclée's life – which is not hard to understand because the professional achievements of Desclée were closely linked to an exemplary career that combined personal suffering with all the rewards of romantic fiction. To grasp Desclée's importance, then, we must too pay some attention to her life. Dumas *fils*'s pronouncement, made in an *éloge funèbre* delivered at her graveside – 'a woman like her has no biography. She knew how to move our hearts and she has died of it: that is the sum total of her story'[6] – is a characteristic piece of mystification. The details of Desclée's life were quite widely known, and soon after her death a short hagiography appeared,[7] later a collection of intimate confessional letters.[8] These letters, in which she professes fidelity to one of her several lovers while insisting that she maintain her professional independence, provided inspiration not just for Duse but, for example, for Marie Bashkirtseff.[9] For younger women, Desclée's story reinforced in complicated ways the reputation for modernity achieved by her acting.

Desclée was born *bourgeoise*, the daughter of a Saint-Simonian lawyer and businessman. Collapse of the family fortunes when she was fifteen made it necessary that she train for a career, and she entered the Conservatoire. From there, she went in 1855 directly to Montigny's Gymnase theatre, where the indisposition of Montigny's wife, the popular Rose Chéri, gave her the chance to act the roles the older actress had made famous. But invidious comparison made her move, in 1858, to the Vaudeville, which offered a less sophisticated kind of entertainment. In 1859 she retired from the theatre and adopted the lifestyle of a true *mondaine*, travelling to Baden, to Hornbourg, to Moscow, and St Petersburg. Finding the fashionable life no more satisfying than the professional, she tried to get back into the theatre. At first unsuccessful (she later described herself as 'a poor creature, bruised, wounded, with a great need for deep affection, friendly, almost paternal'[10]), she eventually joined Meynadier's company bound for Italy. There, guided by a new lover, an older actor named Bondois, *régisseur* of the troupe, she flourished: particularly in the *premières rôles* of Dumas *fils*: *Le Demi-Monde*, *Diane de Lys*, *La Dame aux camélias*. By 1867 she was in Brussels, rehearsing at the Galeries-Saint-Hubert. It was then, according to a celebrated anecdote, that Dumas *fils* himself saw her in *Diane de Lys*, was struck by how she had improved, and sought her for the principal role in the new play he was planning, telling Montigny of her transformation.

Dumas had spotted a physical style that would become commonplace in the gallery of *fin-de-siècle* types: the ambiguous features of the *jolie-laide*, elegance accompanied by a dangerous irregularity in the features, a precarious poise that signified the unpredictable:

A most peculiar voice, drawling and nasal, like that of an Arab singer, which at first appears harsh, rough, and monotonous, with delicate half-tones in it which seem to envelop you in a circle of harmony and intoxicate you . . .

Her outline was graceful, her walk haughty and swift, marvellously supple (she wore no stays), her gestures free but unexaggerated, keeping her well together; a small head, moving easily on a straight neck; large black eyes, dilated nostrils, inhaling life passionately, magnificent teeth, lips made to laugh ironically or sorrowfully in the madness of rage or love – a mask changing rapidly and representing the most opposite expressions, passing suddenly from tenderness to violence, from sarcasm to pity; the cheek-bones rather prominent, cheeks rather hollow, which will never be full again, and which, in spite of paint, showed that they were for ever paled by some internal suffering; thin shoulders and a flat figure.[11]

Before she could return to the Parisian stage Desclée had first to complete her contract with the Meynadier, leaving for Italy in March 1868 for a tour that lasted a year. She returned in June 1869, and promptly collapsed. In the autumn, though, she was able to make her second début at the Gymnase, opening in September in *Diane de Lys*. She was at once hailed as a theatrical revelation. *Diane de Lys* was followed by *Froufrou*, her greatest triumph.

Desclée chose to answer all this acclaim with a show of repudiation, a perverse trait she shared with her mentor, who similarly never missed an opportunity to castigate the audiences he attracted. In 1867 Dumas *fils* slated 'le tout Paris', whose reactions at first nights determined the success or failure of a play.[12] By 1869 he felt so jaundiced with his countrymen that he prophesied 'an invasion of barbarians, of foreign hordes'.[13]

In 1870 the foreigner did enter France: the catastrophe at Sedan in September. Desclée fled to Brussels, but returned to Paris and to her starring roles at the Gymnase. With the fall of the Commune in May 1871 new productions were put in hand – first, Dumas *fils*'s *Une Visite de Noces* in October, an unusual and not especially popular play in which Desclée was nevertheless held to have shown a new side to her talent: 'passionate, steady, ironical, spiritual, delicate'.[14]

La Princesse Georges followed in December, in which Desclée revealed yet more unsuspected resources. 'What a nervous artist!' exclaimed Francisque Sarcey. 'She lives her role! This isn't an actress on stage, it's a woman, a real woman, by turns winning and furious, an exquisite sensibility, a modern feeling that matches today's taste.'[15]

The spring of 1872 was spent performing in Brussels and preparing *Gueule de loup*, to be followed by *La Femme de Claude*, in which Dumas switched his attention to the theme of the adulteress. But even now acclaim did not bring satisfaction. In what was to become a celebrated letter, Desclée wrote to Dumas complaining of her 'empty, monotonous and noisy life':

Why make up one's face until it cries for mercy, cultivate hair down to your nose, make your figure go in here and out there, polish your nails which Nature wishes dull and you bright, and then, half-convinced, study, recite certain things without thinking of the meaning, tell lies, and deceive the ears and eyes of a lot of people so as to amuse them for a few hours?[16]

La Femme de Claude opened in January 1873. In May Desclée left for London where she played a season of thirty performances, including *Froufrou*, but ran into trouble with the censor. She was unable to play either *Le Demi-monde* or *La Dame aux camélias*, and only won permission to perform *Diane de Lys* at the very last minute.

Success was in any case accompanied by deteriorating health, and on her return to France she retired, on doctor's orders, to the country. Dumas was writing a new play for her. He treated her, as he customarily treated her sex in general, with reprimands: she wasn't really ill, and even if she was, she had only herself to blame. In fact she was on her death-bed. Ravaged by pain she begged for someone to help her die, reverting to the religious faith that she claimed had never really forsaken her. 'She has a beautiful soul', the ministering priest observed. Her biographer, romantically banal to the end, describes her death on 10 March 1874 as if 'a page torn from *The Lives of the Saints* became the final reversal in a truly strange novel. The woman of the world suddenly became a martyr.'[17]

There is a clue there none the less. The facts of Desclée's life, in particular the number of liaisons, formed the basis for a cult built on an established set of oppositions: passive woman and resilient female, passionate lover and professional performer, child and (potential) mother (to one of her lovers she was '*la môme*') – to which must be added a more modern combination: expressive artist and self-hating *nerveuse*.

Sarah Bernhardt's explanation of Desclée's secret was simpler: she said that it was 'Truth!'[18] This chapter attempts to explain that 'Truth', that modernity. It asks how the truth was constructed and what that might have had to do with 'the reality of emotion and passion'; it speculates as to why Desclée's posthumous influence should have lasted for so long, and suggests some political answers.

Modern theatre historians say that if the Bancrofts had a French equivalent it was Lemoine Montigny of the Gymnase.[19] Their contemporaries were more cautious and noted significant differences. Reviewing the work of the Bancrofts, *The Times* of 25 April 1870 allowed that, because at the Prince of Wales 'author, actors, and theatre seem perfectly fitted for each other', then 'the Gymnase would be, on the whole, the nearest parallel'. Nevertheless, 'the staple of pieces at that house is heavier and more solid than Mr. Robertson has created for the Prince of Wales' – a euphemistic allusion to the sexual themes of the French drama.

There undoubtedly was a wide gulf between what was available on the Paris and London stages: not only were certain French plays actually banned (as Desclée discovered), but English adaptations invariably tamed the original. When Desclée fought with the Lord Chamberlain in 1873, the most controversial play in London was Wilkie Collins's pious *The New Magdalen*, in which a fallen woman is, after many acts of contrition, rewarded with marriage to a clergyman.

But plays are not the only thing, and, in the long term, the development of nineteenth-century realism was to have more to do with changing theatrical practice, the mutual suitability of 'author, actors, and theatre', than with the propriety of texts. According to André Antoine, Montigny, though he never directed low-life dramas, *rosserie*, and rejected Zola's plays, was one of those who paved the way for the realism of the Théâtre Libre.[20]

Not that Montigny bothered with the humble interiors that preoccupied the Bancrofts. At the Gymnase, French decorum prevailed in style even when, by English criteria, morality was offended. A French critic in London, seeing Mrs Bancroft in Tom Robertson's *Ours*, complained bitterly at having to watch her spend a whole scene preparing a pudding: he did not, he said, go to the theatre to watch women cook. It was a French actor who corrected him, pointing out that the truth of milieu lay precisely there – 'in the white flour and raisins rolled between the slender fingers of Madame Bancroft',[21] the close interaction between body and matter.

In the later nineteenth century, as new methods gained ground, so realism came to be a matter of relative proportions, a principle that does apply equally to Montigny and the Bancrofts.[22] Realism could encompass both domestic interiors (characters in the right relation to furniture) and spectacular landscapes (characters in the right relation to mountains and lakes).

The playwright Victorien Sardou, who came to specialise in grand effects, told the politician Adolphe Thiers, 'My merit, if I have one at all, is that I applied Montigny's theories to the historical drama: I tried to introduce truth into the theatre'.[23]

Little is known about Montigny's exact working methods, but what information there is makes it clear that he stressed above all a character's close relation to things.[24] He also made novel use of the rehearsal period, which he saw as an opportunity for invention and discovery rather than simply for checking cues and moves. For rehearsals he would fill the stage with furniture – 'chairs, sofas, small settees, a piano, footstalls, poufs, console-tables, etc., etc'.[25] – and force the actors to find their way around these awkward obstacles. He would then reduce the number but, the earlier pattern remaining in their minds, actors would no longer instinctively revert to the straight lines and downstage groupings of neo-classical theatre.

Although used as part of a training exercise, the presence of so many solid properties on stage (a central table, surrounded by chairs, upon which the actors might actually sit), the encroachment of the real upon the fictive world had a shock value which a modern critic has been tempted to compare with that of the intrusive nude in Manet's '*Déjeuner sur l'herbe*'.[26] The surprise did not last, of course. By the mid-1860s G. H. Lewes was remarking on the way French actors strive for naturalness:

They still sit upon side sofas, and speak with their faces turned away from the audience, so that half their words are lost; and they will lounge upon tables, and generally comport themselves in a manner which – is not only easy, but free and easy.[27]

What had begun as a tactical deployment of alien objects became naturalised in turn as one of the basic requirements for a convincing *mise-en-scène*.

That is the main reason why it is hard to imagine the impact that Montigny's 'realism' once had. We have, in addition, to recapture the novelty of the text, and in most cases the dramatic vehicles now appear irredeemably old hat. In that respect the most challenging production is the one for which Desclée and Montigny were most famous, *Froufrou*, dedicated to the director, where, according to all who saw her, Desclée was most unmistakably 'the truth'.

Neither melodrama nor outright comedy, *Froufrou* is the not too distant relation of *La Dame aux camélias*. Or, to put that another, perhaps more compelling way: *Froufrou* is an example of the nineteenth-century apprehension and suppression of what would come to be known, in Freudian terms, as 'the family romance'. An aristocratic young woman, Gilberte, marries a neighbouring land-owner, Sartorys, who chooses her over her sister, the more reliable Louise. Soon frustrated by married life, motherhood, and her husband's inability to comprehend her emotional frustrations, Gilberte takes up amateur dramatics, specialising in imitations of Déjazet, the great *soubrette* and *travesti* artiste.

Eventually Gilberte succumbs to an affair with a family friend, Valréas. She encourages Louise to replace her in her wifely and maternal duties while she leaves for Venice with her lover. Sartorys follows her, duels with Valréas, but shows himself incapable of understanding his wife's now considerable remorse. Gilberte falls ill with consumption. As the disease takes hold she returns first to her father, then to Sartorys and to her son. Back in the bosom of the family, dressed in black but pleading to be buried in her white rose-covered ball-gown, she dies clasping her son to herself.

Stock effects – the inevitable consumption, Venice's empty grandeur – provide appropriate motifs for a sexual crisis born of a dashing but oppressive father (who, inevitably, chases actresses), an ineffectual but insensitive husband, and a glamorous but inadequate lover. The basic grouping of three males to one female is now most familiar to us from *Hedda Gabler*, or the child-like bride from *A Doll's House* – though dangerous permutations within the home are alluded to even by Meilhac and Halévy.

The text of *Froufrou* asks that Sartorys be 'paternal, a little too paternal',[28] and Gilberte complains that 'he talks to me as if I were a child, or like a mistress'.[29] Yet, when her sister decides to marry, it's Gilberte who in jealousy 'curls up on her chair like a child'.[30] Her characteristic behaviour pattern is a swirl of misdirected, self-destructive energies, deriving from a general uncertainty about how her sex should conduct itself.

For her first entrance she is dressed 'like an amazon', grasping a riding crop, having raced (and won) against Valréas. She collapses on to a sofa, fans herself with a newspaper, and allows the conversation to turn to the delights of being seen on horseback, and to the origins of Valréas's pet-name for her:

A door opens and down the staircase there comes the sound of swishing petticoats, like a whirlwind . . . Froufrou. . . . You enter, turn, look around, ferret about, put things in order, then disarrange them, chatter, sulk, laugh, talk, sing, strum on the piano, skip around, dance, and then off you go. Froufrou, always Froufrou. I'm sure that when you are asleep your guardian angel gently ruffles his wings to make that lovely noise: froufrou![31]

The actress playing Froufrou has to be volatile, frenetic, self-conscious, to match a largely, if not entirely, ingenuous narrative in which nothing is seriously concealed, so that nothing can therefore be discovered, and, ultimately, nothing can be learned. Which is not much to go on. Yet 'Mdlle. Desclée was Froufrou, and Froufrou is Mdlle. Desclée', insisted the *Morning Post* when she played the part in London.[32]

When spectators write that Desclée 'lived' her part, that she 'became' Froufrou, it is the energetic detail of her acting that they give as the main evidence – 'the twisting-up of the *Moniteur* into a fan, the grace and nature in every movement',[33] or 'Froufrou, when she desires to gain her point, flinging herself about her husband's neck, and as he talks now looking up winningly into his face, now playing with a coat-button, or – just for something to do, and so naturally done – removing a wisp of stray cotton from the coat on which she leans'.[34] Or again, 'watch her lean her head against the pianoforte, crouch and cower, clutch her head in her hands, or wring and crack her fingers in the contractions of nervous excitement'.[35]

Coupled with the admiration for detail is the credit given to Desclée's capacity to react to whatever is in front of her:

Watch her intently, and see the workings in her mind clearly written in her face. When she has nothing to say she is acting. She is never at rest. The eye follows her wherever she moves. She helps on conversation between two others by her marvellous expression.[36]

Minute touches are constantly introduced with admirable effect, and the by-play of the artist is absolutely inimitable. So good, indeed, is it that the spectator dares scarcely let his attention be diverted for a moment, for the purpose even of looking at those on whom the main action of the play depends.[37]

With this combination of detail and reaction, Desclée created a magnetic focus of attention that was well away from the centre of the stage, dividing audience concentration in a tense but commanding way. Her 'realistic' innovations could then lead in two directions simultaneously: towards ensemble acting or towards star acting. They enabled stage groupings to become more complex, and yet they allowed leading players to maintain control, the centre becoming wherever they happened to be.[38]

The reviews of Desclée offer other kinds of evidence of the ways in which realistic acting developed established conventions of the pictorial theatre. They show, for example, that Desclée's ability to be seen to be living her part in no way interfered with the habit of taking calls at the end of scenes or sometimes even within them, a practice that might strike us as incongruous (less so if we think of the conventions of opera), until we realise that, at this stage in its development, realism was still momentary rather than continuous and a matter of demonstration as much as re-creation.

Realistic acting was still the spectacle of identification, a visible rendering of real feelings; its 'truth' lay in the conviction with which the thing was done, and the clarity with which it could be perceived.

But there are signs, too, that this 'realism' of the moment wouldn't last, in the quite widespread worry about sudden changes in behaviour and the growing requirement that conduct should be consistent. The display of technical prowess was beginning to be linked to ideas of psychological process, outer to inner, as in this description of Desclée's method by an English paper:

The artist has not approached her work from the outside, inventing here a gesture and there a bit of 'business', and so composing a structure which may be taken to pieces by a similar menial action to that by which it was put together. The inner being of the character has been seized and understood, and, although, as in all art, the expression of the idea is not given without judicious consideration and selection of means, still those means are the final outcome of a menial process which leaves the artist no choice, so that they appear to the spectator to spring spontaneously from the feeling expressed by them.[39]

What this account does not mention is that the successive stages were marked by up to seven changes of (expensive) costume.[40] At the same time as it hinted at a drama of 'character', *Froufrou* still belonged to the Romantic theatre of display.

We are fortunate in having a record of how Desclée herself saw the challenge of combining a single concept with so many changes in the form of a letter to a young actress about how to approach the part: 'a real back-breaker', as she describes it.[41] For the first two acts, instructs Desclée, 'you are lively, young, gay, calm, carefree'. The significant shift will come with the rehearsal scene in Act II, when Gilberte prepares Déjazet's song, '*Indiana et Charlemagne*'.

Like many another nineteenth-century play with a woman at its centre, *Froufrou* contains rehearsal scenes.[42] Indeed, the play as a whole is saturated with theatricality, almost always seen as a glamorous but trivialising mode. Desclée picks out the rehearsal scene for particular attention because it is Gilberte's difficulty with acting that will prepare the way for her redemption, her amateurishness as an actress preserving her innocence as a woman.

At the rehearsal Gilberte will give a proleptic sign that she has more integrity than the ambience in which she lives. Consequently, says Desclée to her correspondent,

You must be very gauche, very awkward, and say everything in the same tone, like amateurs do. Having given the script to the baroness and said 'I'll begin', move away as if you were going to an imaginary window; open your mouth as if to deliver the lines and say 'I'll begin', once more. We discovered that one evening; do it properly and the scene will come to life.[43]

Yet the rehearsal scenes do allow some disruptive self-awareness to emerge. That there are two manipulators, two candidates for the role of Gilberte's *régisseur* – her lover, Valréas, and her pandering mother, the Baroness – brings a double irony to the situation. At first it is Valréas who behaves like a *régisseur* – 'Quick, the décor. (Puts two chairs in the middle of the stage.) There's the wall that separates the two rooms . . . there, between the two chairs, the door. (He puts a third chair in position.) Indiana in her place, Charlemagne in his.'[44]

Later, though, it's Gilberte's mother who says that she, as usual, 'will be the *régisseur*'.[45] Later still, when they disagree about the script, Gilberte refers to her mother as '*Monsieur le Régisseur*'.[46] These are deliberate jokes, not only about male *régisseurs* but about the abilities of the *régisseur*, to structure and command, as being male in their very essence.

Likewise there are jokes about all susceptible females being basically like actresses, and vice versa. When her mother tells Gilberte that she has already sold a number of tickets, Gilberte, although she knows the proceeds are to go to charity, observes that it is the first money that she has ever earned, yet another casual remark that cuts two ways.

Not that the re-enactment of the rehearsal procedures of the professional theatre is ever allowed to become truly subversive, because the theatrical analogy merely reinforces the underlying direction of the play, with its naturally weak women and instinctively manipulative men. And Gilberte has more serious role-playing difficulties to come, outside theatrical performance. These are to do with her role as mother. In the third act, she and her sister Louise confront each other over the question of Gilberte's child. According to Desclée,

In the third act, as soon as the curtain goes up, you must have nerves and more nerves and yet more nerves. Rumple your dress, your handkerchief, tap on the piano or on what you are carrying. Your body must be on edge. Then prepare for the final violence that we are waiting for. Never be still. Treat it as a scene composed entirely of movement, plenty of movement. Walk up and down, agitated the whole time. Curl up on the sofa, follow your sister and your husband with your eyes, play with your hands, look as if you might break your fingers in trying to control the anger that will very shortly explode. Everything that you can find in yourself of fury, rage, violence, eyes popping out of your head, a little demon. Only madness can excuse the dreadful things that she utters.[47]

This is the scene that everyone remembered, Squire Bancroft among many others, as 'a whirlwind of dramatic art in its highest form'.[48] The *Daily Telegraph* thought it sufficiently important to go through stage by stage:

> See her biting and tearing at the letter of her lover whilst some friend is giving her stereotyped advice; notice her shudder when the pure kiss of her sister is taken for a Judas embrace; watch her rocking and fuming like a spoiled child on the sofa . . . and, best point of all, prior to the great outburst of the storm, look well at the Froufrou on the sofa, when eagerly, craftily, with hunger, and partly with hate, she hears her husband put the one important question to Louise concerning the marriage which may remove the sole obstacle to Frou-frous happiness . . . Now scornful, now violent, now with a face white with rage, now laughing with hysterical contempt; calm at one moment, furious at the next; now moving rapidly about the furniture on the stage, now hissing the most terrible sarcasm into her sister's ear.[49]

There are, though, two acts still to come. For the fourth, Desclée recommends 'a slightly monotonous inflexion, a kind of singsong, a vague look, no movement, sobs in the throat only for the final words'. Changes in pitch, in delivery, will take the audience inexorably towards the pathetic *dénouement* of the fifth act, in which the actress should at first have 'no voice at all, then a great cry as she receives the child, then the words coming with difficulty, the phrases broken up'.[50]

She should, says Desclée, wear a long dressing-gown of black wool with a large hooded shawl, also black, which should be over her head when she enters. She should look black around the eyes; lips should be pale, cheeks hollow. The performance will end on 'childlike smiles' coupled with 'nervous movement'. According to the *Morning Post*:

> This creature, for a moment resuscitated, is the old Froufrou. Her dying request is to be borne to the grave in her bright clothes, and not in the horrid pomp of funeral gear. With a wish that is at once pagan and childlike on her lips, she dies, and Froufrou, with all her tempers and sorrows and offences, is at rest.[51]

In other words, awareness of role-playing has failed to bring about any radical change. And it is this pathetic stasis which, in historical retrospect, confirms *Froufrou* as transitional between the presentational theatre of the mid-nineteenth century and a more modern kind of theatre that is concerned with self-knowledge and motivation.[52] Desclée's contribution to the new theatre, however 'modern' she seemed at the time, could be no more than transitional because her minute physical detail signalled not so much revelation as compulsion: it remained neurotic.

The term is precise, clinical. 'By making herself available for examination, for intimate scrutiny, Desclée joined those other women whose
closely observed displays of unstable behaviour defined their particular
modernity – their *nervosité*.' Desclée was, on more than one occasion, to be
described as 'une Ophélie', a staple comparison in the nineteenth century.[53]
Gilles de la Tourette, in a lecture at the *Salpétrière* hospital, was to admire
her Froufrou for being 'like a singularly precise and well observed type of
worldly hysteria',[54] and Desclée herself said that having 'nerves' was like
seeing in yourself,

> only lies, deception, cowardice; to see yourself as young, soiled, disillusioned, alone
> in the world, working against everyone and everything; in the middle of a thousand
> troubles, a thousand boredoms, finding ways of squandering one's devotion, love,
> happiness on a heap of individuals who are not to your liking and who turn their
> back on you; happy when they don't give you a thousand bad turns.[55]

'Nerves' are signs of the self-division of modern woman. The *nerveuse* is
the site at which the confusion of modern life can be studied. She's victim
and scourge, a dangerous, contagious symptom.

Because they offered themselves up for scrutiny in their professional
life, all nineteenth-century actresses ran the risk of this identification; but
Desclée became the epiphenomenon because her kind of theatre, for the
most part the 'realist' theatre of Dumas *fils*, drew upon the conditions
of female oppression in its very making. It was Desclée, above all, whose
success was held to be due to the powerfully creative insights of those men
who saw what lay within her.

Several men could claim responsibility for having discovered Desclée,
for having brought her out. Bondois, Meynadier's *régisseur*, and Montigny
obviously had good cases, and Dumas *fils* too, for not only did the playwright rediscover her, he also assumed many of the rights that we would
associate with the modern director, in particular when it came to rehearsing
women.[56]

The most famous record of Dumas's intervention concerns a rehearsal
of his play *Une Visite de Noces*. The moment is one in which the heroine
is required to express her full disgust for adultery. 'Sometimes', discloses
Dumas of Desclée, 'so as to reserve her strength, she would not put on the
power in rehearsals which she intended for public representation'.

> I, who knew her, often felt that she was keeping back her powers, and as I liked
> to see everything just as it should be at night, I insisted on her going into the very
> depths of her heart for the sentiment, the intonation, the *cry* that I wanted. This
> was not only a great effort to her, but a real physical *shock*.

One day, the *actress* only was playing, not the *woman*, and we had a regular squabble. She feared the result of giving full swing to the power I exacted of her, and tried all sorts of *ruses* to get out of it. I would not give in, and sense brought out the cry scream from the depths where I knew it was to be found. 'There it is', she said, in an exhausted voice. 'You know where it comes from. You will kill me!' 'What does that matter if my play succeeds?' Then she sat down, half fainting, with her two hands on her heart. 'He is right', she added after a pause; 'that is the way to treat me; otherwise I should be good for nothing.' This cry scream which I had forced from her is the one in the *Visite de Noces*, which, with a movement of the handkerchief . . . precedes the 'Pouah', that brought down the house on the first night, with three rounds of applause and a call in the middle of the act. 'There', she said to me, 'there is your *howl (cry)*. You know where it came from don't you?' She knew what she was saying, and she spoke the truth.[57]

The 'truth', that is, which Dumas knew to be there: the truth of her life as a woman. When *Froufrou* made her a sensation, fêted by audiences, critics, the Emperor himself, Desclée admitted that there was a rift in her life: enormous public success but an unfulfilled capacity for love. 'You are suffering at the moment', Dumas explained, 'from the fatal and logical consequences of your position as an independent woman, the most wretched of all the conditions a woman can know. Women are born to be subordinate and obedient, first to their parents, then to their husbands, last of all, to their children. They are always slaves to duty.'[58]

La nerveuse, divided by self-denial: Desclée becomes expressive as a result of pressure, of suffering, and of guilt. What emerges is 'woman', but 'woman' as negation, a predetermined image discovered by the male *régisseur*. The 'realism' of Desclée's acting becomes more apparent: its underlying principle is simply what men can make of women.

If Rachel, regenatrix of Corneille and Racine, gave theatrical voice to the political passion of 1848 – instinctive, irrepressible, ultimately unfulfilled – then the capricious *nervosité* of Desclée represented the instability of the Second Empire, the national uncertainty that foreshadowed the battle of Sedan, the siege of Paris, and the Commune. Her contemporaries were struck by the way her performances seemed to embody a presence to be found throughout French society. It was as if she were made of some new material:

It's everything, the expression of a time when aristocracy, monarchy, classical or political tradition, everything is mixed up. Out of the mix she has made something powerful, marvellous, inimitable.[59]

Further complexity was added to this compound by her last major role, which was of a woman turned demonic, over-the-top, a politicised *vierge de mal* who spelled out retribution for recent history.

The Commune collapsed in May 1871, with blood and fire; and among the ruins there were many theatres. According to the brothers Goncourt, the large-scale destruction began at Châtelet, site of the enormous Théâtre du Châtelet and of the Théâtre Lyrique, and carried on from there. They give a picture of spent grandeur and frazzled desire. 'Behind the burnt-out theatres, costumes had been laid out on the ground: carbonised silk in which, here and there, one catches sight of the gleam of golden spangles, the sparkle of silver.'[60] Fake diamonds in real ashes maybe, but still the spark of theatrical life, for within a remarkably short time the Paris theatre was back in its tinsel. Theatrically speaking, the Third Republic was the legitimate child of the Second Empire.

And speak theatrically we should, for that is how the crisis was viewed, by spectators and participants alike. The spirit of Karl Marx's classic observation prompted by the Revolution of 1848 – that historical events occur first as tragedy, then as farce[61] – is preserved in his own description of Paris in 1871 as 'the Paris of the *francs-fileurs*, the Paris of the Boulevards, male and female . . . considering the civil war but an agreeable diversion . . . swearing by their own honour and that of their prostitutes, that the performance was far better got up than it used to be at the Porte St Martin'.[62]

In Lissagaray's *History of the Commune*, however (a book Marx professed to admire), the theatrical metaphor is reversed. 'It is true the *mise-en-scène* was unpretending', wrote Lissagaray, 'but it is the drama of Revolution, simple and gigantic as the drama of Aeschylus'.[63] As Lissagaray saw events, it was hardly surprising that when the theatre of reality was taking place on the streets, all the real theatre could do was offer bright diversion. 'The theatres are opening', he reported in May 1871:

The Lyrique gives a grand performance for the benefit of the wounded, and the Opéra-Comique is preparing another. The Opéra promises us a special performance for the following Monday, when we shall hear Gossec's revolutionary hymn. The artists of the Gaieté, abandoned by their manager, themselves direct their theatre. The Gymnase, Châtelet, Théâtre-Français, Ambigu-Comique, Délassements, have large audiences every night.

'Let us pass to more virile spectacles', Lissagaray concluded, 'such as Paris has not witnessed since 1793'.[64] He was, of course, thinking of revolutionary meetings.

Despite the departure of members of the Comédie-Française for London, a surprising number of Paris theatres did stay open, and they stuck to their normal fare. Desclée was sympathetic to 'Le pauvre empereur, comme il doit souffrir!'[65] Montigny claimed that he wanted to keep the Gymnase open to ensure work for his staff. And so, in May 1871, Desclée found herself hiding from *communards* in the cellar of her home, when only recently she had been at the Gymnase playing, to good audiences, comedies fully intended to stave off horror.[66] Her own letters show her to have been quite aware of this contrast:

'O Parisians', she apostrophised, 'I myself don't bother other people; I talk about fripperies, I try out new hair styles . . . and joke about things. . . . Every evening we "frou-frou" in front of good audiences who laugh heartily. . . . On Sunday, the cannons, the general recall, ambulances, battalions block the boulevards, and we have more than six hundred bookings.'[67]

Cannon could be heard all the time and still the public were gay. In the day requisitions, terror, burials with full ceremonial; and in the evening theatre, farce, jokes, and diversions.[68]

Montigny, the provider of these 'diversions', she excused on the grounds that,

There is a sacred duty that the artist must fulfil; but with what resentment, what repugnance. – It's a cruel metier. One has to laugh when all there is matter for bitter tears. One has to cry, and each tear is stolen from the misery of the day! – More theatre: at last respite. Comedy has been replaced by drama, a military drama that shocks Europe. The artist goes into hiding, awaiting better days.[69]

Sarcey too had praise for Montigny's skill at survival – but this, we have to remember, was not only the Sarcey who wrote repeatedly on the need for theatres in times of emergency,[70] but the Sarcey who wrote when the Versailles soldiers finally entered the city in May and carried off the *communards* of the 'serene joy' with which his eye rested on the 'loyal faces of the brave gendarmes, who marched with sprightly step by the sides of the hideous column'.[71] It was this Sarcey, too, who was to write of the executions which followed that 'the axe should be riveted to the executioner's hand'.[72] For sheer brutishness that remark compares with the notorious, never forgotten, jeer of Dumas *fils* about the partners of the *communards*: 'We shall say nothing about their females, out of respect for women – whom these resemble only once they are dead'.[73]

Soon after the massacres that followed upon the collapse of the Commune, Desclée did well with Dumas's *La Princesse Georges*, which is about an adulterous male, while the playwright set about writing a new play that would express his own exacerbated feelings about the recent chaos, a play in which women would once again bear the brunt of history by becoming its emblem, *La Femme de Claude*.[74]

Here, the libidinous female, known by Dumas generically as '*la bête*', whose vocation is prostitution, is held responsible for France's shame. The play's protagonist is Claude Ruper, a Faustian inventor who harks back to Jules Verne and forward to Shaw's Captain Shotover, and whose single ambition is to develop a super-weapon that will make France impregnable.

Claude works with his adopted son, Antonin, while his wife, Césarine, a woman with a considerable past, lives a life quite her own and does nothing to repay the forgiveness originally lavished upon her by her husband. At the start of the play she has been away on the pretext of visiting her sick mother, while actually indulging herself in Paris. On her return, Antonin finds himself helplessly in love with her, but luckily confides in Claude, who not only forgives him, but hands over a chest containing the secret of his invention. Enter Cantagnac, agent for a foreign power, who blackmails Césarine, threatening her with further disclosures unless she steals Claude's papers. Césarine tries to discover the secret of her husband's invention. Claude sees through her wiles and threatens, 'If you prevent me, from doing what God has commanded, if such a God exists, I'll kill you'.

The last act takes place in Claude's study. Prompted by Cantagnac, Césarine has passed a large sum of money over to Antonin, on the pretext that it will act as insurance should Claude ever be faced with ruin. This he has deposited in Claude's safe. She now tells Antonin that Claude has attacked her and that she is prepared to run away with him using the concealed money. Antonin succumbs and opens the safe, which gives Césarine the chance to seize the precious documents and throw them to the waiting Cantagnac. When Antonin realises her trick a struggle ensues. In the end Claude carries out his earlier threat by shooting his doubly treacherous wife.

Desclée was doubtful about *La Femme de Claude* from the moment she read it. She thought the play 'too bold, too new', and was afraid that 'the people aren't real enough'.[75] In the event, the play was a greater success for the actress, for whom it suggested new possibilities, than it was for the author, for whom it looked like the reheating of old obsessions. Desclée's biographer has no reservations about her achievements:

Greater than ever, as much of a revelation in the shocking as she had been in the beautiful . . . she made a sublime monster of this frightening creature which we would never have seen if any other actresses had played her. One had never seen that face animated with such a strange passion where the madness of love had left his mark, where the most shameless and the most frightening emotions were alternately reflected. Hell was released in her, and her voice, her look, her smile, her language expressed at the same time the frightful desire of someone pursued by a divine course. This wasn't a woman, it was a female demon . . . An angel of beauty, she was also an angel of the ugly, a fallen angel, a fatal angel – to degrade and destroy.[76]

As Césarine, Desclée became the ultimate *femme fatale*, developing a new style to match a new type, a style rigid, impervious, unnerving. Dressed as Dumas desired – 'in a slightly old-fashioned way, imperial, without a corset . . . few petticoats, immodest but veiled . . . a costume half modern and half antique, with a revealing neck'[77] – she played the whole of the first act 'with her arms crossed on her chest, without a single gesture'.[78]

Jules Claretie compared her with one of her old rivals. She was 'a Rose Chéri possessed by a devil', who had 'the nerves, the stresses, the necessary madness to present in an irresistible way the unconscious beauties of the contemporary drama'.[79] *La Vie Parisienne* called her 'a sublime viper! all honey and claws, sincere and calculating, chaste and depraved, coquettish, winning, menacing, seductive, shocking'.[80]

Césarine marked a decisive step in the theatrical construction of the vindictive type that Dumas was to develop more successfully in the figure of Mistress Clarkson in *L'Etrangère*, performed by Sarah Bernhardt at the Comédie-Française in 1876 and in London in 1879. The progression was irresistible. Long before defeat by the Prussians, Dumas had made the female the scapegoat for France's misery, and a focus for his own fears and frustrations. History, he could now proclaim, had proved him right: political disaster does indeed follow sexual decadence. Now there need be no pretence. In the preface to *La Femme de Claude* he invoked the *Book of Revelations*:

This Beast was clothed in scarlet and purple, adorned with gold, precious stones, and pearls, and she held in her hands, which were as white as snow, a gold vase full of abomination, the foulness of Babylon, of Sodom, and of Lesbos. Sometimes this Beast, who I thought I recognised as what Saint John had seen, released from her whole body an intoxicating vapour through which she appeared radiating like the most beautiful angel of God, and in which there came, in their thousands, to play, to twist with pleasure, to howl with misery, and finally to evaporate, the minuscule anthropoid animals whose birth had preceded her own.[81]

That is extravagant, not exceptional.[82] Biblical rhetoric and imagery were widely adopted by writers towards the end of the century – in Zola's *The Downfall*, for example, where Parisian entertainments are 'gala gatherings of Sodom and Gomorrah, the music, the flowers, the monstrous pleasures, the palaces bursting with such lust and debauchery, illumining their abominations with such a wealth of tapers that they set themselves ablaze!'[83] 'Woman of Sodom', 'Great Whore of Babylon', '*Vierge du Mal*': these are the dominant images of woman, developing previous versions of the *femme fatale* while responding to the present situation.

And there were others, which Dumas also shared with his contemporaries. 'You are a Messalina, and you will play her', he had said to Desclée when she had hesitated, for reasons partly medical and partly moral, over the part of Césarine.[84] The implication was that guilt over her own sexuality simply proved her suitability for the part. In title and theme, *La Femme de Claude* deliberately invokes the libidinous wife of the Emperor Claudius who, according to Juvenal, had slaked her endless desires by voluntary slavery as a prostitute.

Messalina thus stands for the classic type of female treachery and appetite: an image that was to be reworked in the 1890s, in the exuberant satire of Alfred Jarry, Aubrey Beardsley, and other artists of the *fin de siècle* who used her comically, if not very originally, as a symbol of liberating excess. But already, in the humourless, reactionary plays of Dumas *fils*, open female sexuality had come to signify loss of political will and direction.

Another epithet repeats much the same point. When Cantagnac blackmails Césarine in *La Femme de Claude*, he warns her that any notions that she may have of female freedom are illusory:

I know that you are hard, and said to be free, and that there are free women. There are mothers, wives, and virgins, you have never been a virgin, a wife, nor mother, you are nothing more than an instrument at the disposition of those who know how to use it. It is better to be an honest woman, madam, then I would never have taken hold of you. You have preferred to be Dona Juana, I am the statue of the Commander, and now I have you, you will not escape me.[85]

'Dona Juana': that is to say, a female Don Juan. It is surely not insignificant that the very same image also serves in Rimbaud's great poem *Les Mains de Jeanne-Marie*, although for a quite different purpose, as an indication of the sexual degradation that will not simply be punished but actually replaced, may have already been replaced, by a new kind of woman. Rimbaud makes a specific comparison between a 'Dona Juana' and 'Jeanne-Marie', the heroic *communarde*:

Jeanne-Marie a des mains fortes,
Mains sombres que l'été tanna
Mains pâles comme des mains mortes.
– Sont-ce des mains de Juana?[86]

[Jeanne-Marie has strong hands,
Dark hands tanned by the summer
Pale hands like dead hands.
Are they the hands of Juana?]

Even so, the commitment of Rimbaud's stanza, its uncompromising demand for recognition of the *communarde*, is sustained by a series of negative comparisons – all the things that Jeanne-Marie is not, which include a 'Juana'. In Rimbaud's poem the new heroine has yet to be established in her own right.[87]

Lissagaray, however, thought that he had seen her potential in action, in the sacrificial aid that working-class women gave their men; and he had made another necessary reference. The 'true Parisienne' is now the woman who supports the Commune, while

the unclean and androgyne, born in the mire of the Empire, the madonna of the pornographers, the Dumas *fils* and the Feydeau, has followed her patrons to Versailles, or works the Prussian mine at St Denis.

She, who is now uppermost, is the *Parisienne*, strong, devoted, tragic, knowing how to die as she loves. A helpmeet in labour, she will also be an associate in the death-struggle. A formidable equality this to oppose to the *bourgeoisie*.[88]

The full revelation of revolutionary woman, of woman as revolutionary, will be witnessed in the riddance of past images: the new woman who will be neither a 'Juana', nor the 'madonna of the pornographers' – the creation above all of Dumas *fils*.

Not, of course, that the proletarian heroine, Rimbaud's Jeanne-Marie, could ever assume a central place on the *bourgeois* stage. But she can sometimes be heard in song, in *Carmen*, in the lyrics of Aristide Bruant and Yvette Guilbert. She can even at times be glimpsed in the theatre: refracted in the episodic structure of the Goncourts' 'working-class tragedy' *Germinie Lacerteux*, or made a comic turn in Sardou's *Madame Sans-Gêne*. More often, though, her strength is proved by her absence – in the rhetorical renderings of Césarine offered, in homage to Desclée, by Sarah Bernhardt and Eleonora Duse, in the insurrectionary vehemence of that female passion. Desclée's repertoire, whether Froufrou or '*vierge du mal*', survived on the commercial, international stage as an outlet for displaced political energies. Following her death, whenever French actresses appeared on the English stage, memories of her lost presence were usually close at hand.

CHAPTER 6

'A kind of beauty': Réjane in London

Duped by her lover and exploited by her mistress, the working-class heroine of the Goncourts' exemplary naturalist novel *Germinie Lacerteux* (1864) takes refuge in her room, where she collapses in a delirium:

She spoke in a strange tone, which inspired emotion, fear almost. The vague solemnity of supernatural things, a breath from another world, was in the room. This involuntary, escaping, throbbing, suspended sleep-talk was like a disembodied soul straying upon dead lips.[1]

After a while Germinie is discovered by her mistress, Mademoiselle de Varandeuil, who leans 'with a kind of terror' over 'this abandoned body' and strains to catch at her maid's words:

Her language became unrecognisable as her voice took on a dreamlike quality. It soared beyond her everyday speech and expression, it was as if the language of the people was purified and transfigured by passion. Germinie stressed the forms of words; she gave them their eloquence. Phrases emerged from her mouth with rhythm, with anguish and with tears, as if from the mouth of a fine actress. (180–1)

And so – 'listening as in a theatre' (181) – Mlle de Varandeuil finds herself the uninvited audience to a strangely identifiable kind of performance: 'such acting, such intonation, a sound so dramatic and wracked as this consumptive voice spluttering out its heart, reminded her of none other than Mlle Rachel' (181).

Echoes of Rachel, of an abandoned intensity born of violent emotional turmoil, consecrate the sufferings of a serving maid, elevate the outburst that Germinie delivers in her sleep to tragic utterance: from yet another female body comes the impersonal voice of universal suffering.

The Goncourts needed to employ those echoes if they were to answer the challenge which they had issued to themselves: to write a tragedy about the poor. When Germinie achieves tragedy, she does so unconsciously, and a classical *tragédienne* with a Romantic style was required as a point of reference for her involuntary *tirade*, the theatre supplying an analogy for

Figure 9. Gabrielle Réjane by Downey *c.* 1895

the meeting-place that could never really be found. Mlle de Varandeuil's inadvertent and belated eavesdropping even parallels the origins of the novel in which she appears, since *Germinie Lacerteux* was based upon the posthumous revelations of the squalid secret life led by the Goncourts' own apparently devoted maid. Only, it seems, when delivered in oblivion could the tragic voice of *le peuple* become audible.

When in December 1888 a version of the Goncourts' novel was staged for the first time at the Odéon as 'une pièce en dix tableaux', the title-role of Germinie was taken by an actress best known until that moment for her talents in boulevard comedy: Gabrielle Réjane.[2] The play opened to the kind of response that is the stuff of French theatrical history: the gallery howled at the tedium, the critics squabbled amongst themselves – mainly at the absence of the statutory *scène-à-faire* and the presence of an offending word (*putain*) – and the partisans rejoiced. Réjane triumphed. A double signpost in the course of the late nineteenth century, *Germinie Lacerteux* suggests a new line for a fashionable actress and it prompts André Antoine, the ambitious director of the Théâtre Libre, to advance his naturalist cause with the promise that he will stage, at the earliest opportunity, the Goncourts' grim *La Patrie en Danger*.[3] Through Réjane's unexpected incarnation, a living voice and a vital presence had been found for *le peuple* – an indelible experience. Antoine recalls:

an unexpected, unrecognisable Réjane. Here was the elegant Parisienne, hunched and frumpish, in the clothes of a poor maid – so convincingly transformed into the shape of humanity that she had become Germinie Lacerteux herself . . . Above all in the second part, when Germinie, gradually decaying, growing old, trails her grief – is so truly of the people. It was then that the actress finally achieved greatness.[4]

Elegance transformed into truth: for Marcel Proust a youthful anticipation of Réjane ('I worshipped Réjane, that great woman'), her weaving of opposites ('who wore both masks in turn'), became one of those symptoms of recurrent fever that memory never appeased:

When I first heard Réjane as Sappho and as Germinie Lacerteux, I contracted a recurring sadness, which even now, after so many years, can from time to time overwhelm me again.[5]

Though more than one actress went to make up Berma it was Réjane who contributed the irrecoverable alloy of splendour with strength.

What links all memories of Réjane is enduring admiration for an actress who could somehow achieve the inaccessible at the same time as she retained her already proven power. Their lasting applause recalls a time when the naturalist urge to represent *le peuple* had, in the surfeited post-Commune years, to vie with the undeniable claims of popular bourgeois entertainments.

After *Germinie Lacerteux* Réjane's material varied considerably: in 1890 Meilhac's titillating *Ma Cousine*; in 1891 Porto-Riche's harsh sexual drama *L'Amoureuse*; in 1892 Daudet's equally notorious *Sapho*; in 1893 Becque's *La Parisienne* and Sardou's very different *Madame Sans-Gêne*; in 1894, though briefly, *A Doll's House*. The range, however, was not in itself exceptional. Even the repertoire of the Théâtre Libre remained closely engaged both with its predecessors, *les pièces bien faites*, and its contemporary rivals on the boulevard. The French were, for example, generally less inclined to interpret Ibsen's plays as moral innovations than as daring experiments with conventional dramatic form. Antoine's own enthusiasms were distinctly catholic. The terms of Réjane's success show a like adhesion to the newer naturalism of established mechanics, and critical appreciation of her career rested upon the way in which she transformed, deepened and complicated the predictable workings of her popular repertoire: honesty revealed by vulgarity, beauty discovered in ugliness, articulate expression wrested out of spontaneous action, true love redeemed from professional debasement, even occasionally the tragic reborn through the grotesque.

Among the great actresses of the *fin de siècle*, all of them the wayward daughters of Rachel, Réjane was a link with *le peuple* as they might popularly be imagined. Although their repertoires would occasionally overlap and Réjane, like her rivals, inherited a Romantic tradition of acting, only rarely was she sublime, and only very rarely indeed, only despite herself almost, was she 'tragic'. Mostly she was witty, ironical and wonderfully physical. Arthur Symons made the point in 1901 with characteristic excess:

She is grotesque, she is what you will: it is no matter. The emotion she is acting possesses her like a blind force . . . where Sarah Bernhardt would arrange the emotion for some thrilling effect, where Duse would purge the emotion of all its attributes but some fundamental nobility, Réjane takes the big, foolish, dirty thing just as it is.[6]

Nevertheless, Réjane's skills were blatantly those of a professional actress, because it was only by purely theatrical means that she could demonstrate her natural vitality and her transformative powers. She was never expected to transcend the moment of her performance and, despite her incessant touring, she was always to belong, not to the world, but to Paris. Always, for better or worse, Réjane was to remain a sign of *le peuple*, a volatile signification almost by definition.

And yet signs of the theatrical performer are volatile too, if only because they represent multiple identity. Famous performers, 'stars', may even achieve that complex totality of the image that semioticians have called 'structural polysemy'.[7] Réjane was remarkable because of the changing variety of what she signified: *le peuple* seen through constraining circumstances. Many of her vehicles were like frames which focused only by limiting, though sometimes, with a sudden gesture or a discordant emphasis, she would threaten to break out, much as *le peuple* might intimate their capacity to escape from the bonds that would attempt to fix them as an established quantity.

She 'arrived' in London in 1894 with the play that Sardou had written for her, *Madame Sans-Gêne*, her tumultuous Paris success of the previous year. Thereafter, for a decade or more, she provided London audiences with scenes from the boulevard, sparkling glimpses of French popular theatre, new insights into what the French apparently enjoyed seeing in themselves. From her very first appearance at the Gaiety she was at once perceived to possess an extraordinary but identifiable energy, although in London *le peuple* would always be an alien, specifically French, concept.[8]

London audiences, or at least their more sophisticated members, had certainly been well briefed for what they were about to witness. An article, clearly timed to coincide with the début, translated from the French of Dauphin Meunier by Henry Harland and Ella d'Arcy, appeared in the second issue of *The Yellow Book* in early July. It opened with a prodigal accumulation of epithets, a bulging dossier of aliases, out of which a total picture of the actress might be constructed.

A fabulous being, in an everyday human form; a face, not beautiful, scarcely even pretty, which looks upon the world with an air at once ironical and sympathetic; a brow that grows broader or narrower according to the capricious invasions of her aureole of hair; an odd little nose, perked heavenward; two roguish eyes, now blue, now black; the rude accents of a street-girl, suddenly changing to the well-bred murmuring of a great lady; abrupt, abundant gestures, eloquently finishing half-spoken sentences; a supple neck – a slender, opulent figure – a dainty foot, that scarcely touches the earth and yet can fly amazingly near the ceiling; lips, nervous, sensuous, trembling, curling; a frock, simple or sumptuous, bought at a bargain or created by a Court-dressmaker, which expresses, moulds, completes, and sometimes almost unveils the marvellous creature it envelops; a gay, a grave demeanour; grace, wit, sweetness, tartness; frivolity and earnestness, tenderness and indifference; beauty without beauty, immorality without evil: a nothing capable of everything: such is Woman at Paris: such is the Parisienne: and Madame Réjane is the Parisienne, is all Parisiennes, incarnated.[9]

The plethora of synonyms and antonyms immediately identifies this as the kind of theatrical record that acts as a projection, an advertisement in fact. As each clause leads into the next, so each contributes to the multiple presence that is Réjane.

Madame Sans-Gêne, Réjane's greatest triumph, is an arrangement of styles and scenes rather than a sequential dramatic whole. Its heroine is Cathérine, a washerwoman, Alsatian by birth, Parisian by adoption. The play opens in 1792, at the time of the assault on the Tuileries, with a short scene in which Cathérine demonstrates her innate charity and her persuasive charm by rescuing the Royalist De Neipperg from the insurgents, and even persuading her own fiancé, a revolutionary – Sergeant Lefebure – to turn a blind eye. The rest of the play takes place ten years later. Lefebure and Cathérine are married and he has risen in the ranks of Napoleon's army to become a Marshal of France and Duke of Danzig. Cathérine, however, has failed to take to court life: a famous set-piece, in which she unsuccessfully takes lessons in dancing and deportment, makes this comically clear. Her forthright manner finally brings her into conflict with Napoleon himself: first when she outwits the Emperor's demands that her husband divorce her on grounds of lack of dignity, later when she again defends De Neipperg, this time from accusations of an adulterous affair with the Empress Marie-Louise.

In structuring his play Sardou carefully circumscribed a limited range of moods – sentimentality, comedy, melodrama – so that the effect of the narrative breaks is to highlight the constant animation of the heroine through the relative consistency of her responses. It must surely be this compelling ingredient that has made *Madame Sans-Gêne*, banal in most other ways, one of the great war-horses of the French theatre. When Romain Rolland saw the play at the Théâtre Populaire de Belleville in 1903, he was obliged to note that the audience was so engrossed as to be 'on the point of hissing Napoleon when he reproached the heroine for being a washerwoman'.[10] Much later, in 1941, when that inscrutable actress Arletty called upon German assistance in the making of a film of the play, she found herself an object of deep mistrust.

If the secret of *Madame Sans-Gêne* is Cathérine's semi-comic but entirely heroic failure to adapt to the various circumstances in which she finds herself, then the play was all the more effective in the context of the lavish, detailed (and highly fashionable) Empire sets that Paul Porel, Réjane's manager, husband and Svengali, had provided. And the brilliance of Réjane's interpretation was the manner in which she emphasised Cathérine's ability to remain true to her nature. English reviews claim that by stressing the

shifts between comic high spirits and moral sincerity which Sardou had
created, she not only reconfirmed the essential concomitants of vulgarity –
'How true and moving are her sudden transitions from superficial vulgarity
to the native dignity of the woman and the patriot . . .'[11] – but re-established
the origins of her portrayal:

A woman who is '*peuple*' in the best sense of the word, the sense which would
fain imply that the simpler, the sincerer virtues are the dower and portion of the
daughters of the poor . . .[12]
   . . . a woman of the people, with natural good sense, warm affections, mother-
wit, and instinctive civility.[13]

At the same time, though, the virtues of 'the people', when represented in
such a simple, ebullient character as Cathérine, called for a visible degree
of commitment on the part of the actress who played her, even to the point
of 'exaggeration':

It may be that this lady exaggerates the awkwardness of the ex-laundress in her Court
finery, her kicking and lurching and sprawling. But how fresh and spontaneous,
and sincere is her method! How winning her smile![14]
   Even in the moments when she seemed to exaggerate, exaggeration was of the
very essence of the character, of the very existence of the play.[15]

About all this there was, in 1894, no dispute whatsoever.
   It was all the more extraordinary, then, that three years later, in 1897,
Ellen Terry should have attempted to challenge the French actress's mastery
of this comic technique at the Lyceum. As the press were quick to point out,
might it not be as paradoxical for Terry's vivacious innocence to permeate a
Parisian washerwoman as it would be for Irving's angular stature to embody
le petit caporal? Could either 'adapt'?
   In the event they both triumphed, Irving by affecting a stoop, Terry
with a display of her own versatility in which she reproduced the vulgar 'buoyantly', with 'gusto', 'frankness', 'relish', 'infinite enjoyment' and
'bright joyousness'.[16] 'The queer expressions fall from her lips as though
she had never spoken aught else of a more refined nature', said the *Daily
Chronicle*,[17] though in general the delight that Terry's qualities had survived
their immersion in the lower classes was not entirely displaced by obvious, and repeated, doubts about the social logic of Sardou's play (would
Cathérine really not have changed at all?), nor by the dutiful praise accorded
to Comyns Carr, the translator, for having brought off the near-impossible
feat of transposing Parisian argot into contemporary English slang without
requiring Terry to use a Cockney accent.

Looking back at the response to the Lyceum production of *Madame Sans-Gêne*, it's possible to detect a snobbish unease that is probably confirmed by Shaw's early reaction to the project, which had been to write his own Napoleon play.[18] In *The Man of Destiny*, contra Sardou, accusations of infidelity are true but suppressed (unlike the original, where they are neither suppressed nor true) and there is much Shavian banter about the ineradicable nature of national characteristics, a provocation to Terry and her management which was never taken up.

For all Shaw's scepticism, a play that attracted such lively speculation about an actress's relationship with her audience, and her portrayal of social class, was obviously destined to survive. In 1901, when Réjane's *Madame Sans-Gêne* had become an annual London event and the Lyceum revived the play in the same season, Symons reviewed both productions. Disliking the play's 'false air of honest simplicity',[19] he still found it worth praising Terry because 'she is a delightful person, full of charm, vivacity and kindliness . . . she shares her own enjoyment with you',[20] and Réjane because her acting has 'her distinguished vulgarity, her gross charm'.[21] Even so, he now discerned an unwelcome air of deliberation in Réjane's otherwise appropriate 'exaggeration': 'she plays it sweepingly, with heavy contrasts, an undisguised exaggeration; one eye is always on the audience'.[22]

It was paramount that Réjane's 'exaggeration' and her use of 'contrasts' should continue to cajole by their natural spontaneity since they had made her what she was. The combination of mixed qualities was even seen to infuse the composition of her features: no doubt, as Symons put it, 'one eye' was 'always on the audience', but then among Réjane's more unusual characteristics was something very much like a squint. In Toulouse-Lautrec's marvellous lithograph of the dance scene from *Madame Sans-Gêne*, she has one eye directly staring, the other half-closed, while pugnacious nostrils protrude above an emphatically down-turned mouth. The effect is provocative, somewhere between a wink and a stare, and made all the more comic since her facial expression seems entirely divorced from her awkwardly prancing feet.

As *The Yellow Book* had promised, not just her eyes, but all her features told a story. For William Archer, in 1894, the secret of her art lay less with her eyes, either separately or in unison, than with her mouth:

It contains her art. With a different mouth she might have been a tragedian or a heroine of melodrama, which would have been an immense pity; even for the painters it is not so much a rosebud as a full-blown rose. It has almost the wide-lipped expansiveness of a Greek mask; but it is sensitive, ironic, amiable, fascinating.[23]

Figure 10. Toulouse-Lautrec, 'Réjane and Galipaux in *Mme. Sans-Gêne*, 1894'

This mouth could speak volumes: an ironical channel that could if need be twist and redirect the words that emerged from it in, the point is crucial, a 'confidential' way. Thus 'Madame Réjane strikes one as an eminently "genial" actress, takes you into her confidence, and wins your sympathies from the start'.[24]

Sitting in the audience at the opening night of *Madame Sans-Gêne*, accompanied by his sister, was 'a shadowy young man of two-and-twenty or thereabouts, who Mr Oscar Wilde . . . has aptly described as "a silver hatchet with green hair"':[25] Aubrey Beardsley. A devotee since his visit to Paris the previous year, Beardsley again found Réjane 'ravissante',[26] and expressed his admiration in no less than six drawings, publishing one of them, in the same issue of *The Yellow Book* as the Meunier article.[27] In another of these portraits, eyes and nose perform much the same trick as in Lautrec's lithograph, but the mouth is shaped into a stern grin – with very strange results. Only hints at an Empire dress connect Beardsley's image with Madame Sans-Gêne: a pair of ornate pubic tassles make a quite different reference, just as the rigidly held fan suggests other kinds of instrument. For reasons that may not be immediately apparent, but may be to do with other plays in her repertoire, Beardsley's Réjane looks like a dominating *maîtresse*.

Although that aspect was not of course publicly noted, Beardsley's representations did provide Archer with one of those moments when art retrospectively corrects and clarifies nature. Had he originally called Réjane's mouth 'a Beardsley mouth', Archer later pondered,[28] it 'would have been at once more delicate and more descriptive, these inspirations never arrive at the right time'. Beardsley too, Archer ironically suggests, is the victim of nature, since 'Mme Réjane happens to be the one woman in the world with a Beardsley mouth'. The artist 'invents a mouth, evolves it from his inner consciousness, patents it, and has every right to look upon it as a thing peculiar to himself – a possession, if not a joy, for ever. Then all of a sudden an actress comes along in whom nature has basely anticipated his invention.' The unlucky artist will be accused by his fellows in the avant-garde of having simply imitated nature, says Archer; and in fact one paper did praise one of Beardsley's pictures as an accurate rendering of 'this graceful but ugly actress'. According to legend, however, Réjane herself was not well pleased with her 'Cytherean grin'.[29]

The English reviews of her performances do sometimes seem to suggest that Archer may have been right and that spectators saw Réjane as Beardsley saw her, or even that on seeing Réjane they just saw a Beardsley. Was the artist's response then interpretation, a style to match what he thought

Figure 11. Aubrey Beardsley, 'Portrait of Madame Réjane' from the second number of
The Yellow Book, 1894

Figure 12. Aubrey Beardsley, 'Madame Réjane'

was present, or was it more than that, signification; was what was present inseparable from his particular style? That question might be expanded and rephrased in the aesthetic terms which both actress and artist so frequently invited, and their period so often made use of: was Beardsley's elegant line as fraudulent as the actress's charm, a perverse attempt to present the ugly as the beautiful, a meretricious evasion of the real; or was it the record of the genuine anagnorisis that she brought about, a sign of the beautifully real found in the really ugly? A nineties' cliché equally applicable to Beardsley – 'beauty without beauty', said *The Yellow Book* – neatly summarises the response provoked by Réjane's favoured repertoire, much of which traced an intricate pattern on the borders of decency.

The year 1902, the critic Arthur Symons, the occasion a London revival of *Ma Cousine*,[30] written for Réjane by Meilhac, the part a would-be can-can dancer: 'Last night it seemed to me that she suggested in her costume of the second act, a Beardsley picture: here was the same sort of tragic grotesque, in which a kind of ugliness became a kind of beauty'.[31] To their joint admirers at any rate, Réjane and Beardsley clearly matched each other in that they both practised an art of the grotesque, creating those disturbingly familiar deformations of the natural which tease the spectator with recognition. Though whether the result should, in Réjane's case, be called 'tragic' was another matter. Symons's hesitant 'tragic grotesque' suggests compromise, as if two different kinds of modes could still only uneasily be paired. What, after all, could in any way be tragic about the grotesquely familiar but much sentimentalised story of a modern Parisian actress?

The heroine of *Ma Cousine*, Riquette, actress with a heart, is a model of her kind. If in *Madame Sans-Gêne* Réjane had adapted herself to the obdurate spirit of the servant class, in *Ma Cousine* she showed her other, more frequent side: her representation of the woman to whom adaptability is a professional necessity, morally either a weapon or a weakness. Riquette, who is as yet successful only in minor theatres, persuades another woman's unfaithful husband to forsake his mistress and return to his wife by the device of making up to him herself. This honestly motivated dissembling prompts a moving demonstration of the depths to which Riquette would sink (the Moulin Rouge, no less) if her own lover, a musician, were to be unfaithful to her. As a warning of the degradation involved, Riquette performs the scandalous *chahut*, with its leg-revealing high kick. For Symons, this was a striking moment, which 'summarises the whole art of the Moulin Rouge',[32] and the *Yellow Book* piece had presumably also had it in mind when it noted 'a dainty foot, that scarcely touches the earth and yet can fly amazingly near the ceiling'. An obvious but effective trick of course, to incorporate, within a respectably sentimental drama, the quintessence of everything that it purports to repudiate,[33] but here given a special theatrical frisson by the delighted expertise with which Réjane enacted the notorious kick, having been coached, it was said, by none other than the famous can-can dancer Grille d'Egout herself.

This kind of performance is suggestive in a quite literal sense, as if the theatre is flirting in public with its own resources, though *Ma Cousine* took unusual risks. No matter that when first performed in London the *chahut* was modified to suit local decorum, or that the attention of the lover was switched from a stocking to a shoe, the sheer audacity of the piece still demanded apology. 'It is the manner of the thing, not the matter that pleases. The airy spontaneity, *"gaminerie"*, innocent wickedness, childlike and bland "knowingness" of Mme Réjane as the actress.'[34] All were agreed that Réjane's 'knowingness' survived the risk of contamination without avoiding it and that it tamed the risqué with 'wit':

There is the wit of expression, of interpretation, of the translation of thought by gesture, as well as the wit of the spoken sentence, of the written phrase. Madame Réjane is the living proof that there may be an epigram in a turn of the wrist and an irony that is almost tragic in a toss of the head.[35]

In *Ma Cousine* the acting of a stage actress was wittily surpassed by the actress who acted her: Riquette, as Symons put it, 'who plays a comedy in real life quite in the spirit of the stage', Réjane, who is 'always the cleverest person on the stage . . . a whole theatre in herself'.[36] A significant number of Réjane's vehicles involved theatre people: for instance *Zaza*[37] and *La Montansier*,[38] about the legendary *directrice* who ran a theatre company during the Terror. All, for one reason or another, were deceivers; some were redeemed, some didn't need to be, some were more redeemable than others.

In *Zaza* Réjane played a performer who reverses the process alluded to by Riquette in *Ma Cousine*. The heroine is a sleazy, seductive music-hall singer who, in the course of the play, is transformed by renouncing her ferocious desire for a married businessman. The context of her conversion is, as one might expect, theatre itself. Most of the action in the first scene takes place in Zaza's loge at a *café-concert* in Saint-Etienne. Two doors lead off from an adjoining corridor: one leads outside the theatre, the other to the stage, the back of which we see, and beyond that to the audience area, part of which we also see. There is continual coming and going among performers, stage-hands, waiters, together with hangers-on and admirers from outside. All the mechanisms of stage illusion are revealed, including costumes – Zaza changes clothes in full view on more than one occasion – and make-up – she spends a good deal of time in front of her mirror. The subsequent acts present a progressive series of contrasts: from the singer's own scruffy apartment to the ornate bourgeois salon of the betrayed wife, finally to the pavements outside Les Ambassadeurs on the Champs-Elysées, where Zaza, now an established star, and incidentally a much-improved performer, encounters her lover after a gap of some years and they agree, despite their lasting passion, not to reopen the affair.

That account of the topographical changes is enough to show the blatant sentimentality of the whole endeavour. This is first and foremost a show-business story. Still, if no self-respecting English critic could admit to having been persuaded by Zaza's conversion, he could hardly resist the pull of Réjane's scrupulously self-observant performance. *The Times*, for example:

Watch the music-hall 'artist' at her toilet – how she rubs in the grease-paint, unpins her false hair, dabs the powder-puff over her shoulders, putting on a pinafore the while in order not to soil her skirt. Not a detail is missed. Even when the corset is unlaced, Zaza is careful to go through the pantomime of holding her breath. All the world and his wife have been shown exactly how the 'artiste' dresses and undresses; we feel that the sum of human knowledge has been appreciably augmented. But on the principle that you cannot have too much of a good thing, Zaza does it all, or nearly all, over again. Having combed her hair in Act i, she combs it once more in Act iv, and offers you a further piece of minute realism by removing the loose ends of hair from the comb and throwing them out of the window. Then she dusts the chair with her uplifted petticoats, cleans the wine glasses by blowing into them and giving them a wipe with her dressing-gown, and performs other choice little Bohemian-domestic exploits to which only the pen of a Swift could do full justice.[39]

To a moderately susceptible onlooker the detailed realism of Réjane's performance almost saved a play whose method was to uphold its own sham presentation of moral purity by disclosing the truths that lay behind another, coarser kind of theatrical illusion. The Bohemian alternative of the *café-concert* was obviously intended to ratify the chaste sentiments of the bourgeois romantic theatre with which *Zaza* itself finally belongs. Yet when romantic sentiments, however absurd, were conveyed alongside specific and exciting details of how powerful feelings were elsewhere produced, then the resulting effect was, by a persistent theatrical logic, one of 'spontaneity'. The 'spontaneous' had, in its turn, much to do with the 'vulgar' since, in this ambiguous kind of drama, with its simplified ideology of class and love, it would inevitably, even under the most tawdry conditions, remain inextricable from the vulgar guise in which 'the people', traditional repository of the spontaneous, often presented themselves.

The precedent of *Madame Sans-Gêne* alone was enough to secure the essential superiority of Réjane's 'vulgarity' and to distinguish her from both the English and the French contenders.[40] This applied even in a play like *Zaza*, 'a series of pictures of the uncontrolled and blatant moods of a woman of the gutter':

Madame Réjane is most admirable in every one of these moods, for her acting has just those qualities of volatile suddenness, of emotional directness, and of frank vulgarity which in a finer play enables her to give what is truest and most human in the character of a woman of the people.[41]

In the often prurient atmosphere of *fin-de-siècle* theatre, much depended upon the exploitation of equivocal connections between natural spontaneity and professional deception. But there were also those who didn't need to deceive at all, who calculated instead. Riquette and Zaza, the professional deceivers, were women of Paris; Clothilde, the cool egoist in Henri Becque's play, was *La Parisienne*.[42]

After a career marked by rejection and frustration, Becque had come to typify the newer naturalism: the *rosserie*[43] of the Théâtre Libre. *La Parisienne* opens with a neat trick played upon the staple *ménage à trois* formula, of which the whole play is a critical variation. A couple, involved in what looks like a marital row, are soon revealed as the lovers in the triangle. A similar twist, which carries the play through to its final anti-climax, is that the wife, Clothilde, rarely expresses any of the traditional passions of the adulteress. She simply comments, and calculates her own best interests. There is no final reconciliation since there has been no real disruption: her husband is more engrossed with his career, content to remain a husband in law and nothing more, while her lover grimly picks up the other duties.

Clothilde, as the *Star* put it in 1904, is 'luminous, audacious, daringly cynical, a law unto herself, the consummate egotist . . . now imperious as only the Parisienne conscious of her power can be among modern women, now alluring and seductive'.[44] The *Star* also thought that she was 'all the time a natural woman, full of humorous impulses, seeing with clear eyes the interior comedy of life', whereas in 1901 Symons had described the play as 'a hard, ironical piece of realism, founded on a keen observation of life and on certain precise ideas. It is called a comedy but there is no straight-forward fun in it, as in *Ma Cousine*, for instance; it has all that transposed sadness which we call irony.'[45] 'An air at once ironical and sympathetic' since, as the *Yellow Book* had also put it, 'Madame Réjane is the Parisienne, is all Parisiennes, incarnated'.[46]

Réjane's irony ranged through many different types: cheerful resilience in *Madame Sans-Gêne*, erotic invitation in *Zaza* and *Ma Cousine*, and now cold cynicism in *La Parisienne* – from the *gamine*, a modern version of traditional coquetry, to the *canaille* and beyond. Her presence was so flexible that its 'grotesque' appeal and 'exaggerated' manner could, even in 1902, revert to a naturalistic portrayal on the brink of tragic revelation. In Brieux's *La Robe rouge*[47] she was required to become a peasant woman, the unwitting victim of an ambitious lawyer who discovers an offence committed prior to her marriage, succeeds in turning her husband against her, and finally drives her to murder him. 'After seeing this play', wrote Symons, 'I realise what I have often wondered, that Réjane is a great tragic actress, and that she can be tragic without being grotesque'.[48] That tribute at least registers that Symons had overcome the presuppositions that could result from a union of social type with accustomed technique, a familiarity that did indeed sometimes threaten to reduce Réjane's discomforting ironical regard into a commonplace look.[49]

A danger confronts all stars, even great performers who are also stars, that, unsupported by testing vehicles, they sink back into the matrix which produced them, diluting their own power as they do so. When the point was reached at which the response to plays that were specially written for Réjane controlled the response to her other performances too, then, despite the extreme radical naturalism of *La Robe rouge* or, say, Hervieu's *La Course du flambeau*, she ran the risk of losing her enigmatic force and of becoming a spectacle for theatrical tourists. Because of her repertoire, in England at any rate, Réjane had increasingly come to signify less a type of the intransigence of the people of Paris, less the ambiguous strangeness of 'La Parisienne' than an exotic but recognisable concept: 'Paris' simply, or just 'Frenchness'.

At least one element in this process of familiarisation can be placed in the wider context of dramatic history. In Strindberg's rabidly naturalistic manifesto, the preface to *Miss Julie*, partly inspired, he says, by the psychological realism of the Goncourts' novels, criticism is directed at the habit of 'greeting one's friends' across the footlights, breaking the frame with an appealing stare at the audience.[50] Strindberg's remedy was to demand abolition of the offending lights. But note that his revolt came at the very time when others were confessing to the erotic thrill that accompanied their conviction that a distantly vibrating actress – Bernhardt, for example – had singled out just one member of the audience as the recipient of her special stare.

The critical record shows that Réjane's ambiguous presence straddled the two kinds of response, objective view and private recognition, mixing their techniques. Her winningly insolent looks had seemed to break out of their theatrical (and conceptual) frame, but in a confidential way. Although mysterious, they had been available to everyone, quizzical invitations to a whole audience that it join with her in self-observation. But the look was part of her erotic secret too – recall the 'two roguish eyes . . . lips, nervous, sensuous, trembling, curling' of the *Yellow Book* piece and, as the seasons went by, it became, perhaps inevitably, less mysterious and more 'mystified'.

At her very best Réjane, like some other contemporaries in the popular field, Yvette Guilbert, for example, traversed a schism where realism divided into evocation of a known environment and representation of the unacknowledged forces within it. A vivid discrepancy between character and its material surroundings was sometimes part of her business, ironically less in the solidly naturalistic *Germinie Lacerteux* (never performed in London) than in the popular comedy *Madame Sans-Gêne*, where the authentic resilience of social class was balanced against the stylish authenticity of the set, the sturdy recalcitrance of the body shown to be incompatible with the smoothly opulent clothes that adorned it. But sometimes, in true *belle époque* style, the buttresses smothered the building.

In the Edwardian theatre, notoriously, fame paid lavish tributes to itself, and luxury was an undeniable feature of Réjane's later display, from the couture gowns to the mules given her by the King of Portugal which pulled her carriage to the theatre.[51] Early in 1906 Gaston Mayer reopened the Royalty Theatre in London as a house specialising in French plays. Now 'one of the prettiest theatres in the Metropolis', both stage and auditorium had been enlarged, white and gold mouldings added, and an overall colour scheme of cerise and silver, apparently suggested by Réjane, introduced.[52] The refurbished Royalty epitomises the conspicuous consumption that we think of as characteristic of the new theatres of the period, and for a time it served its purpose, confirming the status of the French stars (pre-eminently Réjane but also Coquelin and Antoine) who appeared there.

Yet fame still had to live up to itself. For years there had been complaints about Réjane's delays and the length of her intervals. More recently, there had been aggrieved objections that she was coarsening her business in a misguided bid to gratify English taste, though that goes back almost to her first seasons. Then there was what some could still say was the inherent innocuousness of her sexuality: always a factor, from 1895: 'one might almost declare her a pattern of girlish – yes, girlish – innocence and fun',[53] through to 1905: 'sex is absent in her performance . . . and a large jolly soul is left'.[54] The grotesque, the *canaillerie*, the 'irony' – those kinds of familiarity had perhaps bred another, removing danger from the glints of recognition.

In London, though, she would keep one firm claim upon realism. Throughout the nineteenth century a major contention between the capitals had been English distaste for classical rhetoric and gesture, and English critics found in their enthusiasm for Réjane's contemporary repertoire and intimate technique a fresh opportunity to express their unease with the formality of French theatre, the tradition often concealed under the abstracted label 'convention'. 'She has no obvious convention at all. It is the triumph of the art of imitation', said *The Speaker*.[55] Even Symons was not entirely exempt from the prejudice, praising Bernhardt's Phèdre, for instance, as 'an art exquisitely balanced between the conventional and the realistic'.[56] The French 'impersonal' manner, surviving even Rachel's Romantic approach to tragedy, still present in Bernhardt, remained a preserve of the alien, from which Réjane's mixture of observation and provocation offered a plausible escape.

So she continued to dazzle into the new century, consolidating her reign in Paris with the inauguration of the Théâtre Réjane in 1906. Later she found success with the new playwrights, Henri Bernstein and Henri Bataille, and masterminded a stunning production of Maeterlinck's *L'Oiseau bleu*. A loyal friend and inspiration to Proust, she remained a totem of *le tout Paris* until her death in 1920, handing on a certain lavish style to Cécile Sorel. And long after the claim had first been heard that in her art working people had been given their due, Réjane was still *le peuple*. The appropriate tribute for this representation of the proletariat was still felt to be that she was able to suggest something beyond what she was merely expected to reveal. In retrospect, though, we may sometimes find it more difficult to applaud her, feeling inclined to question the ostentatious success that her comic talent, her repertoire and seductive style made possible. When Réjane broke faith with the remote vision that the Goncourts had felt the need to evoke, the people of Paris, we may be tempted to think, became one of the sights.

CHAPTER 7

Peacocks and pearls: Oscar Wilde and
Sarah Bernhardt

Of all the French actresses in the Romantic tradition Sarah Bernhardt reigned supreme and for some fifty years. Regal, imperial even, she dominated the repertoire and made innovations – not all of them welcomed by posterity – that were entirely her own. There are more books on Bernhardt than on all the other French actresses put together. Her contacts were extraordinary, stretching across continents; her first visit to London was in 1879, her last in 1921. She inspired women to assert their independence, and she redefined the profession to which she belonged. An artist who became her own model, Bernhardt was one of the great self-fashioners of her age, although for a time she did have a rival, Oscar Wilde. This chapter concentrates upon a single relationship, hoping to catch sight of common elements in the careers of two exceptional personalities and makers of the modern world.

Wilde once described to his artist friend Charles Ricketts a vision of Bernhardt in a play that he would write about Queen Elizabeth the First. 'She would look wonderful', said Wilde, 'in monstrous dresses covered with peacocks and pearls!'[1] Although that play was never written, this was an exceptionally Wildean idea because the story of Elizabeth would not only have involved many love affairs and consequent betrayals, political and familial rivalries, and a potentially marvellous death scene, it would also have brought together, without necessarily synthesising, the assumed characteristics of masculine pride (the peacock) and of feminine delicacy (the pearl) in a figure of dangerously attractive authority, which was just the kind of mixed heroine to whom Wilde was attracted. He did, after all, once say that he would have married any one of Queen Victoria, Sarah Bernhardt or Lillie Langtry with pleasure.[2]

As a young writer, fiercely ambitious to establish himself in the theatre, Wilde paid homage to many actresses, Langtry, Terry, and the Polish star Helena Modjeska among them, but Bernhardt, despite her limited English,

Figure 13. Sarah Bernhardt

was the acme because, even before her international success, she was an historical force. By reviving the roles that the great actresses of the Romantic era, above all Rachel Félix and Mlle Mars, had claimed as their own and by making them hers, Bernhardt retrieved the heroic past and offered it to the present. This was precisely the kind of creative resuscitation that Wilde himself wanted to be engaged in, but he needed to learn how to go about it, starting at the top.

The alignment began in 1879 when Bernhardt appeared with the company of the Comédie-Française for their sensational season at the Gaiety. Along with his friend the actor Forbes-Robertson, Wilde was apparently there at Folkestone when she disembarked, part of a welcoming party that, according to the manager John Hollingshead, was 'not a Barnum organised crowd, but a perfectly spontaneous and enthusiastic mob or "deputation"'.[3] The English actor presented her with a gardenia which she later claimed to have embarrassed her, and a fellow member of her company joked that the crowd would soon make her a whole carpet of flowers. Then, as Bernhardt tells it:

'Here is one!' exclaimed a young man, throwing an armful of lilies on the ground in front of me.

I stopped short, rather confused, not daring to walk on those white flowers, but the crowd pressing on behind compelled me to advance, and the poor lilies had to be trodden under foot.

'Hip, hip, hurrah! A cheer for Sarah Bernhardt!' shouted the turbulent young man.

His head was above all the others heads; he had luminous eyes and long hair, and looked like a German student. He was an English poet, though, and one of the greatest of the century, a poet who was a genius, but who was alas! later tortured and finally vanquished by madness. It was Oscar Wilde.[4]

In fact, there appear to be few, if any, newspaper reports of this event and the various sketches of the scene made by the artist who accompanied Bernhardt could well have been commissioned much later on. We are dealing, as so often, with strategic reminiscence and it is important to be wary, although it is more certain that Bernhardt and Wilde got to know one another quite well that summer. Bernhardt said much later that she had been charmed by the courtesy of his manner. 'Most men who are civil to actresses have an *arrière-pensée*. It was not so with Oscar Wilde. He was a devoted attendant and did much to make things pleasant and easy for me in London, but he never appeared to pay court.'[5]

This is either a tribute to Wilde's deliberate tact or Bernhardt being deliberately disingenuous, pretending against all the evidence that she had no interest in courtiers. Both had strongly developed skills of self-presentation. Wilde, no actor, stood on stage only to lecture or to receive applause, pleased to perform a version of himself; Bernhardt, no amateur, made sure that she never appeared away from the theatre unless in costume, with a guaranteed audience and some good lines. Wilde's friend Robert Sherard (who admittedly could be fanciful) said that Wilde copied Bernhardt's voice: 'The most wonderful things said in the golden voice of the most wonderful woman: that was the conversation of Oscar Wilde'.[6] Even if untrue there is an odd, but not uncommon, kind of gender division at work in this idea: men produce words, women provide the means to make them heard. Later on, at his house in Tite Street, Wilde displayed in his study an etching of Bastien-Lepage's portrait of Bernhardt which tells a rather different story: a profile as firm and as shaped as a *bas relief*. Wilde and Lillie Langtry apparently searched among the Greek coins in the British Museum for a profile that would match Bernhardt's classical outline.[7] It is not known if they succeeded but in Lepage's picture she contemplates a tiny statue of Orpheus the poet, perhaps of her own making, nestling tamely in her cupped hands.

Of all Bernhardt's sensational performances in the year of 1879 her embodiment of Racine's Phèdre was the most electrifying, partly because it could be measured against memories and stories of Rachel in the same part in London in the 1840s. Wilde composed a sonnet inspired by her Phèdre, identifying the role, and perhaps the actress, with Proserpine:

> How vain and dull this common world must seem
>   To such a One as thou, who should'st have talked
>   At Florence with Mirandola, or walked
> Through the cool olives of the Academe:
> Thou should'st have gathered reeds from a green stream
>   For Goat-foot Pan's shrill piping, and have played
>   With the white girls in that Phaeacian Glade
> Where grave Odysseus wakened from his dream
>
> Ah! Surely once some urn of Attic clay
>   Held thy wan dust, and thou hast come again
>   Back to this common world so dull and vain,
> For thou wert weary of the sunless day,
>   The heavy fields of scentless asphodel,
>   The loveless lips with which men kiss in Hell.[8]

By re-enacting the role of Phèdre Bernhardt both invoked Rachel and established the difference between them. She was to bring off a similar feat with two roles in Romantic dramas by Victor Hugo, Dona Sol in *Hernani* and the Queen in *Ruy Blas*, where the precedent was not Rachel but the *tragédienne's* historical counterpart, Mlle Mars, who had introduced these roles in the 1830s. Bernhardt had already proved her ability to make them new. At a gala banquet held to celebrate the successful revival of *Hernani*, hosted by Hugo for 'a hundred and fifty of the most distinguished men in France', where Bernhardt was guest of honour, the poet had publicly announced that as Dona Sol she had actually surpassed her great predecessor.[9]

Yet even as Dona Sol, the London critics saw, and were initially thrown by, the way in which Bernhardt's forceful personality and her discordant delivery made them uncomfortably aware that they were experiencing something new and strange.

As at present existing, she has style, but not dignity; she has grace, but not distinction; she has nerves, but not energy. At moments she appears to become the prey of a kind of daemonic impulse which masters her completely, and hurls her into an attitude of almost cataleptic excellence and impressiveness. Her gestures, in their febrile way, are often instinct with passion. Her diction, albeit the reverse of dramatic . . . is at best and when she has in action that much of her voice which is yet fit for service, monotonously lovely, and fraught with a certain dreamy sweetness for the moment very captivating. In her fury she is hysterical and guttural, and her voice becomes broken and hoarse.[10]

The disconcerting presence of the contemporary actress with her 'nerves' and 'hysteria' was coupled with a sense of what Hugo, famously opposed to Napoleon III, still stood for on the international scene. Another English critic said that the popularity of *Hernani* was attributable not only to the attractions of Bernhardt but 'to the kind of prejudice which successive governments have displayed with regard to the dramas of its author'.[11] For Wilde, at least, the combination of political rebelliousness and intense sensuality, the mood of the high French Romanticism that Bernhardt conjured up in her renderings of Hugo, was irresistible. As an aspirant playwright, Wilde needed dramatic structures (Hugo looked as if he might supply them) and an acting style (Bernhardt's version of melodrama was highly attractive) and he set out to recuperate the Romantic legacy in a thoroughly modern way. This might have looked like a regressive move, but for Wilde the Romantic Movement was unfinished and there was work still to be done.

In the summer of 1880, travelling with his friend, the poet Rennell Rodd, Wilde dropped in on Paris[12] and then, in 1883, having performed himself all over America, partly in the guise of Bunthorne, the character created by Gilbert and Sullivan for *Patience*, flush with money and success, he headed there for an extended stay in which he set about his own public re-enactment of the generation of 1830 by playing all the major parts himself. Rather like Bernhardt, who challenged dead actresses by taking on their roles, this was an act of deliberate Romantic anachronism.

It is still common to speak of the late nineteenth century as 'an age of transition', but an 'age of anachronism' might be more apt. For Wilde, the solution to the contrary demands placed upon the modern writer to be both inspirational and responsive to the instabilities of the time was to look both ways and, with supreme self-confidence, to expect to find the future inherent in the incompleteness of the past. It is, of course, an essential quality of anachronism that it be measured against an agreed pattern, a chronology. But Wilde had an alternative time scheme to propose in place of the official records of progress: a revolutionary pattern of events that had begun with the Romantic Movement and had yet to fulfil itself. The political anachronism was designed to condense this still potent historical energy into a set of attitudes. The past could be – must be – relived because the play was not yet over.

So, from Balzac Wilde borrowed a residential setting (the Hôtel Voltaire on the Quai Voltaire), together with a life-style, working in a dressing gown in his room, sporting a cane when he walked the streets. From Baudelaire and Poe he took his poetics; it was now that he began to compose *The Sphinx*, not to be finished until much later. And from Victor Hugo, the Republican hero, he took his politics. At night he would tramp the sleeping city, pausing at each cross-road to declaim 'Citoyen . . . ma mère, c'est la République'. This is the commitment expressed by the character Enjolras in Hugo's *Les Misérables*[13] and it may have had a special resonance for Wilde whose real mother, Lady Wilde, was indeed a famous republican. But Hugo's monumental novel is full of sentiments and images that would have appealed: the clamour of Paris itself, prisons, barricades, beautiful men, mystery and disguise, tributes to love and to the pathos of revolutionary martyrdom. 'These Christs that die upon the barricades / God knows it I am with them, in some things'[14] – so ends Wilde's 'Sonnet to Liberty', an early poem sometimes mocked for its bathos, but surely a conscious echo of Hugo's novel and a reflection of the great man's own complicated and changing views.[15]

But when Wilde did finally get to visit his idol's home (Swinburne, another Hugophile had been a recent visitor) Hugo promptly fell asleep.[16] He was, after all, quite ancient: eighty-one. When Juliette Druot, his mistress for fifty years, died in May of 1883 the papers reported that, too infirm to join the funeral cortège, he could be glimpsed viewing the spectacle from an upstairs window.[17] Two years later he was dead himself.

From another special hero, that 'most subtle of all modern critics' (Wilde's own phrase for Théophile Gautier[18]) Wilde borrowed a costume with distinctly Hugolian associations: he wore a copy of the famous red waistcoat that Gautier had worn for the tumultuous first night of *Hernani* on 25 February 1830, when opposing Romantics and members of the old school had alternately cheered and barracked Hugo's pioneering play. The legend of that first night had been revived quite recently by Gautier in his *Histoire du Romantisme* of 1874,[19] a book that Wilde knew well. Though the sartorial affectation of the waistcoat began in Paris in 1883 it seems that Wilde was still wearing it in 1891 when William Rothenstein did a pastel portrait that was exhibited in a show with works by Charles Conder. Wilde bought the picture himself but it was later stolen and lost.[20]

Certainly, according to Gautier's memoir published in the 1870s, people were still talking about the original red waistcoat forty years on, indeed Gautier wonders if it is the only thing that would be remembered of him when his poetry, his articles and books are forgotten.[21] If so, he says he wouldn't really mind because the waistcoat has become an emblem of wild ambition and of an attractive ability to rise above ridicule and public opinion. He compares it to the costume of an Andalusian bull-fighter and says that against the greyness of, for example, Voltaire, the Romantics, with their penchant for the colour red, stood for 'life, light, movement, audacity of thought and execution, a return to the splendid periods of the Renaissance and true antiquity' (90). So this is no commonplace shade, it is rather a 'noble colour, now dishonoured by political furies' that needs to be restored to modern life. It is 'blood, life, light, heat'.

At the tailor's fitting for the wonderful waistcoat, Gautier recalls:

We pulled from the cupboard a magnificent length of Chinese cerise or vermilion satin, which we displayed triumphantly before the eyes of the terrified tailor with an air of tranquillity and satisfaction which made him fear for our reason.

The light shimmered and shone on the folds of the material and we rumpled it to show up the sparkling play of colours. We ran through the whole gamut of the colour red – from the warmest to the richest, the strongest and the most delicate. So as to avoid the infamous red of 1793, we admitted a light smattering of purple in our tone; for we were keen not to be accused of showing any political intention. We were not dilettante in the manner of Saint-Just or Robespierre . . . (96)

This, then, is the red of revolution but purged of terror and reimbued with its original poetry, theatricalised. It is nevertheless a declaration of war. Wilde particularly enjoyed Gautier's invocation of the Romantic writer as a fighter who strives 'pour propager sa gloire et ennuyer les philistins' ('to propagate his glory and annoy the Philistines') and he linked himself with Rennell Rodd in another phrase of Gautier's as 'jeunes guerriers du drapeau romantique' ('young warriors bearing the Romantic flag').[22]

In 1880, exactly half a century after the *Hernani* first night, Bernhardt herself had recited François Coppée's tribute, 'La Bataille d'Hernani', from the stage of the Théâtre-Français:

Hernani! . . . cinquante ans sont passeés, mais ce nom
Résonne dans nos coeurs comme un bruit de canon
Et grise nos cerveaux comme une odeur de poudre . . .[23]

'Hernani, fifty years later, the name resounds in our hearts like canon shot and carries us away like the smell of gun powder'; this was poor poetry but, as always in the Hugo connection, fighting talk.

Reading about the première of *Hernani* in Gautier's *Histoire du Romantisme*, Wilde would have learned how 'romantic youth, full of zeal and impassioned by the preface to *Cromwell*, determined to be uplifted like "a mountain sparrow-hawk"'.[24] In the celebrated preface to this unstaged play Hugo had laid down the ground-rules for a Romantic as opposed to neo-classical theatre: *couleur locale, mélange des genres, la théorie du grotesque*. Even Graham Robb, Hugo's best and most recent biographer, has admitted that the preface 'contains a lot of twaddle'.[25] No matter, it makes the right sounds, strikes the right attitudes. Matthew Arnold, who found that Hugo lacked seriousness, may have conceded that 'the tragedy of M. Victor Hugo has always, indeed, stirring events in plenty . . . and yet our poetic sense may remain profoundly dissatisfied'. This was because Hugo's 'brilliant gift for versification is exercised within the limits of a form inadequate for true tragic poetry, and by its very presence excluding it'.[26] Wilde, in contrast, following Swinburne, found in Hugo's plays the blueprint for a theatre that would be fervent and glamorous, spectacular and poetic. They offered a formula for modern playwriting which is what, at the time, Wilde thought he needed.

Further confirmation of the enduring power of Romantic drama came when, in the course of his French residency, Wilde was able to consolidate his friendship with Bernhardt. He saw her in *Fédora*, the first of the plays by Victorien Sardou in which she was able to devise a form of historical theatre that simplified and made even more exotic, the Hugolian precedent. Wilde went backstage in the usual manner and was invited to *soirées* at her house.[27] And, in an extremely well-received talk that he gave to the Paris Pen and Pencil Club in February, he expressed his intense admiration for Bernhardt, praising her supreme judgement and taste in all matters of art.[28]

The main creative effort during the Paris stint was completion of *The Duchess of Padua*, a pastiche Revenge tragedy saturated with echoes of Shakespeare and the Jacobeans, although Hugo is a dominant influence too. The play is Hugolian in style (its moods change rapidly but its locations are quite specific), and even in plot to the extent that, like *Hernani*, it involves a son's frustrated revenge for the murder of his father and a romantic entanglement that ends in the double death of the lovers. In *The Duchess of Padua*, young Guido Ferranti, the hero, is persuaded by the sinister Count Moranzone to settle the murder of his own father by slaying the guilty Duke of Padua. The Duke, the best-written part in the play, is a genial kind of devil with a rather camp line in wit. 'I trust I'll never be a good old man,' he says, 'God would grow weary if I told my sins'.[29] But Guido falls in love with the Duchess virtually on sight and he hesitates. She pre-empts his intended action by killing her husband herself, only to lose Guido, who believes that she has destroyed his trust 'and in its place / Has set a horrible and bloodstained thing, / Whose very breath breeds pestilence and plague, / And strangles Love'.[30] The remainder of the play is taken up with scenes in court and in jail, a complex exchange of the roles of accuser and accused until the pair die together – having learned the perennial Wildean lesson that sins will be forgiven those who 'love much'.

The Duchess follows on from Vera, the heroine of Wilde's first play, the revolutionary nihilist who falls in love with the Czar and saves his life, but she has more pronounced Bernhardtian characteristics. Within the space of a few lines she switches from violent verbal, even physical, attack ('Better you had crossed a hungry lioness') to lyric pathos ('This is the hand he kissed, these are the lips / His lips made havoc of'[31]) and she inspires devotion with a single look. To be gazed at by the Duchess is immediately to be caught up in her power and the play has several carefully placed moments when she is required to glance back over her shoulder as she sweeps off stage, a famous Bernhardt gesture captured in a well-known portrait by Georges Clairin.

Despite the fact that the play has all these Bernhardtian qualities (and even repeats phrases from the sonnet prompted by her Phèdre), Wilde sent it off to the American actress Mary Anderson, with whom he had discussed the proposed play during his American tour. The most obvious reason for this move was that Bernhardt would not have been able to sustain the English language, at least not for a five-act drama. Nevertheless, Wilde told Anderson that *The Duchess* 'would give you the glory of a Rachel, and may yield me the fame of a Hugo'.[32] The manuscript was accompanied by a long letter, inspired by Hugo's preface to *Cromwell*, which argued for a drama of the comic and the grotesque and which stressed the modernity of the antique. '*The essence of art is to produce the modern idea under an antique form*', writes Wilde.[33] Modernity here seems to have two inflections. One is political and Hugolian, the modernity of urban poverty, for example: the duchess speaks of those who 'sleep / under the arches of the public bridges / all through the autumn nights, till the wet mist / stiffens their limbs, and fevers come'.[34] The other kind of modernity is philosophical and Paterian: a modern way of thinking that understands historical development as an evolutionary yet dialectical process.

Ever concerned about theatrical effect, Wilde concludes his letter to Mary Anderson by echoing Gautier on the colour red – and he corrects his own set design, replacing crimson velvet with vermilion silk since the latter will shimmer and, being transparent, when light actually shines through it, 'will suddenly become a door of crimson fire!'[35]

Colour is of tremendous importance within the aesthetic that Wilde, like others, took from Gautier and the Romantics. Although red is significant it is not unique: yellow, mauve, purple and green were all to come in for special treatment in the 1890s. Not only did the late nineteenth century think a lot about colour, it actually thought *through* colour. Colours and emotional ideas were implicated in each other. So, dramatic text and scenic effect must match exactly, the colour must be precisely right for the moment. And red is of primary importance in Romantic visual aesthetics, since its several hues encompass the multitudinous possibilities of passion and authority. Many years later, in 1897, composing *The Ballad of Reading Gaol*, Wilde was again to remember Hugo, this time the theatrical effect of a line at the end of his *Marion de Lorme* which refers to the unforgiving Cardinal Richelieu – 'Regardez tous! Voilà l'homme rouge qui passe!'[36] – and added it to his own description of a heartless British judge: 'The man in red who reads the Law / Gave him three weeks of life'.[37] Even in this highly realistic poem there was still room for a moment of intense Romantic drama.

In fact, in the 1880s, Wilde sometimes used the phrase 'romantic realist' to describe what he called 'the movement of which Hugo is the father',[38] and in 'Shakespeare and Stage Costume', the essay he published in 1885,[39] he quotes from Hugo's 1838 author's note to *Ruy Blas* the edict that:

Les petits détails d'histoire et de vie domestique doivent être scrupuleusement étudiés et reproduits par le poëte, mais uniquement comme des moyens d'accroître la réalité de l'ensemble, et de faire pénétrer jusque dans les coins les plus obscurs de l'œuvre cette vie générale et puissante au milieu de laquelle les personnages sont plus vrai, et les catastrophes, par conséquent, plus poignantes. Tout doit être subordonné à ce but. L'homme sur le premier plan, le reste au fond.[40]

[The little details of history and of domestic life must be scrupulously studied and reproduced by the poet, but solely as a means of adding to the reality of the whole and of instilling into the darkest corners of the work this general and powerful life, in the midst of which the characters are more real and the catastrophes, as a result, more poignant. Everything must be subordinated to this end. Man in the foreground – the rest in the background.]

Unfortunately, *The Duchess of Padua* was turned down by Mary Anderson and not performed until 1891 in New York, under a different title. For a while Wilde turned from plays to other kinds of writing; Bernhardt built on the success of *Fédora*. They must surely have met in London or Paris or at least corresponded in the late 1880s, but there is no firm evidence.[41]

Wilde's aesthetic was changing. Reprinted in *Intentions* of 1891, 'Shakespeare and Stage Costume' now carried a coda:

Not that I agree with everything that I have said in this essay. There is much with which I entirely disagree. The essay simply represents an artistic standpoint, and in aesthetic criticism attitude is everything. For in art there is no such thing as a universal truth. A Truth in art is that whose contradictory is also true. And just as it is only in art-criticism, and through it, that we can apprehend the Platonic theory of ideas, so it is only in art-criticism, and through it, that we can realise Hegel's system of contraries. The truths of metaphysics are the truths of masks.[42]

Most critics see this as typically Wildean perversity,[43] but it's more specific than that. 'Attitudes' now replace 'archaeology'; the need for anachronism, not entirely concealed in the earlier version by any means, is now foregrounded as the key to an energetic aesthetic, since the presence of contradiction admits of change.

When Bernhardt marked Hugo's death in 1885 with a revival of *Marion de Lorme*, her production, despite the great displays of public mourning, was not a success. Romantic tragedy needed to be updated. Asked in the 1890s about the playwrights he admired, Wilde now added the name of Maeterlinck to that of Hugo.[44] This was both a pairing (two French language dramatists) and an opposition (historical versus imagined, rhetoric versus image, climactic versus protracted). Together the twin influences were to produce *Salomé*. Whether Wilde had Bernhardt specifically in mind when he wrote the play is uncertain. He later denied that he had, but it has been suggested that this was playing safe, wishing to hold on to the public presentation of himself as an autonomous genius and that the play was written in French primarily to subvert the rule of the Lord Chamberlain.[45] He did give Bernhardt a copy of his *Poems* (1892) inscribed 'A Sarah Bernhardt. Hommage d'Oscar Wilde . . . Comme la / Princesse Salomé / est belle ce soir! Londres'[46] and he was right to think that she too could see the possibilities in Maeterlinckian symbolism if rightly handled. Wilde's own brand of symbolism would allow the retention of the comic within a tragic structure – Hugolian mixed genres again. And as for the grotesque: at the end of *Ruy Blas* Bernhardt as the Queen, finding 'her lover at her feet, dying at what he takes to be her bidding' had had, according to one account, 'a burst of supreme passion, in which she clasps his head to her bosom, fondles it, and recoils shuddering from the lips already stiffening with death'.[47] There was a similar gesture at the climax of *Hernani*. *Salomé*, in which the heroine notoriously clasps the head of the dead Baptist, would preserve and heighten such perversely Romantic moments. At the same time the Maeterlinckian symbolist style would replace the local colour and extreme detail of Hugo with a more modern use of tonal graduation and new ways of representing the mysteries of subjectivity, particularly in the realm of sexuality. Even the colour red would take on a new vividness.

According to Salomé's erotic tribute, the mouth of Jokanaan is like 'a band of scarlet', 'like a pomegranate', which is 'redder than roses', redder than the 'red blasts of trumpets', redder than the feet of those who tread the wine in the wine-press, redder than the feet of doves, a red that is simultaneously coral and vermilion. 'There is', Salomé finally gasps, 'nothing in the world so red as thy mouth'.[48]

But it was blasphemy not sex that put paid to Wilde's colourful experiment. The story of the Lord Chamberlain's refusal to license the play and of Wilde's threat to go into permanent exile in Paris has been told many times. It marks a significant missing date in the chronicle of the 1890s, the collaboration that was never completed, the dream-team that never played, the supergroup that never appeared.[49]

At least Bernhardt never had to demonstrate her skill in dancing although, unstaged as it was, *Salomé* still offered enough scope for jokes at the expense of its temperamental author and his would-be leading lady. In his illustrations to Wilde's text Aubrey Beardsley portrays Wilde as a lecherous bearded Herod and he draws on Bernhardt for a hideous Salomé. In the cruel world of the 1890s, beautiful women and gay men are rarely permitted to grow old gracefully. In the eyes of another caricaturist, Toulouse-Lautrec, middle age is allowed to suit neither; indeed they seem to be coming to resemble one another, shapeless, genderless. Wilde alludes, camply, to the feminine; Bernhardt assumes the masculine.

Age was a challenge that these two spendthrifts were to handle in different ways. For Wilde the playwright, the best option was the mature medium of the society play. Together with leading male actor-managers (Herbert Beerbohm Tree and George Alexander, both of whom he had known for a decade or more) he found success with *Lady Windermere's Fan* in 1892 and followed that with *A Woman of No Importance* in 1893. Bernhardt, who had told Wilde's friend Robert Sherard back in 1889 that 'forty-five thousand francs a year is nothing, a bagatelle . . . not enough to live upon', opted for lucrative revivals.[50]

Figure 14. 'The Comédie Française at the Gaiety: *Hernani*' (*Illustrated London News*, 21 June 1879)

She toured the world, he ruled the West End – until life and the law caught up with him. In 1895, in Holloway waiting for trial, desperate to raise money for his defence, he communicated with Bernhardt through Sherard, offering to sell her the rights in *Salomé* for a lump sum. She wept (the right response) and then, whether for reasons of financial meanness, not wanting to alienate her English admirers, or because privately she knew that for her the moment of *Salomé* had gone forever (she must have been aware of the performance of *Salomé* at the Théâtre de l'Œuvre in Paris in 1896) – for whatever reason – she refused.[51]

Their final meeting was at Cannes very late in 1898 when she was appearing in *Tosca* and Wilde was staying at nearby Napoule. He went backstage and, as he wrote to Robert Ross, 'she embraced me and wept, and I wept, and the whole evening was wonderful'.[52] Even in that ritual of insincerity, of dressing-room compliments, the tears must have run hot. Professionals both, they knew how to behave on occasion, could suit the style to the scene. That talent they still shared.

The contemporary Irish poet Derek Mahon has written a superbly raffish piece in which he imagines Wilde wandering the streets of the Left

Figure 15. Toulouse-Lautrec, 'Oscar Wilde', 1896 (detail)

Bank in those very last years. Portraits of Wilde in his decline have become something of a sub-genre in recent times: writers from Peter Ackroyd to Tom Stoppard to David Hare have all taken it on, but Mahon's poem, with its surreptitious allusion to Scott Fitzgerald's *The Great Gatsby*, is exceptional in its appreciation of modern failure:

> The morgue
> yawns, as it yawned too for Verlaine, Larforgue,
> nor will you see your wife and sons again.

Figure 16. Toulouse-Lautrec, 'Sarah Bernhardt as Cleopatra', 1898

Gestures, a broken series; performance strain;
judge by appearances and what you get
is an old windbag. Still full of hot air,
still queer as fuck and putting on the style,
you spout in the Odéon given half a chance
for yours is the nonchalance of complete despair.[53]

The Hôtel d'Alsace, which is where Wilde ended up, was only a brisk ten minutes' walk from the Place du Châtelet, where Bernhardt had a new theatre. For Wilde that brief journey must have been out of the question.

At the vast Théâtre Sarah Bernhardt, the gestures were unbroken, the performance strain was concealed, and appearance, as always, counted for almost everything. It is hard to imagine, for another modern personality, the pain of hearing about the scale of that enterprise, the overweeningness of the new century.

In her extraordinarily baroque memoirs, so rich in unlikely detail that it is impossible to distinguish foundation in fact from apocryphal decoration, the actress Cécile Sorel claims to have visited Wilde at the hotel soon before his death: 'a stout, bowed man who looked like a wounded bull. His eyes were glassy, his mouth slack.'[54] Apparently she asked him to her home and threw a party which she recreates in prose as sumptuous as one of her own stage costumes:

An invisible orchestra was to play throughout dinner. Lackeys holding torches stood on the steps of the broad stone staircase. Others in white stockings and knee breeches, with gold epaulettes, awaited the guest they were to announce.

When Wilde arrives the servants, assuming him to be a beggar, move to turn him away. He enters the salon, strokes the marble torsos of Greek statues. Sorel, in her emerald jewellery and a gold Egyptian gown, sails towards him:

Beautiful in his hideousness and corpulence, he drew his heavy body up for an instant upon his too-thin legs. Already he was reviving beneath his poor worn clothes.
'Ah', he said, 'this is the woman of whom I have often dreamed. . . . It is a shame to show myself to you in this pitiful state'.

Questioned by Sorel as to why he had never visited her before, Wilde replies that he did not dare, since 'You are the image of the woman whom I have brought to life in my books. You had become a myth which I could no longer approach.'[55]

Sorel was in some ways Bernhardt's successor (it seems they became friends just before the older woman's death). Much as Bernhardt, her career but not her fame in decline, had chosen to take her turn among the other variety acts at the London Coliseum in the 1920s, Sorel was to make a move from the Comédie-Française to the Casino de Paris in 1933. Had he survived his Parisian purgatory beyond 1900 it is not entirely inconceivable that Wilde, born in 1854, could have witnessed these heroic accommodations to changes in the business of theatre, these recognitions of 'la folie moderne'. He certainly understood all too well the demands that an audience makes upon the performing artist. In a prose poem called 'The Disciple' he has the fatal pool of myth mourn Narcissus, the dead man it loved, because 'as he lay on my banks and looked down at me, in the mirror of his eyes I saw ever my own beauty mirrored'.[56] This reciprocity is replicated in the mutual dependence of personality (that very modern word) and his or her audience. They need each other, are sustained by each other. When one disappears, both die.

But if Narcissus is modernity's myth of doom, Echo is its recurrent sound of survival. 'I like hearing myself talk. It is one of my greatest pleasures.' That is Wilde in fact,[57] but in a famous photograph Bernhardt is shown listening with entranced self-delight to the sound of her own voice as it emerges from a recording machine: a sound that returns from the moment of utterance, defying time, revisiting from the dead, as early recorded voices were often said to do.

A recording exists (it sometimes surfaces on radio programmes even now) which purports to be of Wilde reciting 'The Ballad of Reading Gaol' into Edison's machine at the Paris exhibition of 1900. It is almost certainly a fake though the urge to believe that it is genuine is hard to suppress.[58] In fact, that exhibition was Bernhardt's affair: she even made a short film of herself as Hamlet to be shown along with the other marvels celebrating France's up-to-dateness. Endless return was what Wilde had praised Bernhardt for in the sonnet of 1879, dedicated to her, recasting Phèdre as Prosperine – 'Ah! Surely once some urn of Attic clay / Held thy wan dust, and thou hast come again / Back to this common world so dull and vain'. Technology almost made it possible: the urn of attic clay turned into the horn of a phonograph.

Within months of the exhibition he was dead; she went on for another twenty-three years as it turned out, filled with films, music-hall appearances, work for the war effort, an amputation, new lovers, but few new plays. People no longer wrote for her as they once had done. She became a bit of a joke; but then she always had been: 'Sarah Barnum', the one-woman freak show, a sight to see, to hear, and to mimic. Now more than ever, she survived as much in parodies and pastiches as in the records of her own performances. Already the pre-postmodernists of the early twentieth century, doubting the evidence of their own eyes and ears, distrusted the real, acknowledged instead the truth of imitations.

When, for example, Lettie, the New Woman character in D. H. Lawrence's *The White Peacock* of 1911, feels stressed and confused she breaks into Bernhardtese. Here is a typically over-blown passage from early on in the novel as she engages with her potential lover, the farmer George Saxton.

Figure 17. Sarah Bernhardt listening to her own voice in the Bettini Recording
Laboratory, NY

At last she rose, gathered the books together, and carried them off. At the door she turned. She must steal another keen moment: 'Are you admiring my strength?' she asked.

Her pose was fine. With her head thrown back, the roundness of her throat ran finely down to the bosom which swelled above the pile of books, held by her straight arms. He looked at her. Their lips smiled curiously. She put back her throat as if she were drinking. They felt the blood beating madly in their necks. Then, suddenly breaking into a slight trembling, she turned around and left the room.

Following that histrionic exit Lawrence allows for a dramatic pause during which George sits, 'twisting his moustache'. And then,

She came back along the hall talking madly to herself in French. Having been much impressed by Sarah Bernhardt's 'Dame aux Camélias' and 'Adrienne Lecouvreur', Lettie had caught something of the weird tone of this great actress, and her raillery and mockery came out in little wild waves. She laughed at him, and at herself, and at men in general, and at love in particular. Whatever he said to her, she answered in the same mad clatter of French, speaking high and harshly. The sound was strange and uncomfortable. There was a painful perplexity in his brow, such as I often perceived afterwards, a sense of something hurting, something he could not understand.

'Well, well, well, well!' she explained at last. 'We must be mad sometimes, or we should be getting aged. Hein?'

'I wish I could understand,' replies poor George, 'plaintively',[59] but it's not just the 'mad clatter' of the French language that he fails to understand, it is the 'strange and uncomfortable' sound itself: the high Romantic, entirely theatricalised, madness that counters ordinary living: Lettie's parody is an intimate homage, invited by the star herself.

Bernhardt did eventually play the part of Queen Elizabeth, but the text was not by Wilde and though there may have been some pearls, no peacocks were in sight. In 1912 she made a film based on a play about the Queen. A flop in Europe, it was an unexpected hit in the US where, bought by Adolph Zukor, it laid the foundations for what was to become Paramount Pictures. Viewing it now, perhaps even at the time, Bernhardt's gestures all through appear over-conventionalised and limited. Certainly, compared with some other films of the period, this one is stuck in a style of the-atrical *tableau* that already seems old-fashioned. The famous profile and pose are lost in the middle distance and the absence of close-up makes it difficult to appreciate or judge the power of Bernhardt's voiceless pres-ence. Other actors and actresses learned very quickly how to make the medium work for them, but it is not clear that Bernhardt did. Was the

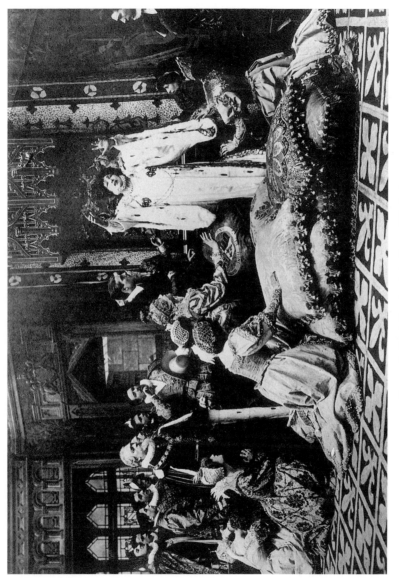

Figure 18. Sarah Bernhardt in *Queen Elizabeth*

twentieth-century art already too modern for the ageing actress? Or was it insufficiently developed to know how to recapture her nineteenth-century brilliance? *Queen Elizabeth* now looks like a mismatch of style, of moment and of medium. As Bernhardt's co-conspirator, Oscar Wilde, had always maintained, the past comes in and out of focus only at the appropriate time. The film of *Queen Elizabeth*, a material demonstration, proves him right.[60]

CHAPTER 8

The greatest actress in the world: Edwige Feuillère and her admirers

> *Estelle*: The *Sunday Times* was quite good.
> *Almina*: Yes, but I couldn't understand half of it, too many French
> words and that Edwigger what's her name being dragged in all the
> time.
> *Estelle*: Not Edwigger, dear. Edveege. Edveege Fooyare.
> Noel Coward, *Waiting in the Wings*, 1960[1]

BREAK OF NOON

In the autumn of 1951, the year of the Festival of Britain, Edwige Feuillère, temporarily a member of the Renaud-Barrault Company, appeared in London in Claudel's *Partage de Midi* for the very first time. The French company had been invited to the St James Theatre by Laurence Olivier and Vivien Leigh, who had seen Jean-Louis Barrault's production in Paris in 1948. As well as making a nice complement to the Festival celebration which the Oliviers had marked with a not entirely successful programme of 'the two Cleopatras' (Shakespeare's and Shaw's), the French visit contributed to the spirit of post-war *entente cordiale* in the theatre. This had begun in 1945 with a two-way exchange between the Old Vic Company (so named for the occasion) and the Comédie-Française and had continued, in England at any rate, with the considerable interest shown in contemporary French plays. Anouilh, Giraudoux, Cocteau, together with the rather more demanding Sartre and Camus, had all been quickly translated and professionally performed. Yet alongside respect for the impressive intellectuality of the new work there ran an ancient ambivalence towards French convention: those interminable speeches, the dominance, verbal and spatial, of single characters.

She 'talks and talks and talks', complained a new critic on the *Sunday Times* named Harold Hobson when Eileen Herlie delivered the stupendous monologue, almost thirty minutes long, in Cocteau's *Eagle with Two Heads*

Figure 19. Edwige Feuillère

at the Lyric Hammersmith in September 1946.[2] Five years later Hobson's estimation of French theatre was wonderfully reversed by the Renaud-Barrault *Partage de Midi*, starring Feuillère. Writing in his memoirs in the 1970s, by then retired, he would recall that he immediately hailed 'the dazzling Edwige Feuillère' as 'the greatest actress in the world'.[3] Although true in spirit, this memory is not strictly accurate in fact. What the young Hobson had actually written about Feuillère in the *Sunday Times* was this:

Her voice is miraculously soft, and comforting, and caressing; she wears her Edwardian costumes with a supple grace; has apparently the gift of being able to make her eyes swim with tears at will; at every moment is in complete control of her performance; can utter words as simple as 'Qu'il fait chaud' with such languor, such a sense of voluptuous suffocation that the air of the theatre seems heavy with heat.[1]

The underlying point being, as Hobson was at pains to stress at the time, that Feuillère was 'an actress too resplendent in her own right to be fobbed off on us as a mere reincarnation of some star of the past', in other words, that although she obviously belonged to the tradition of Rachel, of Bernhardt, of Réjane even, she enhanced that legacy in distinctive ways. And just like her great predecessors, Feuillère had, in at least one critical mind, contemporary rivals against which her own talent could be measured, specifically Madeleine Renaud, Barrault's wife, a very considerable performer in the classic repertoire. Renaud played Araminte in Marivaux's *Les Fausses Confidences* in London in 1951, enabling Hobson to make the comparison that would eventually confirm Feuillère's superiority: 'Into both pain can enter. But whereas with Mme Renaud one knows the pain will soon pass and sunshine return, with Mme Feuillère the pain is always there, though the rippling laughter often hides it.'

It was not until two years later, 1953, when he edited a volume called *The Theatre Now* that Hobson actually wrote that he considered Feuillère to be 'without exception, the greatest and most moving player I have ever seen'.[5] By the time of her second visit, to the Edinburgh Festival and the Duke of York's Theatre in London in 1955 with *Partage de Midi*, the phrase was firmly in place: 'This actress, whom I think to be the greatest in the world . . .'[6] And, when it came to her final London season, which was in 1968, Hobson was so confident in his judgement, and of his own critical position, that he was able to mock himself and his now famous tribute: 'Even I, who have made myself hoarse proclaiming that she is the greatest actress in the world, was a little nervous for her before last Monday's performance began'. Fortunately, 'It was a base and craven fear; for from the moment of her entrance it was evident that she was as radiant as we remembered . . . I do not think we shall see such a performance again in our lifetime'.[7]

The St James season of 1951 that started it all off was an occasion of some considerable theatrical significance, and not just for Hobson: 'The moment that she swept on to the stage like a fluttering bird released from a cage there was dead silence', remembers someone else who was there: 'No applause. No shuffling. No striking matches or lighters. No unwrapping of chocolates. For an hour and a half this audience was mesmerised by a beautiful woman who had the power to communicate the most complex words and thoughts to a foreign audience.'[8]

Feuillère was forty-three years old and already an established star of the French theatre. After training at the Conservatoire and a brief period in light comedies at the Palais-Royal, she had joined the Comédie-Française in 1931, making a great impression as Susanne in *Le Mariage de Figaro* and in two other pieces from the established repertoire: *La Parisienne* by Henri Becque and, almost inevitably, *La Dame aux camélias* by Dumas *fils* (1939). In the same period she achieved a more public name for herself in films, in two of which she briefly appeared naked: Abel Gance's *Lucrèce Borgia* (1935 with Antonin Artaud) and Max Ophuls's *Sans lendemain* (1939). Identified both with Réjane (Feuillère claimed never to have forgotten someone remarking about her that 'Réjane was ugly too') and with Bernhardt, with whose voice her own was often compared (by Jean Cocteau, for one), Feuillère's career already pointed in two directions at once – back to the nineteenth century and forward into the twentieth. She continued to perform during the occupation and in the 1940s worked closely with Cocteau, starring in both the original French stage and film versions of *L'aigle à deux têtes* (1946 and 1947) and with Jean Giraudoux, who wrote *Sodome et Gomorrhe* (1942) for her. When, late in the decade, Jean-Louis Barrault finally persuaded the poet and playwright Paul Claudel to allow him to produce a version of *Partage de Midi*, an autobiographical play about adulterous romance which, though written in the 1890s and first published in 1905, the increasingly religious author had never allowed to be performed, Feuillère was an obvious first choice for the dominant, indeed the only, female part.

Partage de Midi involves just four characters. In the first act, which takes place in the blaze of noon on the deck of a ship heading East, Mesa, a colonial official troubled by religious doubts, finds himself tempted by the prospect of an affair with the beautiful Ysé who is married to de Ciz, also on board. In the second act, which takes place at midnight in a Hong Kong cemetery, their affair is almost consummated following an exchange of erotic protestations, and Mesa contrives to send de Ciz off to his death by offering him a post in the Chinese hinterland, where cholera is rife. But this murderous trick fails to lead to the consolidation of his relationship with Ysé since, in the third act, which also takes place at night, she deserts him for a more overtly masculine lover, Almaric. Rebellion breaks out among the Chinese and Almaric and Ysé find themselves trapped. Mesa arrives with a safe pass for Ysé, which she refuses; Mesa and Almaric fight and

Mesa is struck unconscious by Almaric who seizes his pass. The two lovers flee, leaving Mesa for dead.

Then, in the most haunting moment of the whole play, Mesa recovers consciousness and, the stage now penetrated by an intense beam of silver moonlight, breaks into the 'Cantique de Mesa' a long poetic address to the heavens in which he recognises that his rejection, first apparently by God and secondly by Ysé, are both part of a divine plan to bring him to the recognition that sacrifice and surrender are the necessary preconditions of faith. Mesa finally achieves love.

Harold Hobson had been brought up as a Christian Scientist and he remained deeply religious all his life. What impressed him most, even on that very first encounter with *Partage de Midi* in 1951, was the thought that here was a profoundly Christian play fully deserving of its place in the modern repertoire:

> It is M. Claudel's brilliant theatrical achievement in this play, and it outweighs all his defects that he springs on us the surprise which he makes absolutely convincing, of saving Mesa, not by resisting temptation, but by falling into it. For by the agony he then suffers, the heart of Mesa, which till then, despite its rectitude, had remained a little cold, is burst open to a full realisation of what love really means, the love of Christ no less than the love of men and women.[9]

In addition, the extraordinarily luminous mood of *Partage de Midi*, the collaborative achievement of Barrault's precise *mise-en-scène*, Christian Bérard's perfectly white costumes and Félix Labisse's airy atmospheric settings, all of which managed to be both ethereal and intensely sensual, made religion dramatically real. In a unique demonstration of material theatre as spiritual revelation, physical beauty and divine presence merged with one another. Hobson again, this time from his autobiography:

> The vision of the white boat-deck lit by the blazing midday sun of the tropics; the white-dressed, seductive Edwige languorously sitting in the centre of the stage; the glittering waves shimmeringly reflected in the white sails of the ship; Edwige's ringing peals of laughter marvellously timed and regulated in pitch and volume before the absolute silence that was not broken again until the tolling of the ship's bell at noon; and the white-clothed figure of Barrault standing rigid and motionless as, amongst all this whiteness, he contemplated the blackness of murder, were something that, in their combination of visual and dramatic impact, London had not seen the like of before: nor indeed of the enormous swell of rhetoric with which at the end of the play, Barrault comes to God in the same splendour of noonday as in Donne God comes to man.[10]

While Ysé is evidently in the line of *la grande coquette*, her role and function is aggrandised by association with the notion of the *l'éternel féminin* as in

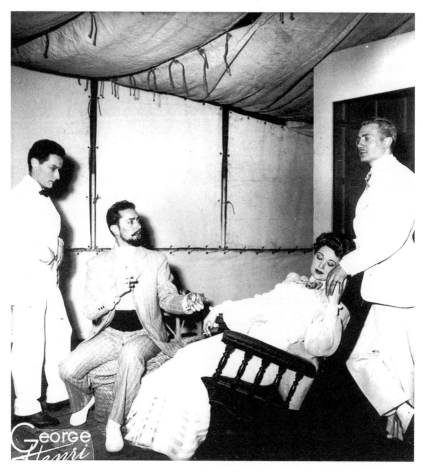

Figure 20. Jean-Louis Barrault (far left) and Edwige Feuillère in *Partage de Midi*

Symbolist theatre. This subtle development is even tacitly acknowledged within the text itself. 'I believe her to be impudent coquette', says Mesa. To which Almaric replies, 'As you wish. Though you misunderstand her completely. My dear friend, she is a superb woman.'[11] Fittingly, Barrault drew on gestural means to convey those moments of intense sexual attraction (and, perhaps, because Claudel himself continued to have grave doubts about the second act, given its 'erotic frenzy').[12] When Barrault's Mesa imagined making love to Ysé he did so with a piece of business apparently inspired by Nijinsky: his hands passing all around her body, never touching, 'as Sergeant Troy's sword flickered round Bathsheba Everdene', as Hobson was to describe it later.[13] Always alive to ways in which French theatre relied upon the expressive possibilities of bodily movement, Hobson found in the *mise-en-scène* for *Partage de Midi* an ideal combination of sacred and secular, in which the latter was never, as in certain contemporary playwrights he admired such as Jean Genet and Samuel Beckett, allowed to purloin and obliterate the former. For all the play's strong sexual nuance, aesthetic propriety was maintained throughout.

We can learn more about how these effects were actually achieved from Feuillère herself, who was by this time an artist of considerable experience with strongly developed ideas. Indeed, there are hints that she was not always at one with the production, including the gestural love-making which she found superfluous to the verse.[14] For Feuillère language and the body intersect, as lovers might: the sound of Claudel's verses, she said later with startling directness, 'penetrated me as a woman might be penetrated, you see . . . The word and the sound have guided my happiness in living and my most profound blossoming. All these things have been given to me by the wonderful texts that are the gifts of life.' Feuillère felt the most intense bond with the characters she played, and she took pains to stress that when she played Ysé she gave herself over to the language of the part completely, that it liberated her and that, though she personally was naturally modest, she still put more of herself into the shameless Ysé than into any other part.[15]

Feuillère further believed that in life the body instinctively expresses emotional priorities in advance of their articulation in language and that actors should repeat this process in their art. In a late volume of interviews she speaks of the importance of preceding thought with gesture, even when this might run counter to conventional ideas of acting: 'For me the *gesture* instinctively comes before the thought. How many times have I said that a movement of the hand released and expressed a thought – when the reverse should be the case.' Similarly, in preparing for speech, she made the fullest use of silence: 'I have always taken the time to "listen to the silence before speaking" – consciously at first, then I made it my method; I heard my voice speaking the words ahead of me and I followed it, it led me.'[16]

There are few signs of these kinds of professional insight in Harold Hobson's palimpsestic tributes to Feuillère; nor, perhaps, should we expect to find them there, since they lie outside his self-imposed critical brief, which is to explicate the effect of the play in line with his own moral awareness. Of course, the opportunity for relentless proselytising that Claudel legitimately provided for Hobson was not often taken up by other critics, most of whom found rather different matters upon which to comment. Kenneth Tynan, soon to become Hobson's great rival, distanced himself from the play's doctrinal import ('the harsh growth of Claudel's own Catholicism') while admitting the rare theatrical beauty of Barrault's production: 'as lovely and mysterious to watch as a tank of tropical fish . . . a hothouse of canvas awnings, alive with reflected ripples'. But even Tynan was aware of the tradition to which Feuillère belonged: 'Her moment of union with Mesa, in the second act, left one line quivering in my mind like a dagger: "Il n'y a plus d'Ysé!" She speaks it as Bernhardt is said to have spoken Pelléas' "*Moi! Moi! Et Moi*" in the tones of a strangled dove.'[17] This was a telling comparison since Claudel's play connects not only with Maeterlinck but also with the lyrically tormented side of Sarah Bernhardt, an actress always highly conscious of the sexual potential of vocal delivery. But, yet again, one finds little detailed recognition of that complex history in Hobson, whose adoration of Feuillère is more perversely anachronistic than perhaps he realised, slipping very easily from the erotic to the spiritual, occluding any overt recognition of the theatrical, as well as psychological, truth that these twin poles can depend upon each other in violently profane ways.

To bring that point more fully home, Hobson's transcendent piety might be compared with a text roughly contemporaneous with the heyday of Barrault's revival of *Partage de Midi*: George Bataille's *Eroticism* (1957) which insists throughout that 'flights of Christian religious experience and bursts of erotic impulses are seen to be part and parcel of the same movement'.[18] In Hobson's reading of Claudel the guilt of murder replaces the guilt of adultery, evading Bataille's perception that sexual and religious ecstasy are closely intertwined. Hobson understands the religious paradox that sin precedes redemption but he never gets close, at least not in public, to the sexual conundrum that the force of human desire depends upon the boundaries it must transgress. As a Christian apologist he underestimates the deviance of desire altogether, a precondition of his personal admiration for Claudel and for the actress who had brought this buried play back to life.[19]

'The greatest actress in the world': attempting to understand the terms on which that extraordinary claim could be made, the conditions that made it possible, implies no questioning of Edwige Feuillère's achievements as an actress, nor indeed of Harold Hobson's integrity as a critic. The significance of the global title depended upon circumstance, upon the availability of star parts for women and a suitable repertoire, upon respect for style and for virtuoso display: a tradition, a way of doing things, that was national in origin but internationally respected. Just as Rachel had stood for Romantic revolution, Desclée for mid-century hysteria, Bernhardt for an energetic *fin de siècle*, so Feuillère too was emblematic, but this time of theatrical history itself, of a whole line of French actresses – a cause for celebration but, inevitably, for revaluation as well.

'CHAMPAGNE AND TEARS'

Feuillère returned to London with *Partage de Midi* in 1955, which she now played alongside Dumas *fils*'s *La Dame aux camélias* costumed by Pierre Balmain. For Harold Hobson, there was no holding back: 'Mme Feuillère enters from the centre like the sun at noon to illustrate all shadows, like the sheaves in harvest to fill all penuries', he proclaimed, drawing upon John Donne's vision of God's mercy.[20] Not surprisingly, this brought a response: letters to the *Sunday Times* complaining about Hobson's elevation of Feuillère, pointing out that whereas Hobson was willing to claim that the best male actors were English (a composite creature including Gielgud, Olivier, Guinness and several others), the title of world's greatest actress was 'bestowed whole and entire on Mme Feuillère, a Frenchwoman'.[21]

Easing himself out of a difficulty largely of his own making, Hobson replied with his own definition of the critic as 'the historian of what happens to his own heart and mind when he is subjected to a certain artistic experience. He undergoes an emotion, and then searches for reasons to justify it.' This makes the critic both less and more 'arrogant' than is often supposed; less because he does not appeal to any higher authority, more because he puts his response above that of other people, unless of course they happen to agree with him. Fortunately, in the case of Feuillère, this seemed largely to be so. 'The impact which Madame Feuillère's performance . . . made on me; and, I must conclude, on all people of taste (of whom the theatre, as I have indicated, was remarkably full) was tremendous'.[22]

For Harold Hobson, Feuillère's Marguerite Gautier (which she repeated in London in 1957) was always 'an unrivalled demonstration of beauty and sadness',[23] the courtesan being a woman 'gay, frivolous, pathetic, heroic, wicked, charming and unfortunate. The actress who plays her can delight the audience with her beauty, and make the audience weep over her misfortunes.'[24] As played by Feuillère, her death 'unites two qualities apparently exclusive of each other, I mean quietness and sensationalism. The quietness is in Mme Feuillère's marvellous voice, which is softer than the cooing of doves, or the murmur of a far-off stream; the sensationalism in her fall.'[25] Where Tynan found Marguerite's famous death-fall ('as sudden as the departure of a ghost at dawn') to be 'mortally shocking',[26] Hobson found it 'miraculously moving'. For Hobson, the strength of *La Dame aux camélias* lay in its chief character, Marguerite Gautier, 'by a dramatic act of self-abnegation, thrusting her happiness from her'.[27] For Tynan, recalling records of Eleonora Duse in the same part, the play had 'a springtime charm' that Feuillère's 'riper, sweeter melancholy' somewhat threatens: '"all champagne and tears," Henry James called it, but Mme Feuillère gives us a riper, sweeter melancholy – Yquem and tears, perhaps'. Feuillère's Marguerite showed her to be (and Tynan's qualification of Hobson's tribute is entirely deliberate) simply 'the best romantic actress I have ever seen', a restriction taken further by Caryl Brahms writing in *Plays and Players*, for whom the actress was merely 'without doubt the greatest Edwige Feuillère in the world',[28] and to its end point by Milton Shulman, whose headline in the *Evening Standard* brusquely announced, 'No, Edwige is not the best'.[29] But, as Hobson said, Feuillère's performance as Marguerite did attract an unusual amount of attention. There was even a tabloid row between the impresario Peter Daubeny and the theatre critic of the *Daily Express* John Barber (who had championed Edith Evans as 'the greatest actress alive') over the status of the courtesan in French culture.[30]

Strangely, all this fuss was about a role and a play that, as the years of touring and revivals went by, Feuillère herself came to hate, calling it a 'prison'.[31] Nevertheless, it was partly thanks to her efforts that, *La Dame*, both play and myth, remained a safe haven. In the early 1960s Vivien Leigh, who had perhaps noted her success, turned in that direction and in 1962 toured the play in Australia and South America. Called in to discuss the possibility of directing her in a new production in 1967, John Dexter was struck on their first meeting by Leigh's natural appropriateness for the role of a consumptive beauty: 'a strange beautiful woman. Stretched tight, almost transparent, pink and white, she seemed ethereal – no other word.'[32] Sadly, when she succumbed to tuberculosis herself at the age of fifty-three in the same year, this was her final image. Visitors to what was to become her death-bed found her 'sitting up in bed, in a ravishing nightgown, looking very frail and more beautiful than I can remember, her skin pink and white, her eyes large and lustrous; it was like a scene from *La Dame aux camélias*'.[33]

In theatrical history *La Dame* had always been a touchstone for deathly beauty, for memories of romantic love, and for an idea of theatre as the place where audiences can experience, however vicariously, the emotional turmoil of special people.[34] Ever respectful of its power Terence Rattigan, finding himself in 1958, like Vivien Leigh, trapped in a past that had come sooner than expected, and inspired by the well-known affair between another middle-aged actress, Margaret Leighton, and a much younger lover, the actor Laurence Harvey, rewrote Dumas's play under the frankly honest title of *Variations on a Theme*. Directed by John Gielgud in 1958, costumed by the Queen's dressmaker, Norman Hartnell, the play transposes Dumas's Paris to the south of France and an unresolved affair between Rose, a middle-aged woman dying of consumption, and her young lover, a working-class ballet dancer heavily involved with his male mentor. Critics then and since have accused Rattigan of a fudged attempt to write about a gay relationship under the cover of a heterosexual affair, though the play may be read, perhaps more interestingly, as an attempt to treat different kinds of sexual possession according to an overall social morality.[35] Rattigan revises nineteenth-century morality: Rose's daughter rehearses a scene from *La Dame* and there are even invocations of Bernhardt. But this was hardly enough for a generation that knew little about French courtesans and French actresses. So appalled was she by the over-dressed unreality of what she had seen in *Variations on a Theme*, on her very first trip to the theatre, that a young Salford schoolgirl, named Shelagh Delaney, felt driven to write her own play. Rattigan's play was neither a critical nor a commercial success; *A Taste of Honey*, Delaney's working-class drama, was picked up by Joan Littlewood's Theatre Workshop and later transferred to the West End where it ran for many months.[36]

Marguerite Gautier had become a vision of lost elegance in a vista of broken dreams. When Blanche du Bois, the heroine of Tennessee Williams's *A Streetcar Named Desire* and Vivien Leigh's greatest role, tries acting out the romantic life, there is still only one part to play:

'We are going to be very Bohemian. We are going to pretend that we are sitting in a little artists' café on the Left Bank in Paris.' [*She lights a candle stub and puts it in a bottle.*] '*Je suis la Dame aux Camélias! Vous êtes – Armand!*' 'Understand French?'

'Naw, Naw, I . . . ,' her would-be *beau* stutteringly replies.[37]

La Dame aux camélias: Blanche's fantasy, Vivien Leigh's final role, the inescapable prison of Edwige Feuillère.

'A TUBE OF FACE-CREAM' / 'SHE LACKS THE TRAGIC MASK'

It was probably inevitable that Feuillère should attempt Racine's Phèdre, but her decision in 1957 to play the part for the first and only time in London is striking. One or two Parisian critics crossed the Channel simply to witness the occasion. Given her own previous successes, and the precedents of Rachel and Bernhardt in the same part, the English capital must have looked like the fitting place for an important début.

For an actress working at the tail-end of the great nineteenth-century tradition of romantic Phèdres, decisions concerning the relation of sexuality to spirituality were crucial. When she came, in the 1980s, to write a first-person novel based on the life of another actress, the eighteenth-century tragedienne Hippolyte Clairon, who in 1743 played Phèdre at the age of twenty, Feuillère had her heroine confess, 'I did not know then – happily for me – that Phèdre was, in its totality, an un-actable part'. The reason for this was simply that 'From her first entrance on the breath of a woman who knows that she is going to die for her sin, to her final exit on the breath of liberating death, there is a bitter struggle between the gut and head, between passion and reason; her instincts play havoc with the rights and the duties that come with greatness'.[38]

All great roles ultimately escape the individual performer, which is why they must be endlessly reattempted, as Feuillère knew well. Startlingly costumed in contrasting tones of blood red, with a black wig and white mask-like make-up, her visual appearance was much admired, even if its tragic garishness seemed at times to conflict with the mellifluous, regretful sound of her voice. Hobson who must have been thinking of G. H. Lewes, in awe of Rachel, and of James Agate, in thrall to Bernhardt, reminded himself that some of the greatest actresses in the history of the European theatre have seized the opportunity afforded them by Racine's 'condemnation of uncontrolled passion to provide a display of lust and sex which in the name of art, has made the hair of dramatic critics stand on end, and their innocent hearts thump in their chests'. He went on to endorse Feuillère's refusal to take that route, to praise the way in which she plays a text that 'shows us a woman oppressed by a feeling of mortal sin', a reading justified by the author's own preface.[39]

Other critics concurred with his understanding of the interpretation, though with rather less enthusiasm. Caryl Brahms, for instance: 'Phèdre-Feuillère might have been squeezed out from a tube of face-cream, so smooth, so rich in texture, so carefully regulated, so cleansing and so moral was it all. Here one felt, was the full *femme bien élevée* held back by horror at her own mortal sin, rather than hag-driven by the need to fulfil it.' Brahms did concede that 'in this, of course, Madame Feuillère has her author with her'.[40] Like Hobson, Tynan also looked back to Bernhardt and to Lewes on Rachel, but he complained that critics were wrong to cite Racine's preface as evidence of the play's purely moral intention:

Here, surely, the author was simply insuring himself against possible charges of immorality, being fully aware that the woman he had created was not only the prey of Venus, but an active collaborator as well . . . With Mme Feuillère one gets no sense of danger. Her performance is an immensely graceful apology for Phèdre, a sort of obituary notice composed by a well-wishing friend; but is never a life lived nakedly before our eyes . . . The hunted, ravaged look of the great sufferers is beyond her means. She lacks the tragic mask.[41]

Hobson had found support for his sin-laden religious understanding of the play, which required Racine to betray signs of imminent Jansenist conversion in his portrayal of the heroine, in the works of an academic critic, Martin Turnell. Unusually for English journalism, due deference was paid to scholarly expertise throughout Feuillère's London season. John Weightman, a highly reputable academic, was called in by the *New Statesman*. Weightman's review (which begins by noting the 'regrettable' Marguerite Gautier of the previous week) contrasts 'the easy pathos' of one role with the visceral pain of the other. As Phèdre, Feuillère is 'full of the leaden pregnancy of unrequited love': 'On *Ah, Dieux!* which marks her full realisation of Hippolyte's love for Aricie, she clutched her midriff with both hands, as if the cancer had suddenly swelled intolerably.' Weightman didn't admire the opening scenes nearly so much – 'the stage was intense but not sufficiently volcanic' – and he complained that Feuillère missed 'one of the most beautiful e mutes in French literature' at the end of the line, 'Soleil, je te viens voir pour la dernière fois'.[42]

But Feuillère also had to face a challenge to her English stature from within the French theatre itself. In 1960 the tragedienne Marie Bell returned to London as Phèdre, a role she had first played there in 1945, this time under the auspices of the World Theatre Season. The Season's organiser, Peter Daubeny, who had invited Feuillère three years earlier, would later concede that though Feuillère had been 'magnificently moving, a figure of sumptuous passion in her sombre crimson robe', nevertheless 'she lacked the ferocity of the true Racinian tragic heroine'. Consequently, 'while I have called Edwige Feuillère our finest romantic actress, for me the greatest tragédienne of our time is Marie Bell'.[43] Even Hobson, although still loyal to the theory that *Phèdre* is Racine's Jansenist confession of personal guilt, the basis of Feuillère's interpretation, acknowledged that 'Mme Bell can find plenty of justification for the very different interpretation which she is now offering London play-goers. Conscience, remorse, the sense of sin enter very little into her powerful projection of this woman who loved her stepson and poisoned herself in disgust and horror.'[44] Bell was to visit London quite regularly in the 1960s, setting new criteria for French tragedy; Feuillère never repeated her Phèdre experiment again and, on her last visit to London in 1968, played safe with *Partage de Midi*.

Although Feuillère was very likely unaware of it, there had been another, even more radical challenge to her supremacy, this time from within the English theatre. Only a few months after her performances in the vast Palace Theatre in the West End, the distinguished English actress Margaret Rawlings (1906–96) had for two nights only played the role in a 'Theatre in the Round' production at the rather more humble Mahatma Gandhi Hall in Fitzroy Square. This was a brave move in several ways. Surrounded on all sides by her audience, Rawlings challenged the orthodoxy that the hieratic authority of the role should be reflected by a commanding positioning on stage (English critics had complained that Feuillère repeated the same entrance every time she came on) and, by playing the piece in translation, Rawlings was effectively offering *Phèdre* up for revaluation by English audiences.

Both Tynan and Hobson, though they relegated her to a minor place in their weekly portmanteau reviews, recognised the importance of what she was trying to do. 'Theatre in the Round theoretically demands an intimate style of acting; Racine, among other things, is a collection of bursts of rhetoric', said Hobson. Nevertheless, Rawlings 'dominated by a sense of monstrous sin, unites these two apparent irreconcilables with astonishing skill. Her paroxysms of anguish do not shatter the conventions of Theatre in the Round; and her moments of quietness give to Racine a new poignancy.'[45] 'A Phèdre of daunting majesty, Margaret Rawlings is conceivably the only actress in England with the guns for the part', wrote Tynan, adding, perhaps for the personal irritation of Hobson, 'After one glare from that basilisk eye, Mme Feuillère would be lucky if she were allowed to creep back and play Oenone'.[46] And there were others among her audiences who could appreciate the significance of what she was trying to do. The young Alan Bates, later to become an actor of great power and sensitivity in both modern and classical roles, wrote her a fan letter in which he praised her performance as 'infinitely better than the much-vaunted one given by Edwige Feuillère last year in London', even if, as a fellow professional, he added a few notes of his own: 'I don't say it was perfect; occasionally it writhed a bit too much, arms were moved about a little excessively at times, despairing hands went to the brow rather more often than was necessary'.[47]

Rawlings herself found the experience of playing Phèdre simultaneously rewarding and frustrating. As an actress she had scaled one of the peaks of the European repertoire, but she had done so in a late nineteenth-century translation by Robert Bruce Boswell that because of its anachronisms and its ponderous and stilted inversions, was in every way inadequate.[48] She put matters right as far as she could by reworking Boswell to such an extent that a new translation under her own name eventually appeared in 1961.

Rawlings chafed against Phèdre's situation from inside the character, looked for chances to express that inner experience, and yet remained determined to work closely with the text itself. Her foreword to the published version is notable because, in contrast with the male critics, academic or otherwise, it approaches the play from the view of a female performer. There is comparatively little reference to theological context and almost none to the 'condemnation of uncontrolled passion' (Hobson's phrase), merely a note that as a modern woman she is free of the 'pruderies' of her Victorian predecessors. Where Hobson was apt to be concerned about the age of Racine, Rawlings, more logically, was concerned about the age of Phèdre.

With a confidence that today's Early Modern scholars might find naïve, but which made a serviceable point at the time, she insists that 'one of the reasons why there are great actors in the English drama, and great actresses in the French, is that Shakespeare was writing for men and boys, while Racine was writing for women'.[49] Unlike other translations, hers would be 'speakable and actable'; declaring that 'Racine was writing for actors'; she says that she 'began this translation during rehearsals' (9). But Rawlings' most passionate claim is that her translation should allow the main parts to be taken by much younger players than has normally been the case. (Though Rawlings was herself a year or two older, in fact, was she thinking of Feuillère, who was fifty in 1957?) 'The play must have been far more exciting in Racine's own time, or when Rachel played Phèdre at the age of twenty-two, and Bernhardt at twenty-eight' (13). In the present day it is assumed that only the most experienced players will be able to match the demands of verse-speaking, though for anyone young in the audience this has the effect of making the whole plot 'indecent or at least laughably unlikely' (13). Rawlings longs

to see the play done with a Phaedra of not over thirty-five, a Theseus of not over forty-five, and a Hippolytus of not under twenty-five. Theramenes is a little older than Hippolytus, indeed the same age as Phaedra or a little younger. What we forget is how young people died of old age in those days . . . If Phaedra is not a day over thirty-five, married to a handsome forty-five much away on business (including helping a friend to steal a neighbouring dictator's wife), and if her stepson is about five to – at the most – ten years younger than herself, there is no difficulty whatever for an audience to get caught up in excitement and sympathy with her tragedy. (13–14)

For all Racine's protestations in his preface that the play serves above all a moral function, this translator knows that Phèdre's prime motivation 'was love: just violent sexual passion, and if the actress is too old for a young audience to believe in it – then it's just too bad – they have not seen the play' (14).

Admitting to only a few local difficulties when it comes to reading the play in this light, Rawlings confesses her one or two offences against the text. One is Phèdre's soliloquy in Act IV, scene 5 that comes after the shock of learning that Hippolyte loves Aricia. Racine gives her some ten lines, which Rawlings finds psychologically redundant. These, she believes, should be cut, so that 'Theseus goes, leaving Phaedra and the audience with the shock of her realisation that Hippolytus was not insensible to love; that, in fact, *he loved another*'. In performance Rawlings simply dropped the passage so that 'after a ghastly, deadly pause, during which the audience does not know what she will do – an almost unbearable suspense – to say the line: Hippolytus can feel, but not for me'. Again, 'from an actress's point of view it is infinitely more effective' (15).

Rawlings' predecessors had tended to conclude Phèdre's dying speech on a downward movement (as for instance Boswell's 'Death from mine eyes, veiling the light of heav'n / Restores its purity that they defied). Rawlings, in contrast, opts for a more assertive note, a rising syntax that she matched in performance by dying from a standing position:

> The light from eyes which have defied it, so –
> Restores to daylight all its purity.   (169)

Rawlings' remarkable bid to create, on both stage and page, a resistant, sexually convincing woman has been forgotten by critics, probably because, for all her protestations, her versification is insufficiently modern, still too close to Boswell's sub-Shakespearean iambics. Even so, it has remained in print for many years and is much used for teaching purposes and for the occasional performance. It is the only English translation by a woman, the only translation by an actress who has actually played the part.

Later English Phèdres have attempted the difficult transition from one century to another, one culture to another, in more obviously risky ways, both linguistic and scenic. Tony Harrison's *Phaedra Britannica*, played at the National Theatre in 1975, transposed the play to the British Raj in India, although its director, John Dexter, wished that he 'could bring a French company into the other theatre for, at least, the opening week to do the original in the original, as I don't think anyone will appreciate what Tony has done without a direct cross-reference'.[50] With this play, however strong the poetic personality of the translator – not just Harrison but Ted Hughes, Derek Mahon, Robert Lowell – all new versions run the risk of remaining mere shadows of the original. Defending Lowell's translation from the accusation that it made blatant what in the original was muted and implied, the critic Christopher Ricks has said that 'Lowell translated *Phèdre* as he did because of an unignorable historical change in the modes of life and the habits of thought . . . This crucial and undisputed change is our unremitting consciousness of and self-consciousness about sexuality.'[51] Ricks was surely right: sexuality is historical in that it lives in language. Edwige Feuillère, renowned for grace and poise, may well have known this, but she made her decisions within the narrow confines of theatrical tradition. Unlike her English contemporary, Margaret Rawlings, she couldn't look to translation for help – and even Rawlings could not go beyond her own historical moment.

BREAKDOWN

Throughout the 1950s and into the 1960s an envious distrust of French theatre was maintained; in some circles it was actually intensified. At Peter O'Toole's famously *louche* parties a drunken male guest was apparently in the habit of reciting awesome phrases – 'C'était pendant l'horreur d'une profonde nuit' – from Act II of Racine's tragedy, *Athalie*. Not only was this 'acting' and, as such, inappropriate behaviour at a party, complains O'Toole in his memoirs, it was 'French acting, at that, which is a sin'.[52] For a new generation of actors and directors, however inspired they may originally have been by Barrault in *Les Enfants du paradis*, the great post-war film commemorating the Romantic heritage of French theatre,[53] respect for the declamatory tradition stood in the way of immediacy, of 'relevance' and of the development of an English theatre which would give pride of place to what the director Lindsay Anderson, with his New Left inclinations, would call a 'common culture'. In an exasperated polemic published in 1957, directed at the cosy ways of British academic critics, Anderson cites John Weightman's complaint in the *New Statesman* that Feuillère's Phèdre missed 'one of the most beautiful e mutes in French literature' as evidence of a 'languid, over-sophisticated, salon voice' that could never 'touch the conscience or inspire the heart to make new affirmations'.[54] What hope was there for change when the country's supposed intelligentsia was preoccupied with such privileged niceties as the speaking of French verse?

The problem, as Dan Rebellato neatly puts it in his revisionist history of the period, was that 'expelling the French meant doing battle with an enemy within',[55] so deeply embedded was the habit of imitation, the lack of national confidence. Even Peter Brook, later to become a tyro of experimental theatre, began with Anouilh, directing *Ring Around the Moon* (1950) and *Colombe* (1952), the latter set in the Paris theatre world of 1900, and featuring *une monstre sacrée* obviously based on Bernhardt. Any lasting break with this ingrained deference would be easier for men to achieve than it would be for women, and easier by far for those who had not been brought up in a theatrical atmosphere where grace and style were priorities typified by French ways and means.

This was partly a matter of generation. Now in her forties, uncertain about roles, distracted by illness and the break-up of her marriage to Laurence Olivier, alone professionally as well as personally, Vivien Leigh would instinctively turn to the old repertoire, considering both *Froufrou*, a success for Desclée, Bernhardt and Réjane more than three-quarters of a century earlier (the impresario Binkie Beaumont was against the idea) and *La Parisienne*, introduced by Réjane some four decades before Feuillère took it up in 1937. And, in some ways, contemporary Paris did still seem to show the lead. In April 1958 Leigh starred in an English version of Giraudoux's *Pour Lucrèce*, which had been a notable hit for Feuillère and Madeleine Renaud there the previous year. Translated by Christopher Fry, it was now titled *Duel of Angels*. Leigh followed that in 1959 with Noel Coward's anglicisation of Feydeau's *Occupe-toi d'Amélie*, renamed *Look after Lulu*. Her choice of these plays with their French origins, star vehicles in which her success, though limited, was real enough, makes her decision in 1962 to take *La Dame aux camélias* on an international tour alongside *Duel of Angels*, also set in the mid-nineteenth century, look quite pragmatic.

Duel of Angels takes place in Aix-en-Provence. Armand, husband of Paola, falls for the sweet but prudish Lucille, wife of a judge. Paola decides to take revenge, and to teach Lucille the nature of sexual reality, by drugging her and by persuading her, when she awakes, that she has been violated by Marcellus, the local libertine. Lucille insists that she is now effectively married to her abuser but, on learning that her husband holds her responsible for what has happened, she poisons herself and dies on lines that seem to echo the final words of Phèdre. The heart of a static piece (John Osborne was to slate its 'fog of French bombast and twaddle'[56]) lies in the set-piece exchanges between the two women, in which Lucille stands up for a conventional morality that denies desire while Paola argues for a feminist promiscuity that punishes men by entrapping them in their own lusts.

Vivien Leigh was cast as Paola with, as Lucille, Claire Bloom – who was nearly twenty years younger, still starting out, and anxious to develop her own style. Neither was entirely happy with their role. When Jean-Louis Barrault directed the London production of the Giraudoux play as he had done in Paris, he found it hard to persuade Leigh of the logic of a part she seemed to loathe.[57] Even Feuillère conceded that Paola has a 'masculine temperament'[58] while Bloom, aware of changes in the English theatre, was, according to her 1996 autobiography, beginning to fear that she was 'considered to be part of the genteel West End Theatre'.[59] It was, perhaps, with Vivien Leigh's relative failures at the St James in 1951 in mind that Bloom complained that 'the blandness of English female acting was at that time almost universal. The need to be a "lady" had hindered the development of English actresses. There were no great Cleopatras, the one great tragic role in Shakespeare equal to the roles of the male actors . . . I had no interest in being a lady.'[60] Yet, as Bloom has also admitted, the older star taught her a good deal even if she 'influenced me much more as a woman than as an actress'.[61]

For *Duel of Angels* Vivien Leigh insisted that her Dior costumes were stitched in Paris, and as a result they fitted her perfectly.[62] There was nothing whimsical about this demand, which was not only to do with a certain idea of disciplined perfection, always hard to maintain, but with establishing a crisp, knife-edged silhouette that would invite an audience's wonder at the emotional state of the woman within. *Couture* theatre had a long history;[63] the ideal of sartorial elegance had underpinned the white Edwardian-style dress Feuillère wore for the role of Ysé and, even more so, the Balmain ball-gowns she chose for Marguerite Gautier. Increasingly this kind of self-presentation would seem posed, cold and static, like the formal catwalk shows and the rigid fashion photography that were soon to be swept away by a new approach, less symmetrical and much more relaxed, developed by David Bailey and his fellows. But in the early 1960s Leigh understood *couture* theatre better than any other English actress, and she had shown on at least one occasion, as Blanche du Bois, what lack of style could do to a woman. Her later decision to return to tradition, to become, as it were, the English Feuillère, though not entirely unsuccessful, is not simply to be blamed on her own innate conservatism, or that of her advisors. There was a professional interplay among her roles in that her studies of breakdown were defined in opposition to the immaculate poise, the preserved outline of a great Romantic actress. Recovery meant reclaiming that lost ground even when as Blanche and as Scarlett O'Hara she had brilliantly demonstrated what it might hide.

Claire Bloom was surely also right to have sensed sense in Leigh's fragile precision, her defensive commitment to sartorial and theatrical correctness, evidence of something about to become old-fashioned. For Bloom herself wasn't like that; she knew that although the world of Vivien Leigh might overlap with her own (they would in fact, both play Blanche du Bois) she would survive and go on to new ventures – including Nora Helmer and Hedda Gabler. Leigh must have felt the air of change herself but professionally she found it hard to develop accordingly, even when she found herself a middle-aged niche with Tennessee Williams's *The Roman Spring of Mrs Stone* and at her death was planning Edward Albee's *A Delicate Balance* to have been directed by John Dexter – a play in which Edwige Feuillère had appeared in Paris.

Feuillère had much better luck in her later years, partly because the Parisian stage was more respectful of the established repertoire (she was able to star in a successful revival of Giraudoux's *Madwoman of Chaillot*) but also because she was able to feature in French adaptations of Tennessee Williams's *Sweet Bird of Youth* and the French version of the Katharine Hepburn vehicle, *On Golden Pond*. In extreme old age, burdened with honours from the French state, she devised an authoritatively retrospective one-woman show that won her even more esteem.

ENTR'ACTE?

Paris may have been respectful, but London was moving on, and rapidly. Of all the plays that are commonly said to define the fifties 'revolution' in British theatre, including *Look Back in Anger, Waiting for Godot, The Birthday Party*, only Arnold Wesker's *Roots* and Delaney's *Taste of Honey* have a woman at their centre, and both heroines are young and working-class. Reduction in the number of mature female parts was not simply a by-product of change; it was at the heart of theatrical innovation at the mid-century because it was part of a deliberate repudiation of the past. Critics have accounted for changes in the representation of women in the 1950s according to displacements within the model of the nuclear family;[64] they have explored implications for playwriting in the contradictions between a professionally based homosexual sub-culture and a publicly expressed homophobia.[65] But the French theatrical canon that Edwige Feuillère and Vivien Leigh knew best had little to say about the family other than in terms of inheritance, often bourgeois and strictly financial, and the homoerotic was hardly a surface presence either, unless enforced emotional deprivation is seen as a common condition, as it sometimes is, in which women and gay men can substitute for one another. This repertoire – it can even be called the Feuillère repertoire – had at its heart the emotional and sexual needs of mature women and yet, despite the innovations of Ibsen nearly a century before, their representation was still enveloped within a cultural context made up of class, of luxury, of artificial charm, and, not least, of Frenchness itself – so much so that the plays inevitably came to look like the deadening enemies of reform. Unravelling that legacy would take time and opportunity. We are not done yet. Edwige Feuillère may indeed have been the 'greatest actress in the world': the championship title was vacant when she came into her prime. She has, though, remained its last recipient.

Notes

INTRODUCTION: THE GOLDEN AGE OF ACTING

1 Henry James, *Autobiography*, ed. F. W. Dupee (London: W. H. Allen, 1956), p. 204.

2 For English actors in France see J.-L. Borgerhoff, *Le Théâtre anglais à Paris sous la restauration* (Paris: Librairie Hachette, 1913) and V. Leathers, *British Entertainers in France* (Toronto: University of Toronto Press, 1959).

3 *The Theatre*, which ran under Clement Scott's editorship from 1880 to 1897, had an article on the French theatre in almost every issue.

4 Clement Scott, *The Drama of Yesterday and Today*, 2 vols. (London: Macmillan and Co., Ltd, 1899), 2, p. 437. All subsequent references to this edition are to Scott and are given within the text.

5 S. J. A. Fitzgerald, *A Chronicle of the St. James's Theatre from its Origin in 1835* (London: Guild of Women Binders, 1900), p. 7. For the economic context of the *Monte Cristo* riots and of contemporary claims for a 'national drama' see Tracy Davis, *The Economics of the British Stage 1800–1914* (Cambridge: Cambridge University Press, 2000), especially pp. 57–9.

6 Introduction to Henry Morley, *The Journal of a London Playgoer* (1866; Leicester: Leicester University Press, 1974), p. 17. Allardyce Nicoll asserts that 'Fully one half of the plays written between 1800 and 1850 must have been suggested by Parisian models'; Allardyce Nicoll, *A History of English Drama 1660–1900* (Cambridge: Cambridge University Press, 1955), 4, p. 79.

7 Oxford: Oxford University Press, 1982, pp. 311–12.

8 For information on the differences between English and French attitudes to the profession and on the social origins of French performers see F. W. J. Hemmings, *The Theatre Industry in Nineteenth-Century France* (Cambridge: Cambridge University Press, 1993), especially chapters 9, 10 and 13.

9 Marie Desmares Champmeslé (1642–98), actress and mistress of Racine for whom he wrote several tragic roles, including Phèdre.

10 Adrienne Lecouvreur (1690–1730), tragedienne and pioneer of a less declamatory style of acting.

11 Hippolyte Clairon (1723–1803), much admired by Voltaire, and another notable Phèdre.

12 'We can make the fortunes of a Mademoiselle Rachel, whom not half of her auditors really understand, and who, if it were not a new and fashionable entertainment, would send the other half to sleep . . . and at the same time our theatres, at which our beautiful dramas might be found if encouragement would bring on proper management, are in fact sinking . . .' William Robson, *The Old Play-Goer* (1846; Sussex: Centaur Press, 1969), p. 167.

13 I have discussed a typical example, comparisons between Rachel Félix and Sarah Bernhardt, in my 'Aspects of Bernhardt', *The Yearbook of English Studies*, 11 (1981), pp. 143–60.

14 Among the best modern sources for French theatre in the nineteenth century are Marvin Carlson, *The French Stage in the Nineteenth Century* (Metuchen, NJ: The. Scarecrow Press, Inc., 1972); F. W. J. Hemmings, *Theatre Industry and Theatre and State in France 1760–1905* (Cambridge: Cambridge University Press, 1994).

15 For information on the immediately previous periods see Martin Meisel, 'Napoleon; or, History as Spectacle', in *Realizations. Narrative, Pictorial and Theatrical Arts in Nineteenth-Century England* (Princeton: Princeton University Press, 1983); Jane Moody, *Illegitimate Theatre in London, 1770–1840* (Cambridge: Cambridge University Press, 2000); George Taylor, *The French Revolution and the London Stage 1789–1805* (Cambridge: Cambridge University Press, 2000).

16 Ian McIntyre, *Garrick* (London: Penguin Books, 2000) pp. 166–8. All subsequent references to this edition are to McIntyre and are given within the text. Also see Frank A. Hedgcock, *David Garrick and his French Friends* (London: Stanley Paul & Co., 1911) and Jean Benedetti, *David Garrick and the Birth of Modern Theatre* (London: Methuen, 2001).

17 Hedgcock, *David Garrick*, p. 97.

18 See Herbert F. Collins, *Talma: A Biography of an Actor* (London: Faber and Faber, 1964).

19 See Hemmings, *Theatre and State*, p. 71.

20 *Morning Post*, 31 May 1819. There are reports of French plays at the Argyll Rooms throughout the spring and early summer of 1819 and 1820. Also see Marcel Moraud, *Le Romantisme Français en Angleterre de 1814 à 1848* (Paris: Librairie Ancienne Honoré Champion, 1933).

21 *The Times*, 30 June 1817. Also see Collins, *Talma*, ch. 38.

22 Frances Ann Kemble, *Record of a Girlhood*, 3 vols. (London: Richard Bentley and Son, 1878), 1, p. 108.

23 John Scott, *Journal of a Tour to Waterloo and Paris in Company with Sir Walter Scott in 1815* (London: Saunders and Otley, 1842), pp. 140–1. Also see *An Englishman at Home and Abroad 1792–1828, With Some Recollections of Napoleon: Being Extracts from the Diaries of J. B. Scott of Bungay, Suffolk.* ed. Ethel Mann (London: Heath Cranton Limited, 1930).

24 *William Charles Macready: Reminiscences and Selections for his Diaries and Letters*, ed. Sir Frederick Pollock, 2 vols. (London: Macmillan and Co., 1875), 1, p. 237.

25 Henry Gibbs, *Affectionately Yours: Fanny Kemble and the Theatre* (London: Jarrolds, 1947), p. 145.

26 For evidence of this see the memoirs by two French actors: Frédéric Febvre, *Journal d'un comédien*, Tome Premier 1850–1870, Tome Deuxième 1870–1894 (Paris: Paul Ollendorf, 1896) and Bouffé, *Mes Souvenirs 1800–1880* (Paris: E. Dentu, Editeur, 1880).

27 Hemmings, *Theatre and State*, p. 174.

28 *Ibid.*, p. 193.

29 Hemmings, *Theatre Industry*, p. 3.

30 See Hemmings, *Theatre and State*, p. 194.

31 See Barry Duncan, *The St. James's Theatre: Its Strange and Complete History 1835–1957* (London: Barrie and Rockliff, 1964), ch. 3 *passim*.

32 *Morning Post*, 28 January 1845.

33 René Delorme, *Le Musée de la Comédie-Française* (Paris: Paul Ollendorf, 1878), p. 184.

34 John Hollingshead, *My Lifetime*, 2 vols. (London: Sampson Low, Marston and Company, 1895), 2, p. 111.

35 John Hollingshead, *Gaiety Chronicles* (London: Archibald Constable and Co., 1898), pp. 362–3.

36 *My Lifetime*, 2, p. 111. For accounts by foreign visitors to Paris see Hemmings, *Theatre Industry*, p. 81.

37 For some typical nineteenth-century accounts of the Comédie-Française see Georges d'Heylli, *La Comédie-Française à Londres (1871–1879)* (Paris: Paul Ollendorf, 1880); Georges d'Heylli, *Journal Intime de la Comédie-Française (1852–1871)* (Paris: E. Dentu, Editeur, 1879); J. Brander Matthews, *The Theatres of Paris* (New York: Charles Scribners and Sons, 1880); J. P. [presumably Juliet Pollock], 'The French Stage', *Macmillan's Magazine*, 21, March 1870, pp. 400–4.

38 John Hollingshead, 'The First Theatre in Europe', in *Plain English* (London: Chatto and Windus, 1880), pp. 16–22. For conditions at the Théâtre-Français and elsewhere see Hemmings, *Theatre and Industry*, ch. 2, 'The Auditorium'.

39 *The Complete Tales of Henry James, vol. 5 1883–1884*, ed. Leon Edel (London: Rupert Hart-Davis, 1963), p. 13. All subsequent references to this edition are within the text.

40 *Henry James: A Life in Letters*, ed. Philip Horne (Allen Lane: The Penguin Press, 1999), p. 95.

41 Arthur Pougin, *Dictionnaire Historique et Pittoresque du Théâtre* (Paris: Librairie de Firmin-Didot, 1885), p. 304. All subsequent references are to Pougin.

42 *Autobiography*, pp. 44–5.

43 See Hemmings, *Theatre and State*, pp. 186 and 191.

44 *Ibid.*, pp. 153–9.

45 The Comédie-Française was in London in 1922, 1924, 1934, 1939, 1945, 1948, 1959 and as part of the World Theatre season that ran at the Aldwych from 1964 to 1973.

46 J. Comyns Carr, *Stray Memories by his Wife* (London: Macmillan, 1920), p. 1.
Also see *Mrs. J. Comyns Carr's Reminiscences*, ed. Eve Adam (London: Hutchinson, 1926), p. 23.

47 *Stray Memories*, p. 2.

48 A letter to *The Times* on 21 October 1913 remembers Desclée's début: 'I was
sitting next to a man who was notorious among those who knew him as a man
absolutely without heart or feeling. To my surprise, I saw the tears streaming
down his face, and like myself he was quite unable to control his emotion. I
turned to him and said, "Well, I should think those are about the first tears
you have ever shed." He said to me, "If I had seen that woman when I was a
lad it would have changed the course of my life".'

49 Programme for the French Theatre Season, National Theatre, 1997.

50 The background to the *Paradoxe* is well known but complicated. In 1770
Diderot read a pamphlet entitled *Garrick; ou, les acteurs anglais* by Antoine
Fabio Sticotti, an adaptation of John Hill's *The Actor; or, A Treatise on the Art
of Playing* (1755). So taken was Diderot by Sticotti's pamphlet and, presumably,
by his own conversations with Garrick, that he produced his own *Paradoxe
sur le Comédien*. However, this was not to be published until 1830, an English
translation finally appearing in 1883.

51 See George Taylor, *Players and Performances in the Victorian Theatre*
(Manchester: Manchester University Press, 1989), especially ch. 11, and Joseph
R. Roach, *The Player's Passion: Studies in the Science of Acting* (Newark: Uni-
versity of Delaware Press, 1985).

52 Marie-Françoise Dumesnil (1713–1803) a rival and contemporary of Clairon,
and a favourite of Voltaire.

53 *Morning Chronicle*, 21 June 1817.

54 *Morning Post*, 20 June 1817.

55 *The Times*, 20 June 1817.

56 'Notes of a Journey through France and Italy', in *The Complete Works of William
Hazlitt*, ed. P. P. Howe (London: J. M. Dent, 1930–34), 10, p. 154. All subsequent
references are to Hazlitt, *Complete Works* followed by volume number.

57 *Atlas*, 1 July 1827.

58 Charles Hervey, *The Theatres of Paris* (Paris: Galignani and Co.; London: John
Mitchell, 1846), pp. 99–100.

59 *Macready: Reminiscences* (London: Macmillan, 1875), p. 180.

60 See, for example, Janet Beizer, *Ventriloquized Bodies: Narratives of Hyste-
ria in Nineteenth-Century France* (Ithaca and London: Cornell University
Press, 1993); Elin Diamond, 'Realism and Hysteria: Towards a Feminist
Mimesis', *Discourse*, 13 (Fall–Winter 1990–91), pp. 59–92; Joanna Townsend,
'Elizabeth Robins: Hysteria, Politics and Performance', in *Women, Theatre and
Performance: New Histories, New Historiographies*, ed. Maggie B. Gale and Viv
Gardner (Manchester: Manchester University Press, 2000), pp. 102–20.

61 For a more theoretical exploration of this trope see *Embodied Voices: Representing Female Vocality in Western Culture*, ed. Leslie Dunn and Nancy A. Jones
(Cambridge: Cambridge University Press, 1994). Kaja Silverman's *The Acoustic*

Mirror (Bloomington: Indiana University Press, 1988), although primarily concerned with film, is also very relevant.

62 J. Comyns Carr, *Coasting Bohemia* (London: Macmillan and Co., 1914), pp. 233–4 and 236–7.

63 Gay Gibson Cima, *Performing Women: Female Characters, Male Playwrights, and the Modern Stage* (Ithaca and London: Cornell University Press, 1993), p. 3.

64 Jules Clarétie, *Profils de Théâtre* (Paris: Gaultier-Magnier, 1902), p. 220.

65 *The Complete Letters of Oscar Wilde*, ed. Merlin Holland and Rupert Hart-Davis (London: Fourth Estate, 2000), p. 600. Subsequent references are to Wilde, *Complete Letters*.

66 Martha Noel Evans, *Fits and Starts: A Genealogy of Hysteria in Modern France* (Ithaca and London: Cornell University Press, 1991), p. 40.

67 See Gail Finney, *Women in Modern Drama* (Ithaca and London: Cornell University Press, 1989), *passim*.

68 *The Times*, 28 May 1924.

69 *The Times*, 2 June 1924.

70 Richard Schechner, *Performance Studies: An Introduction* (London and New York: Routledge, 2002), p. 209.

71 Good sources for information are Emile Abraham, *Les Acteurs et les Actrices de Paris* (Paris: Michel Lévy Frères, 1861); George Cain, *Anciens théâtres de Paris* (Paris: Librairie Charpentier et Fasquelle, 1906); Henry Lyonnet, *Dictionnaire des Comédiens Français*, 2 vols. (Paris: E. Jorel, 1908); F. Sarcey, *Comédiens et Comédiennes*, 2 vols. (Paris: Librairie de Bibliophiles, 1884).

72 Letter to the Countess of Blessington, 27 January 1847, *The Letters of Charles Dickens. Vol. 5. 1847–1849*, ed. Graham Storey and K. J. Fielding (Oxford: Clarendon Press, 1981), p. 14.

1 MADEMOISELLE MARS, THE ENGLISH AND ROMANTIC LOVE

1 *Evening Mail*, 29 July 1827.

2 For information on Mars see Francis Ambrière, *Mademoiselle Mars et Marie Dorval au théâtre et dans la vie* (Paris: Seuil, 1992); Roger de Beauvoir, *Mémoires de Mademoiselle Mars*, 2 vols. (Paris: Gabriel Roux et Cassanet, Editeurs, 1849); Micheline Boudet, *Mademoiselle Mars l'inimitable* (Paris: Terres des Femmes, Perrin, 1987); Maurice Descotes, *La drame romantique et ses grands créateurs (1827–1839)* (Paris: Presses Universitaires, 1955); Maurice Descotes, *Les grands rôles du théâtre de Marivaux* (Paris: Presses Universitaires, 1972); Marcel Pollitzer, *Trois reines de théâtre* (Paris: La Colombe, 1958). In 1902, at the Imperial Theatre, Lillie Langtry took the name part in a drama based on her life: *Mademoiselle Mars* by Paul Kester. For Mars's contractual negotiations with the Comédie-Française see Hemmings, *Theatre and State*, pp. 188–9.

3 [Not signed] 'The Drama', *New Monthly Magazine*, Historical Register, 25 (1828), pp. 342–4, esp. p. 342.

4 *The Spectator*, 19 July 1828.

5 'Not a whisper escapes the ear, even in the immense area of Covent Garden Theatre. She would not sacrifice the sense of feeling of the moment to any consideration of applause. She speaks to convince and to excite, and the heart and the judgment are yielded to her in voluntary subjection. Tenderness and pathos dwell in her tremulous accents, conviction in her earnest tones, and cheerfulness and conscious power in the play of her features, and the graces of her motion.' *Atlas*, 22 July 1832.

6 *Examiner*, 15 July 1832.

7 *Morning Herald*, 10 July 1832.

8 *The Times*, 1 July 1828.

9 *Examiner*, 6 July 1828.

10 *France*, 3rd edn, 2 vols. (London: Printed for Henry Colburn, 1818), 2, p. 195. All subsequent references are to *France*.

11 *The Times*, 28 June 1828.

12 *France*, pp. 197–8.

13 *Atlas*, 29 June 1828, p. 200.

14 *France*, p. 200. Back in Paris a year later Lady Morgan was to glimpse Mars at a reception: 'a simple and elegant-looking woman, no longer young, and plainly dressed in white silk, without a single ornament, and only a bandeau binding her beautiful black hair; but such eyes! Once seen they were never to be forgotten.' A footnote adds, 'This mild and matronly-looking lady, three years after, was enchanting the dramatic world by her performance of "Valérie", the blind girl of eighteen, in one of the most popular of M. Scribe's thousand and one dramas, perhaps since Molière, the most popular of all French dramatists, and deservedly so.' Morgan, Lady Sydney, *Passages from My Autobiography* (London: Richard Bentley, 1859), pp. 130–1.

15 Augustus William Schlegel, *Course of Lectures on Dramatic Art and Literature* (London: Henry G. Bohn, 1846).Translated by John Black, Esq., Revised according to the last German edition, pp. 316–17.

16 *The Times*, 13 July 1832, p. 3.

17 *The Spectator*, 211. For the week ending Saturday 14 July 1832, pp. 657–8. The critic continues 'Her *Valérie* we shall not again attempt to describe. It is the very *antipode* of *Célimène* – it is all nature, sweetness and pathos; and he must be either more or less human who can witness it with dry eyes.'

18 *The Spectator*, 19 July 1828, p. 43.

19 See, for example, Madame Blaz de Bury (née Stuart), *Molière and the French Classical Drama* (London: Charles Knight, 1846), p. 187.

20 Adam Phillips, *On Flirtation* (London: Faber and Faber, 1994), p. xxiii.

21 *On Flirtation*, p. xix.

22 The continuing and changing engagement with flirtation shown by nineteenth-century novelists has been amply documented by Richard Kaye in *The Flirt's Tragedy: Desire Without End in Victorian and Edwardian Fiction* (Charlottesville and London: University of Virginia Press, 2002). Kaye traces the English *coquette* back to Millamant in Congreve's *Way of the World* but nevertheless

claims the 'realist novel's generic superiority to the theatre' (p. 15). All subsequent references are to Kaye, *Flirt's Tragedy*.

23 Stendhal [Beyle, Marie-Henri], *Œuvres intimes*, 2 vols. (Paris: Gallimard, 1981), 1, p. 81. All subsequent references to this edition are within the text.

24 Stendhal [Beyle, Marie-Henri], *Correspondance*, 3 vols. (Paris: Gallimard, 1962–8), 1, p. 623.

25 Stendhal [Beyle, Marie-Henri], 'Racine et Shakespeare', in Stendhal, *Œuvres complètes* (Geneva: Edito-Service, 1970), 37, pp. 34 and 38.

26 Beyle, Marie-Henri [Stendahl], *Chroniques pour l'Angleterre*, 4 vols. (Grenoble: Publications de l'Université des langues et lettres de Grenoble, 1982), 2, p. 68.

27 'Leave a lover with his thoughts for twenty-four hours, and this is what will happen:
    At the salt mines of Salzburg, they throw a leafless wintry bough into one of the abandoned workings. Two or three months later they haul it out covered with a shining deposit of crystals. The smallest twig, no bigger than a tom-tit's claw, is studded with a galaxy of scintillating diamonds. The original branch is no longer recognisable.
    What I have called crystallization is a mental process which draws from everything that happens new proofs of the perfection of the loved one.' *Love*, trans. Gilbert and Suzanne Sale (Harmondsworth: Penguin, 1945) p. 45.

28 'Myself: "Love, even unrequited love, provides a sensitive soul, for whom what is imagined really exists, with a fund of enjoyment of the same kind; sublime visions of happiness and beauty enwrap oneself and one's beloved. How often has Salviati not heard Léonore telling him, like Mademoiselle Mars in *Les Fausses Confidences*, with her bewitching smile, Now these are illusions a prudent man never has"'. *Love*, pp. 251–2.

29 Jonathan Keates, *Stendhal* (London: Minerva, 1995), pp. 245–6. Also see Robert Vigneron, 'Stendhal et Hazlitt', *Modern Philology*, 35 (1937–8), pp. 375–414.

30 Tom Paulin, *The Day-Star of Liberty: William Hazlitt's Radical Style* (London: Faber and Faber, 1998), pp. 290–1.

31 Hazlitt, *Complete Works*, 10, p. 148. All subsequent references to this edition are within the text.

32 *Ibid.*, 12, p. 324.

33 Pasta, Giuditta, 1797–1865: soprano who made her London début at the King's Theatre in 1817 and returned throughout the 1820s. Rossini's favourite singer, she also excelled in Bellini and Donizetti and was famous for the naturalness of her acting style.

34 'On the Universal Tendency to Debasement in the Sphere of Love', in *The Penguin Freud Library*, 7, 'On Sexuality', trans. James Strachey (London: Penguin Books, 1991) pp. 342–60, esp. p. 258.

35 Compare Crabb Robinson in 1828: 'went to the Opera House to see Mlle Mars in *Le Mariage de Figaro* – The piece gave me no great pleasure. Mlle Mars is no longer fit for the *Soubrette* if she ever were – She wants youth and vivacity and she has too much dignity – Still her grace and fine delivery are very

gratifying'. *The London Theatre 1811–1866, Selections from the Diary of Henry Crabb Robinson*, ed. Eluned Brown (London: Society for Theatre Research, 1966), p. 124.

36 *The London Magazine*, February 1825 in *Chroniques pour l'Angleterre*, 1988, 5, 1824–5, p. 78.

37 *Chroniques pour l'Angleterre*, p. 82.

38 *An Intimate History of Humanity* (London: Sinclair Stevenson, 1994), pp. 102–3.

39 For an extended discussion of flirting in novels from just this vantage point see Kaye, *The Flirt's Tragedy, passim.*

40 Signed 'M' [probably T. C. Morgan], 'Coquetry', *New Monthly Magazine*, 38 (1830), pp. 397–402, esp. p. 399. The Stendhalian epitaph is 'Un homme ne peut presque rien dire de sensé sur ce qui se passe au fond du coeur d'une femme tendre: quant à une coquette, c'est différent; nous avons aussi des sens et de la vanité' ('A man is almost incapable of saying anything sensible about what goes on in the inmost heart of a sensitive woman; as for a coquette, that's another matter, for men, too, have senses and vanity.') *Love*, p. 55.

41 *France*, I, p. 317.

42 Jane Austen, *Emma* (Harmondsworth: Penguin, 1966) pp. 361–2.

43 Later she appeared in Hugo's *Angelo, Tyran de Padoue* (1835) and, playing the part of a much younger woman, in Dumas's *Mademoiselle de Belle-Isle* (1837).

44 *Observer*, 8 March 1830. Also see Kenneth Ward Hooker, *The Fortunes of Victor Hugo in England* (New York: Columbia University Press, 1938) and Marcel Moraud, *Le Romantisme Français en Angleterre*. In 1831 there was a production at Drury Lane of an English adaptation of *Hernani* entitled *The Pledge* in which Macready appeared. Although the play was quite well received the run was short and Macready himself was unimpressed: 'Victor Hugo was a man of vast genius, but he could not think him a man of dramatic genius'. Lady Pollock, *Macready as I Knew Him* (London: Remington and Co., 1884), p. 24.

45 Morgan, Lady Stanley, *France in 1829–30*, 2 vols. (London: Saunders and Otley, 1830), I, p. 167.

46 *Ibid.*, I, p. 170.

47 'The French Drama: Racine and Victor Hugo', *Westminster Review*, 34 (1840), pp. 287–324, esp. p. 322.

48 G. H. Lewes, 'The State of Criticism in France', *British and Foreign Review*, 16 (1844), pp. 327–62, esp. p. 337.

49 'The State of Criticism in France', p. 360. Lewes's dislike of Hugo continued into the 1850s, see *Dramatic Essays: John Forster and George Henry Lewes, Reprinted from the "Examiner" and the "Leader"*, with notes and an introduction by William Archer and Robert W. Lowe (London: Walter Scott Ltd., 1896), esp. pp. 191–8.

50 'The State of Criticism in France', p. 343.

51 [George Eliot], 'Arts and Belles Lettres', *Westminster Review*, 65 (1856), pp. 625–50, esp. p. 642. Kaye, *Flirt's Tragedy*, p. 223, suggests that Eliot may have drawn upon Stendhal in *Middlemarch*.

52 *Atlas*, 15 May 1841.

53 Frances Ann Kemble, *Record of a Girlhood*, 3 vols. (London: Richard Bentley and Son, 1878), 3, pp. 281–2.

54 Mrs Trollope, *Paris and the Parisians in 1835*, 2 vols. (London: Richard Bentley, 1835), 1, p. 18. A notable prude and firm admirer of Louis-Philippe Mrs Trollope nevertheless recorded her disgust at finding Mars acting in Hugo's 'trash' and described her performance in *Angelo Tyran de Padoue* as 'like watching the painful efforts of a beautiful racer pushed beyond its power – distressed, yet showing its noble nature to the last', 2, p. 285.

55 For other examples of the legend of Mars see C.S.C. [Clement Scott], 'The First Dona Sol', *The Theatre*, 3rd ser. 6 (1882), pp. 1–10; Théophile Gautier, 'Mademoiselle Mars', in *Portraits Contemporains* (Paris: Charpentier, 1874), pp. 416–18; Lady Pollock, 'The Comédie-Française', *The Contemporary Review*, 18 (1871), pp. 43–55; Ernest Legouvé, *Sixty Years of Recollections*, trans. with notes by Albert D. Vandam (London and Sydney: Eden, Remington and Co., 1893), pp. 74–101.

2 RACHEL'S 'TERRIBLE BEAUTY': AN ACTRESS AMONG THE NOVELISTS

1 *The Poems of Shelley, Volume Two, 1817–1819*, ed. Kelvin Everest and Geoffrey Matthews (Harlow: Longman, 2000), p. 489.

2 'Sir Walter Scott, Racine, Shakespear', Hazlitt, *Complete Works*, 12, p. 346. All subsequent references to this edition are within the text. It has been suggested that Hazlitt never read Racine in the original. See Katherine E. Wheatley, *Racine and English Classicism* (Austin: University of Texas Press, 1956).

3 There are innumerable lives of Rachel. The best biography, by far, is Rachel M. Brownstein, *Tragic Muse: Rachel of the Comédie-Française* (Durham, NC, and London: Duke University Press, 1995). Among the other modern books in English are Bernard Falk, *Rachel the Immortal* (London: Hutchinson, 1935), Joanna Richardson, *Rachel* (London: Max Reinhardt, 1956), and Henry Knepler, *The Gilded Stage* (London: Constable, 1968). Also see John Stokes, 'Rachel Félix', in *Three Tragic Actresses*, ed. Michael Booth, John Stokes and Susan Bassnett (Cambridge: Cambridge University Press, 1996), pp. 66–116. All subsequent references are to *Three Tragic Actresses*. The essential contemporary source is Jules Janin, *Rachel et la tragédie* (Paris: Amyot, 1859), which is compiled from his original *feuilletons*, including his famous accounts of her performances in 1838:

> The moment she arrives on stage she seems ten times bigger; she has the stature of an Homeric hero; her head is higher and her chest broader; her eyes light up, her feet regally command the ground; her gestures are like music from the soul, her words resonate vibrate from afar, consumed by the passion in her heart (p. 54). She is like a pythoness: she speaks like an oracle. She enters hesitant, pale, wild, panting; she trembles, she is cold, afraid, disturbed; she wants to flee. (p. 75)

Janin is the source for all encomiums of Rachel, English as well as French.

4 For further biographical information on Lewes, see Rosemary Ashton, *G. H. Lewes: A Life* (Oxford: Oxford University Press, 1991) and Alice Kaminsky, *George Henry Lewes* (Syracuse: Syracuse University Press, 1968) – all subsequent references are to Kaminsky.

5 *On Actors and the Art of Acting* (London: Smith, Elder, & Co., 1875), pp. 23–7. All subsequent references are to *On Actors*.

6 Here, for instance, are four uses by the critic of the *Morning Post*. On *Bajazet* (1842): 'Replete with a more refined, and yet almost as terrible a beauty, was the third scene in the fourth act. . . .' (5 July); on *Adrienne Lecouvreur* (1850): 'the impression of the terrible beauty of the scene' (18 July); on the same play in the following year: 'Nothing can be more beautiful than her frank devoted love . . . nothing more terrible than the desperate struggle' (3 July 1851); finally, on *Phèdre* (1853): 'As an instance of the grand and terrible beauty with which the genius of Rachel lights up the pages of French classical tragedy, *Phèdre* is, perhaps, not surpassed . . .' (2 June).

7 Compare each of Lewes's observations with the following from other critics: 'Her gestures are also most appropriate and graceful, and never partake of the violence which so few French tragic actors can abstain from' (*Morning Post*, 11 May 1841); 'her appropriation of emphasis whenever she is determined (which she is not always) to give a phrase its full meaning' (*The Times*, 22 May 1841); 'the tortured look and trembling frame, surcharged to bursting' (*The Era*, 23 May 1841); 'Mlle Rachel, as all who have observed her performances seem to agree, expresses gentle and tender feelings less felicitously than jealousy, rancour, wounded pride, and dissembled rage' (*Morning Post*, 22 May 1841).

8 'The glaring wrath of the panther Roxane' he wrote in his review of *Bajazet* (*Atlas*, 8 August 1846), remembering Hazlitt on Kean: 'His hurried motions had the restlessness of the panther's.' Lewes's contributions to the *Atlas*, which have never been listed, can be identified on the internal evidence of words and phrases that he habitually repeated in later years. *The George Eliot Letters*, ed. Gordon S. Haight (London: Oxford University Press, 1956), 8, Appendix II, p. 367, shows that Lewes received payment for writing about Rachel in the *Atlas* in 1846. All subsequent references are to *George Eliot Letters*.

9 'Racine and Corneille', *Atlas*, 22 August 1846. Lewes's early and unfashionable commitment to Racine is demonstrated in his first major article, 'French Drama: Racine and Victor Hugo', *Westminster Review*, 34 (1840), pp. 287–324. His belief in identification makes him an importantly transitional figure in the process whereby Romantic ideas of acting developed into naturalistic theory. For Lewes's influence on Stanislavski, see Joseph R. Roach, Jr., 'G. H. Lewes and Performance Theory: Towards a Science of Acting', *Theatre Journal*, 32 (1980), pp. 312–28.

10 'Foreign Actors and the English Drama', *Cornhill Magazine*, 8 (1863), p. 177; rpt. *On Actors*, p. 170.

11 *Atlas*, 8 August 1846.

12 The Earl of Beaconsfield, K.G., *Tancred or The New Crusade* in *The Collected Edition of the Novels and Tales of the Right Honourable B. Disraeli* (London:

Longmans, Green and Co., 1886), 4, pp. 314–36. All subsequent references are to Disraeli.

13 Disraeli, p. 149.

14 And this is precisely what Arnold did see in Rachel. In 1863, five years after her death, he wrote three sonnets about the actress who had so moved him in the 1840s. The third ends with an apostrophe to her ability to exceed racial difference:

> Germany, France, Christ, Moses, Athens, Rome.
> The strife, the mixture in her soul, are ours;
> Her genius and her glory are her own.

The Poems of Matthew Arnold, ed. Kenneth Allott (London: Longmans, 1965), pp. 482–5, also see Park Honan, *Matthew Arnold: A Life* (London: Weidenfeld, 1981), pp. 109–10.

15 Review of the fifth edition of *Coningsby*, *British Quarterly Review*, 10 (1849), rpt. *Disraeli's Novels Reviewed, 1826–1968*, ed. R. W. Stewart (Metuchen, NJ: Scarecrow Press, 1975), p. 198.

16 Charlotte Brontë, *Villette*, ed. Mark Lilly (Harmondsworth: Penguin Books, 1979), p. 339.

17 The most obvious reason for identifying character with author is that Vashti is described by Lucy Snowe in very similar terms to those in which Rachel was described by Brontë. When Brontë saw Rachel she said that the actress had sold her soul to 'Beelzebub', and that she 'made me shudder to the marrow of my bones: in her some fiend has certainly taken up an incarnate home. She is not a woman – she is a snake – she is the –.' Thomas James Wise (ed.), *The Brontës: Their Lives, Friendships and Correspondence* (Oxford: Basil Blackwell, 1980), 3, pp. 245 and 251. All subsequent references are to Wise.

18 *The Brontës: The Critical Heritage*, ed. Miriam Allott (London and Boston: Routledge and Kegan Paul, 1974), p. 84. All subsequent references are to Allott.

19 Wise, *The Brontës*, 2, p. 153.

20 Allott, *The Brontës*, p. 161. Lewes may not have been personally responsible for some of the more detrimental remarks in this review, as it had been revised by Lord Jeffrey. See Kaminsky, *Lewes*, p. 99.

21 Wise, *The Brontës*, 3, p. 67.

22 *Ibid.*, 3, p. 245. Compare *Villette*, p. 338: 'I longed to see a being of whose powers I had heard reports which made me conceive peculiar anticipations'.

23 'Rachel and Racine', 7 June 1851. Published on the day that Brontë saw Rachel in *Adrienne Lecouvreur*, this article is, for the most part, a reprinting of Lewes's review of Rachel in *The Leader*, 6 July 1850. Most, but not all, of 'Vivian'ʼs dramatic criticism from *The Leader* is collected in *Dramatic Essays: John Forster and George Henry Lewes*, with notes and an introduction by William Archer and Robert W. Lowe (London: Walter Scott Ltd., 1896).

24 See 'Performing Heroinism: The Myth of *Corinne*', in Ellen Moers, *Literary Women* (London: W. H. Allen, 1977), pp. 173–210, which refers to Lewes, Brontë and George Eliot.

25 *Leader*, 12 July 1851.

26 Wise, *The Brontës*, 2, pp. 208–9.
27 *Ranthorpe*, ed. Barbara Smalley (Athens, OH: Ohio University Press, 1974), p. 97.
28 *Rose, Blanche and Violet* (London: Smith, Elder and Co., 1848), 1, p. 101.
29 Wise, *The Brontës*, 2, p. 210.
30 Rpt. Allott, *The Brontës*, pp. 184–6 and 208–11.
31 *George Eliot Letters*, 1, pp. 245–6, and 3, p. 93.
32 *Leader*, 4 June 1853.
33 *George Eliot Letters*, 3, p. 104.
34 George Eliot, *Daniel Deronda*, ed. Barbara Hardy (Harmondsworth: Penguin Books, 1967), pp. 82–95. All subsequent references are to *Daniel Deronda*. The episode has also been discussed by Joseph Litvak, *Caught in the Act: Theatricality in the Nineteenth-Century Novel* (Berkeley, Los Angeles and Oxford: University of California Press, 1992); Gail Marshall, *Actresses on the Victorian Stage* (Cambridge: Cambridge University Press, 1998); Brian Swann, 'George Eliot and the Play: Symbol and Metaphor of the Drama in Daniel Deronda', *Dalhousie Review*, 52 (1972), pp. 191–202; Hugh Witemeyer, *George Eliot and the Visual Arts* (New Haven: Yale University Press, 1979); and Joseph Mazo, 'The Artist as Actor in English Fiction' (Harvard dissertation, 1971).
35 *George Eliot Letters*, 3, p. 98.
36 *Pall Mall Gazette*, 10 March 1865.
37 Sir Theodore Martin, *Helena Faucit (Lady Martin)* (Edinburgh and London: William Blackwood and Sons, 1900), p. 266. All subsequent references are to Martin.
38 Martin, *Faucit*, p. 340.
39 *Daniel Deronda*, p. 56.
40 'Shakespeare's Women: By One who has Impersonated Them: Hermione', *Blackwood's Edinburgh Magazine*, 149 (1891), pp. 1–37. Also see Dennis Bartholomeuz, *The Winter's Tale in Performance in England and America 1611–1976* (Cambridge: Cambridge University Press, 1982).
41 Carol Jones Carlyle's comprehensive life of Faucit (*Helen Faucit: Fire and Ice on the Victorian Stage*, London: The Society for Theatre Research, 2000) includes sensitive discussions of her relationship with Macready and of the possibility that she suffered from a form of hysteria. She also shows that comparisons between Faucit and Rachel were complicated and, at times, even contradictory.
42 *Daniel Deronda*, p. 730.
43 This crucial rupture is discussed by Catherine Belsey, 'Re-reading the Great Tradition', in *Re-Reading English*, ed. Peter Widdowson (London: Methuen, 1982), pp. 21–35.
44 *On Actors*, pp. 264–78.

3 MEMORIES OF PLESSY: HENRY JAMES RESTAGES THE PAST

1 *The Tragic Muse* (London: Hart-Davis, 1948), p. 91. All subsequent references to this edition (which is based on the first edition published in London by

Macmillan in 1890) are within the text. The Penguin edition of 1995, which includes an excellent introduction and annotations by Philip Horne, prints the New York edition of 1908.

2 Emile Augier, *L'Aventurière*, Nouvelle Edition (Paris: Michel Lévy, 1870), p. 70.
[Yes, I have things in my life to feel guilty about, yes, my heart has failed me
But you do not know what blows I have suffered!
How could you know, you with your chaste, tranquil soul
To whom life is sweet and goodness comes easily,
You, child, who as guardians of your tender honour
Have a family and above all happiness!
How could you know how on cold evenings
Poverty murmurs in young ears?
You do not understand, never having been hungry,
That people renounce honour for a bit of bread.]

3 See *Three Tragic Actresses*, pp. 73–7.

4 Georges d'Heylli, *Madame Arnould-Plessy, 1834–1876* (Paris: Tresse, Editeur, 1876); Charles Hervey, 'Madame Arnould Plessy', *The Theatre*, 9 (1 April 1887), pp. 194–200; Eugène de Mirecourt, *Plessy-Arnould*, in *Les Contemporains* (Paris; chez l'auteur, 1858); Eugène de Mirecourt, *Mme Arnould-Plessy* (Paris: chez Achille Faure, 1867); Georges d'Heylli, *Journal Intime de la Comédie-Française* (Paris: E. Dentu, 1879); F. Sarcey, *Comédiens et Comédiennes*, 2 vols. (Paris: Librairie de Bibliophiles, 1884).

5 Pougin, *Dictionnaire historique*, p. 243.

6 See Hemmings, *Theatre Industry*, p. 185.

7 See Maurice Descotes, *Les grands rôles du théâtre de Marivaux* (Paris: Presses Universitaires de France, 1972).

8 *The Complete Plays of Henry James*, ed. Leon Edel (London: Rupert Hart-Davis, 1949), p. 37.

9 *The Scenic Art* (London: Rupert Hart-Davis, 1949), p. 317. All subsequent references are to *Scenic Art* and pages are given in the text.

10 'To which George Sand immediately replied: "I will not accept Mlle Plessy until I have seen her act and obtained confirmation of the talent that you ascribe to her. I would rather withdraw my play than see it acted simperingly. Mlle Plessy has the reputation of being the most affected actress in the world."' Boudet, *Mademoiselle Mars l'inimitable*, p. 352.

11 D. J. Gordon and John Stokes, 'The Reference of *The Tragic Muse*', in *The Air of Reality: New Essays on Henry James*, ed. John Goode (London: Methuen, 1972), pp. 61–168. This essay says that a reference to Mlle Bartet made in James's *Notebooks* makes it possible that the novel is set in 1879. However, deliberate historical imprecision elsewhere suggests that it may be better to think of the time scheme as more generalised: the '1870s'. It has often been said that James's friend Fanny Kemble made her own contribution to Madame Carré. For more recent discussion of the novel's theatricality see Brownstein, *Tragic Muse: Rachel of the Comédie-Française*; Litvak, *Caught in the Act: Theatricality in the Nineteenth-century Novel*; Marshall, *Actresses on the Victorian Stage*. For

demonstrations of how *The Tragic Muse* is infused with references to French literature, including plays, see Pierre A. Walker, *Reading Henry James in French Cultural Contexts* (Dekalb: Northern Illinois University Press, 1995) and Edwin Sill Fussell, *The French Side of Henry James* (New York: Columbia University Press, 1990).

12 *The Letters of Charles Dickens, Vol. 7: 1853–1855* (Oxford: Clarendon Press, 1993), p. 750.

13 *The Letters of Charles Dickens*, ed. by his sister-in-law and his eldest daughter (London: Macmillan, 1893), p. 740.

14 See T. Edgar Pemberton, *Charles Dickens and the Stage* (London: George Rodway, Covent Garden, 1888); Dutton Cook, 'Charles Dickens as a Dramatic Critic', *Longman's Magazine*, 2 (May 1883), pp. 29–42; Sylvère Monod, 'Une Amitié Française de Charles Dickens: lettres inédites à Philodès Régnier', *Etudes Anglaises*, 2 (1958), pp. 119–35, and 3 (1958), pp. 210–25.

15 A short essay called 'A Flight' has Dickens sharing a train carriage from London to Paris with a 'Compact Enchantress', a 'French actress, to whom I yielded up my heart under the auspices of that brave child, "MEAT-CHELL," at the St James's' Theatre the night before last'. *Reprinted Pieces* (London: Chapman and Hall, 1911), p. 128.

16 *The Letters of Charles Dickens, Vol. 6: 1850–1852* (1988), p. 120.

17 *The Letters of Charles Dickens, Vol. 5: 1847–1849* (1981), p. 588.

18 See George Taylor, *Players and Performances in the Victorian Theatre* (Manchester: Manchester University Press, 1989), p. 95, for a discussion of Lewes in this context.

19 *On Actors*, pp. 123–4. All subsequent references to this edition are given in the text.

20 For further accounts of the Paris visit see Carol Jones Carlyle, *Helen Faucit: Fire and Ice on the Victorian Stage* and Richard Foulkes, *Performing Shakespeare in the Age of Empire* (Cambridge: Cambridge University Press, 2002), pp. 22–31.

21 Helena Faucit, Lady Martin, *On Some of Shakespeare's Female Characters* (Edinburgh and London: William Blackwood and Sons, 1885), p. 234.

22 *Morning Post*, 4 January 1845.

23 Anon. [Sarah Austin], 'Shakespeare in Paris', *Edinburgh Review*, 83 (1846), pp. 47–63, esp. p. 48.

24 *Morning Post*, 21 January 1845.

25 See B. Juden and J. Richer, 'Macready et *Hamlet* à Paris en 1844', *La Revue des lettres modernes*, 74–5 (1962/3), pp. 3–35.

26 *Macready's Reminiscences*, ed. Sir Frederick Pollock (London: Macmillan, 1875), 2, p. 251. When, in the course of his Paris season, Macready visited the Conservatoire, he observed, 'I . . . saw the inefficiency of the system clearly; it was teaching conventionalism – it was perpetuating the mannerism of the French stage, which is all mannerism', Alan S. Downer, *The Eminent Tragedian: William Charles Macready* (Cambridge, Mass.: Harvard University Press, 1966), p. 272. My account of the French visit is made up from these two books together with

William Archer, *William Charles Macready* (London: Kegan Paul, 1890); Victor Leathers, *British Entertainers in France* (Toronto: University of Toronto Press, 1959); and various newspaper reports.

27 *The Times*, 22 January 1845.

28 *Morning Post*, 29 May 1845.

29 Boudet, *Mademoiselle Mars*, p. 273.

30 E.g. *Illustrated London News*, 12 April 1845.

31 25 April [1845]. *The London Theatre 1811–1866, Selections from the Diary of Henry Crabb Robinson*, p. 176.

32 *Morning Post*, 24 May 1845.

33 *The Era*, 13 April 1845.

34 *Morning Post*, 10 May 1845.

35 *The Times*, 2 April 1845.

36 *Daily Telegraph*, 8 May 1873.

37 Maurice Descotes, *Les grands rôles du théâtre de Molière* (Paris: Presses Universitaires de France, 1960).

38 24 July 1847.

39 *Morning Chronicle*, 28 April 1845.

40 See Frédéric Febvre, *Journal d'un comédien, Tome premier 1850–1870* (Paris: Paul Ollendorf, 1896), pp. 107–9.

41 See D'Heylli, *Madame Arnould-Plessy, 1834–1876*, pp. 15–16.

42 George Eliot, *Adam Bede* (Harmondsworth: Penguin), p. 321. However, as Richard Kaye has shown (*Flirt's Tragedy*, pp. 118–41), elsewhere, particularly in *The Mill on the Floss*, the *coquette* motif was used with considerably more subtlety.

43 Haymarket Theatre, 14 January 1869 – with E. A. Southern.

44 *The Principal Dramatic Works of Thomas William Robertson* (London: Sampson Low, 1889), I, p. 272.

45 Gustave Planché, 'Molière à la Comédie Française', *Revue des Deux Mondes*, 2 (15 April 1856), p. 903.

46 *Comédiens et Comédiennes*, p. 16.

47 *Scenic Art*, pp. 62–3.

48 Boudet, *Mars*, pp. 295–300.

49 *Le Figaro*, 20 April 1880.

50 See 'The Comédie-Française and Sarah Bernhardt', in *The Era*, 25 April 1880, p. 3.

51 *The Era*, 25 April 1880, p. 3, and 9 May 1880, pp. 4 and 6. Shortly after, Geneviève Ward gave an admired performance of the role in London which, it was said 'inclines to that given by Mdlle. Sarah Bernhardt, who to obtain her ends, uses the seductions and wheedling graces of the courtesan, and not the commanding airs of "La Grande Dame" which Madame Arnould Plessy assigned to the character.' *The Era*, 9 May 1880, p. 11.

52 *The Era*, 25 May 1880, p. 4.

53 Peter Brook, *The Melodramatic Imagination* (New Haven and London: Yale University Press, 1995), p. xi.

54 See Elaine Aston, *Sarah Bernhardt: A French Actress on the English Stage* (Oxford: Berg Publishers, 1989), p. 31.
55 See *The Times*, 5 April and 6 May 1873.
56 *The Era*, 11 May 1873, p. 10.
57 Emile de Molènes, *Desclée. Biographie et souvenirs* (Paris: Tresse, 1874), p. 101.
58 *The Spectator*, 7 June 1873, p. 726.
59 *The Era*, 25 May 1873, p. 11.
60 *Scenic Art*, p. 247, also see p. 250.
61 *The Academy*, 20 May 1876, p. 497.
62 *Scenic Art*, p. 7.
63 *Ibid.*, p. 90.

4 DÉJAZET/DÉJA VU

1 London: Penguin Books, 1988, p. 45.
2 The main sources for information about Déjazet are Frank Archer (pseudonym of Frank Bishop Arnold), *An Actor's Notebooks* (London: Stanley Paul, 1912), pp. 140–3; Jules Claretie, *Profils de Théâtre* (Paris: Gaultier Magnier, 1902); Jules Claretie, *La vie moderne au théâtre. Causeries sur l'art dramatique* (Paris: Georges Barba, 1869); L. Deutsch, *Déjazet* (Paris: Editions du Laurier, 1928); Georges Duval, *Virginie Déjazet* (Paris: Tresse, 1876); L.-Henry Lecomte, *Une Comédienne au XIXe siècle: Virginie Déjazet* (Paris: Léon Sapin, 1892); L.-Henry Lecomte, *Virginie Déjazet: D'après ses papiers et sa correspondance* (Paris: Librairie Illustrée, Montgredien, 1902); Eugène de Mirecourt, *Déjazet* (Paris: Gustave Havard, 1855); E. Pierron, *Virginie Déjazet* (Paris: Bolle-Lasalle, 1856). The Bibliothèque de l'Arsenal in Paris has a file of cuttings on her. Articles in English include Anon., 'Déjazet', *Galaxy*, 4 (June 1867), pp. 179–90; Anon., 'Déjazet', *The Englishwoman's Domestic Magazine*, 9 (1 Dec. 1870), pp. 350–1; Anon., 'Virginie Déjazet', *Temple Bar*, 59 (May 1880), pp. 108–13; and a long obituary in *The Daily News*, 3 December 1875.
3 Fanny Kemble, *Records of Later Life*, 3 vols. (London: Richard Bentley, 1882), 2, p. 224. All subsequent references are to Kemble. Whewell was later Master of Trinity, author of *Elements of Morality* (1845) and many other books.
4 *Morning Post*, 7 May 1842.
5 Kemble, *Records*. Letter dated 7 May 1842. *Morning Post*, 7 May 1842, lists the Whewells as being in the audience on the 6th and makes no reference to them on subsequent nights.
6 Kemble, *Records*, 2, pp. 243–4.
7 *Ibid.*, 3, pp. 322–3.
8 15 June 1844.
9 For further discussion of the representation of sexuality in the Victorian theatre see Tracy C. Davis, *Actresses as Working Women* (London and New York: Routledge, 1991).
10 John Russell Stephens, *The Profession of the Playwright: British Theatre 1800–1900* (Cambridge: Cambridge University Press, 1992), p. 102.

11 See Kathy Fletcher, 'Planché, Vestris and the Transvestite Role: Sexuality and Gender in Victorian Popular Theatre', *Nineteenth Century Theatre*, 15 (1987), pp. 9–33.

12 Charles J. Mathews, *Letter from Mr. Charles Mathews to the Dramatic Authors of France* (London: J. Mitchell, 1852), p. 22. The play is *L'Idiote* by Teaulon et Nezel which Déjazet had introduced in Paris in 1834.

13 Introduction to *The Queen of the Frogs*, in *The Extravaganzas of J. R. Planché, Esq.* (London: Samuel French, 1879), 4, p. 132.

14 *Parisian Sketches*, ed. with an introduction by Leon Edel and Ilse Dusoir Lind (London: Rupert Hart-Davis, 1957), p. 22.

15 For modern discussion of cross-dressing see Marjorie Garber, *Vested Interests: Cross-dressing and Cultural Anxiety* (New York and London: Routledge, 1992); *Crossing the Stage: Controversies on Cross-dressings*, ed. Lesley Ferris (London and New York: Routledge, 1993); Laurence Senelick, *The Changing Room: Sex, Drag and Theatre* (London and New York: Routledge, 2000). For discussion of the French tradition see Gerda Taranow, *The Bernhardt Hamlet: Culture and Context* (New York: Peter Lang, 1996), pp. 83–4.

16 Lecomte, *Comédienne*, p. 2.

17 For information on the place of *vaudeville* in French theatrical history see Hemmings, *Theatre and State in France*, pp. 17–19.

18 Lewes, *Dramatic Essays*, p. 184.

19 Quoted in de Mirecourt, *Déjazet*, p. 25.

20 12 May 1842, p. 5.

21 It seems that the French plays, when politically sensitive, were frequently modified to suit English circumstances. In 1850 Planché adapted Emile Souvestre's *Enfant de Paris* as *Day of Reckoning*, but changed the clash between a young French working man and a corrupt aristocrat because it appeared too 'republican'. Even so, the play apparently stirred British theatre-goers. See William W. Appleton, *Madame Vestris and the London Stage* (New York and London: Columbia University Press, 1974), p. 180.

22 See, for example the *Atlas*, 27 May 1843.

23 From a letter to the *Gazette des Théâtres*, 3 July 1870.

24 Charles Osborne, *The Complete Operas of Mozart: A Critical Guide* (London: Victor Gollanz, 1978), p. 247.

25 Lecomte, *Comédienne*, p. 145.

26 See Gerda Taranow, *Sarah Bernhardt: The Art within the Legend* (Princeton: Princeton University Press, 1972), pp. 211–13.

27 Pougin, *Dictionnaire Historique*, p. 681.

28 *Ibid.*, p. 659.

29 Laurence Senelick, 'The Evolution of the Male Impersonator on the Nineteenth-Century Popular Stage', *Essays on Theatre*, 1 (1982), pp. 31–44.

30 See J. S. Bratton, 'Beating the Bounds: Gender Play and Role Reversal in the Edwardian Music Hall', in *The Edwardian Theatre*, ed. Michael R. Booth and Joel H. Kaplan (Cambridge: Cambridge University Press, 1996), pp. 86–110.

31 Pougin, *Dictionnaire Historique*, p. 659.

32 *Ibid.*, p. 740.
33 Lecomte, *Comédienne*, pp. 441–2.
34 Charles Baudelaire, *Œuvres complètes* (Paris: Aux éditions du Seuil, 1968), p. 82.
35 Lecomte, *Comédienne*, p. 59.
36 For more on the semiology of smoking see Richard Klein, *Cigarettes are Sublime* (Durham, NC, and London: Duke University Press, 1993) and G. Cabrera Infante, *Holy Smoke* (London: Faber, 1985).
37 Carlson, *The French Stage in the Nineteenth Century*, p. 121.
38 Lecomte, *Comédienne*, p. 444.
39 Charles Hervey, 'Napoleon the Third and the Stage', *The Theatre*, 9 (1887), pp. 10–15.
40 Theodore Zeldin, *France 1848–1945* (Oxford: Clarendon Press, 1973), 1, p. 362. Also see E. J. Hobsbawm, *The Age of Revolution, 1789–1848* (London: Weidenfeld and Nicolson, 1962). For impersonations of Napoleon on the French stage see Hemmings, *Theatre and State*, p. 211.
41 *Morning Post*, 4 June 1842.
42 By Bayard and Dumanoir, written as an accompaniment to their *Richelieu*, first introduced at the Palais-Royal in December 1839, brought to London in 1843.
43 *Vested Interests*, pp. 55 and 396.
44 Victorien Sardou, *Théâtre complet* (Paris: Albin Michel, 1950), p. 594.
45 *Morning Advertiser*, 22 November 1870.
46 *The Englishwoman's Domestic Magazine*, 9 (1 December 1870), pp. 350–1.

5 THE MODERNITY OF AIMÉE DESCLÉE

1 Squire Bancroft, *Empty Chairs* (London: John Murray, 1925), p. 24. Also see Frank Archer (pseudonym of Frank Bishop Arnold), *An Actor's Notebooks* (London: Stanley Paul, 1912), pp. 149–51.
2 *Le Naturalisme au théâtre* (Paris: Charpentier, 1923), p. 146. Unless otherwise stated all translations are my own.
3 *Scenic Art*, pp. 9 and 78.
4 'The Life of an Actress', *The Theatre*, 4 (1 July 1884), pp. 1–29, esp. p. 29. All subsequent references are to Scott, 'Life'. Also see Scott, *The Drama of Yesterday and Today*, 2, pp. 439–41.
5 Félix Duquesnel, 'Ombres Parisiennes', *Figaro*, 2 October 1894.
6 Alexandre Dumas *fils*, 'Desclée', in *Entr'actes*, 2nd ser. (Paris: Calmann Lévy, 1878), p. 381.
7 Emile de Molènes, *Desclée. Biographie et souvenirs* (Paris: Tresse, 1874); all subsequent references are to de Molènes. This is the main source for information about Desclée, but also see Pierre Berton, 'Desclée: Souvenirs de la vie de théâtre', *La Revue de Paris*, October 1913, pp. 513–36; Rienzo de Renzis, *Aimée Desclée: artista e amante* (Rome: Cremonese Editore, 1935); and André Maurois, *Three Musketeers: A Study of the Dumas Family* (London: Cape, 1957). The Bibliothèque de l'Arsenal in Paris has a dossier of cuttings relating to Desclée at Rt. 7019.

8 Paul Duplan, ed., *Lettres de Aimée Desclée à Fanfan* (Paris: Calmann-Lévy, 1895). All subsequent references are to *Fanfan*.

9 *The Journal of Marie Bashkirtseff* (London: Virago, 1985), p. 560.

10 *Fanfan*, p. 12.

11 Scott, 'Life', p. 18.

12 'Les Premières représentations', in *Paris-Guide* (Paris: Lacroix, 1867), pp. 785–98.

13 Preface to *L'Ami des Femmes*, in *Théâtre complet*, 4 (Paris: Calmann-Lévy, 1922), p. 54.

14 De Molènes, *Desclée*, p. 81.

15 *Ibid.*, p. 93.

16 Scott, 'Life', p, 22.

17 De Molènes, *Desclée*, pp. 193–4.

18 *Empty Chairs*, p. 25.

19 See Carlson, *The French Stage*, p. 124.

20 Antoine quoted in Toby Cole and Helen Krich Chinoy (eds.), *Directors on Directing* (Indianapolis and New York; Bobbs-Merrill, 1963), p. 90.

21 Frédéric Febvre, *Journal d'un comédien*, 1, pp. 259– .

22 See Martin Meisel, *Realizations: Narrative, Pictorial and Theatrical Arts in Nineteenth-Century England* (Princeton: Princeton University Press, 1983). Interesting contemporary opinions can be found in Percy Fitzgerald, *Principles of Comedy and Dramatic Effect* (London: Tinsley Brothers, 1870).

23 Germain Bapst, *Essai sur l'histoire du théâtre* (Paris: Hachette, 1893).

24 See Marvin Carlson, 'French Stage Composition from Hugo to Zola', *Educational Theatre Journal*, 23 (1971), pp. 363–78.

25 Albert Lambert, *Sur les planches* (Paris: Flammarion, 1894), pp. 112–14. Also see Hemmings, *Theatre and Industry*, pp. 215–16.

26 Bert O. States, *Great Reckonings in Little Rooms* (Berkeley, Los Angeles and London: University of California Press, 1985), pp. 41–3.

27 *On Actors*, p. 116.

28 *Froufrou*, nouvelle édition (Paris: Calmann-Lévy, 1885), p. 94.

29 *Ibid.*, p. 101.

30 *Ibid.*, p. 112.

31 *Ibid.*, pp. 4–5.

32 13 May 1873.

33 *Daily Telegraph*, 13 May 1873.

34 *Ibid.*

35 *Morning Post*, 13 May 1873.

36 *Daily Telegraph*, 13 May 1873.

37 *Morning Post*, 13 May 1873.

38 There is no doubt that Bernhardt was to organise her *mises-en-scène* on this principle. See my essay in John Stokes, Michael Booth and Susan Bassnett, *Bernhardt, Terry, Duse: The Actress in Her Time* (Cambridge: Cambridge University Press, 1988). All subsequent references are to *Bernhardt, Terry, Duse*.

39 *Examiner*, 24 May 1873.

40 De Molènes, *Desclée*, p. 140.

41 The letter appeared in *Entr'acte*, 29 January 1892, and was reprinted in part by Jules Clarétie in *Profils de Théâtre* (Paris: Gaultier Magnier, 1902), pp. 345–6.

42 The tradition includes *Adrienne Lecouvreur* by Scribe and Legouvé, and *Zaza* by Berton and Simon, as well as *A Doll's House*. Actress heroines are innumerable, from *Fanny Lear* by Meilhac and Halévy to Clorinde in Augier's *L'Aventurière*.

43 *Profils de théâtre*, p. 345.

44 *Froufrou*, p. 69.

45 *Ibid.*

46 *Ibid.*, p. 73.

47 *Profils de théâtre*, p. 346.

48 *Empty Chairs*, p. 25.

49 13 May 1873.

50 *Entr'acte*, 29 January 1892.

51 13 May.

52 See Gay Gibson Cima, *Performing Women*.

53 See de Molènes, *Desclée*, p. 58. For the nineteenth-century image of Ophelia see Elaine Showalter, *The Female Malady* (London: Virago, 1987).

54 *Profils de théâtre*, p. 220.

55 De Renzis, *Aimée Desclée*, pp. 68–9.

56 This, I am aware, may seem to equate the *régisseur* with a modern director too easily, but the functions of the *régisseur* shifted a good deal at this time. Pougin (p. 643) says that there were no 'fixed and invariable rules'. The best consideration of this important subject is Michael Hays, *The Public and Performance: Essays in the History of French and German Theater, 1871–1900* (Ann Arbor, Mich.: UMI Research Press, 1981).

57 Scott, 'Life', p. 26.

58 *Three Musketeers*, pp. 380–1.

59 De Molènes, *Desclée*, p. 102.

60 Robert Baldick (ed.), *Pages from the Goncourt Journal* (Oxford: Oxford University Press, 1978), p. 193.

61 'The Eighteenth Brumaire of Louis Bonaparte', in *Marx and Engels: Selected Works* (London: Lawrence and Wishart, 1968), p. 96.

62 Marx and Engels, *Selected Works*, p. 297.

63 Lissagaray, *History of the Commune of 1871* (London: Reeves and Turner, 1886), p. 207.

64 *Ibid.*, pp. 300–1. For information on the theatres during the Commune, see the anonymous *An Englishman in Paris* (London: Chatto and Windus, 1892); Gustave Labarthe, *Le Théâtre pendant les jours du siège et de la commune* (Paris: Fischbacher, 1910); André Tissier, 'Les Spectacles pendant la Commune', *Europe*, Nov.–Dec. 1970, pp. 179–98; Françisque Sarcey, *Paris during the Siege* (London: Chapman and Hall, 1871). For Commune decrees regarding the theatre, see Stewart Edwards (ed.), *The Communards of Paris, 1871* (London: Thames and Hudson, 1973), pp. 150–5.

65 *Fanfan*, p. 143.

66 Ludovic Halévy, *Notes et souvenirs* (Paris: Calmann-Lévy, 1889), pp. 84–6.

67 *Fanfan*, p. 152.

68 *Ibid.*, p. 158.

69 De Molènes, *Desclée*, pp. 74–5.

70 Labarthe, *Le Théâtre*, pp. 40–1.

71 Lissagaray, *History*, p. 382.

72 *Ibid.*, p. 439.

73 Edith Thomas, *The Women Incendiaries* (London: Secker and Warburg, 1967), p. xii.

74 For the history of Dumas's polemics on the sexual mores of his time, including the notorious pamphlet *L'Homme-Femme*, see *Cahiers Renaud-Barrault*, 45 (November 1963); André Lebois (ed.), *Le Dossier 'Tue-la!'* (Avignon: Edouard Aubanel, 1969); Dumas's own *Une Lettre sur les choses du jour* (Paris: Michel Lévy, 1871) and *Nouvelle lettre sur les choses du jour* (Paris: Michel Lévy, 1872).

75 De Molènes, *Desclée*, p. 157.

76 *Ibid.*, pp. 160–1.

77 *Fanfan*, p. 206.

78 *La Vie Parisienne*, quoted in de Molènes, *Desclée*, p. 165.

79 De Molènes, *Desclée*, p. 164.

80 *La Vie Parisienne*, quoted in de Molènes, *Desclée*, p. 165.

81 'A. M. Cuviller Fleury', *La Femme de Claude* (Paris: Michel Lévy, 1873), p. xlii.

82 See Paul Lidsky, *Les Ecrivains contre la commune* (Paris: Francis Maspero, 1970), and *Les Ecrivains français devant la guerre de 1870 et devant la commune*, Colloque 7 (Paris: Publications de la Société d'Histoire Littéraire de la France, 1972).

83 *The Downfall* (London: Chatto and Windus, 1892), p. 515.

84 De Molènes, *Desclée*, p. 156.

85 *La Femme de Claude*, p. 42.

86 *Œuvres complètes* (Paris: Gallimard, 1972), p. 49.

87 'When woman's unmeasured bondage shall be broken, when she shall live for and through herself, man – hitherto detestable – having let her go, she, too, will be poet!', Rimbaud declared when the Commune was at its height. 'Woman will find the unknown! Will her ideational worlds be different from ours? She will come upon strange, unfathomable, repellent delightful things; we shall take them, we shall comprehend them.' Quoted by Simone de Beauvoir, in *The Second Sex* (Harmondsworth: Penguin Books, 1987), pp. 723–4.

88 Lissagaray, *History*, pp. 207–8.

6 'A KIND OF BEAUTY': RÉJANE IN LONDON

1 Edmond et Jules de Goncourt, *Germinie Lacerteux* (Paris: Charpentier, 1864), p. 179. All subsequent references to this edition are within the text.

2 There is only one book on Réjane and it is wholly inadequate: Camillo Antona-Traversi, *Réjane* (Paris: Editions le Calame, 1930). François Baudot, *Réjane: la reine du boulevard* (Paris: Editions 7L/Steidl, 2001), offers a superb collection of photographs. Worth noting among the many English articles and newspaper

reports are interviews with the actress in the *Sketch*, 4 July 1894, pp. 520–1, and the *World*, 27 June 1894, p. 8, and two extended features: Albert D. Vandam, 'The Real Madame Sans-Gêne', *New Review*, 62 (July 1894), pp. 24–34, and an essay by Oscar Wilde's friend Robert H. Sherard in the *Lady's Realm* (July 1899), pp. 293–301.

3 See André Antoine, *Mes Souvenirs sur le Théâtre Libre* (Paris: Arthéme Fayard, 1921), pp. 125–31; Francis Pruner, *Les Luttes d'Antoine* (Paris: Lettres Modernes, 1964), pp. 273–82; Harold Hobson, *French Theatre since 1830* (London: John Calder, 1978), pp. 93–6.

4 Antona-Traversi, *Réjane*, p. 55. The book prints several other similar tributes.

5 *Réjane*, p. 70.

6 *Star*, 18 June 1901. The play was Daudet's *Sapho*. The same point is made, more concisely, by *The Speaker*, 26 June 1904, in a comparison between Réjane's repertoire and Bernhardt's *La Dame aux camélias*: 'Réjane stands for sheer, raw truth; Sarah for the transforming passion of poetry'.

7 I take the term from Richard Dyer, *Stars* (London: British Film Institute, 1979) which, although about performance on film, has much that is also relevant to theatre.

8 Among the other plays in her 1894 season was *L'Amoureuse* by G. de Porto-Riche.

9 'Madame Réjane', *The Yellow Book*, 2 (1894), pp. 197–206, esp. p. 197. See Katherine Lyon Mix, *A Study in Yellow* (Lawrence, Kan.: University of Kansas Press, and London: Constable, 1960), p. 113.

10 *The People's Theater*, trans. Barrett H. Clark (London: Allen & Unwin, 1919), p. 94.

11 A. B. Walkley, *The Speaker*, 30 June 1894.

12 *Pall Mall Gazette*, 25 June 1894.

13 *The Era*, 30 June 1894.

14 A. B. Walkley, *The Speaker*, 30 June 1894.

15 *Pall Mall Gazette*, 25 June 1894.

16 Taken from *The Era*, 17 April 1897; *Pall Mall Gazette*, 12 April 1897; and *The Speaker*, 17 April 1897.

17 12 April 1897.

18 See *Our Theatres in the Nineties*, 3 vols. (London: Constable, 1948), 1, pp. 177–8; 3, pp. 105–10; Martin Meisel, *Shaw and the Nineteenth-Century Theatre* (Princeton and London: Princeton University Press, 1963), pp. 356–9; Dan H. Lawrence (ed.), *Bernard Shaw: Collected Letters 1874–1897* (London: Max Reinhardt, 1965), pp. 701–2, 740–1, 776.

19 *Star*, 22 June 1901.

20 *Star*, 11 June 1901.

21 *Star*, 22 June 1901.

22 *Ibid.*

23 *The Theatrical World of 1894* (London: Walter Scott, Ltd., 1895), pp. 184–5.

24 All this, and more, must have been seen by the many artists who tried to capture her appeal. Charles Conder and Augustus John both made portraits,

their whereabouts now unknown. In France the most acclaimed picture was, unfortunately, Albert Besnard's chocolate-box 'Portrait de l'actrice moderne', first exhibited in Paris in 1898. Symons liked to compare her to a Forain.

25 *Star*, 25 June 1894.

26 *The Letters of Aubrey Beardsley*, ed. Henry Maas, J. L. Duncan and W. G. Good (London: Cassell, 1970), p. 71.

27 Beardsley either gave or sold a picture of Réjane to Henry James. *The Letters of Aubrey Beardsley*, p. 69.

28 *The Critic* (New York), 18 August 1894, p. 108.

29 Mix, *A Study in Yellow*, p. 113.

30 First performed in Paris in 1890, and in London in 1895.

31 *Star*, 29 May 1902.

32 *Ibid.*

33 Cf. Shaw: 'Integrity consists in obeying the morality which you accept; and neither Meilhac nor Réjane pretend for a moment to accept the morality which they both disregard in *Ma Cousine*', *Our Theatres in the Nineties*, I, p. 176.

34 *Star*, 2 July 1895.

35 *Pall Mall Gazette*, 2 July 1895.

36 *Star*, 20 June 1901.

37 By Pierre Berton and Charles Simon. First performed in Paris in 1898, banned in London in 1901, permitted in 1902.

38 By de Caillaret, de Flers and Jeoffrin, performed in London in 1904.

39 *The Times*, 27 May 1902.

40 *The Speaker*, 7 June 1902, compares Réjane's Zaza with Mrs Lewis Waller's English interpretation.

41 *The Speaker*, 7 June 1902.

42 First performed by Réjane in Paris in 1893, in London with Antoine in 1901.

43 Neatly, if contentiously, defined by Augustin Filon in *The Modern French Drama* (London: Chapman and Hall, 1898), p. 78, as 'a vicious sort of ingenuousness'.

44 *Star*, 24 June 1904.

45 *Star*, 21 June 1901.

46 The 'Parisienne' type unites different occupations and, to some extent, different classes, in a manner which implicates them in each other, placing the whole under a sexual heading. The extraordinary string of books on French women and French fashion produced by Octave Uzanne (some of them translated into English) demonstrates the process. *La Femme à Paris. Nos Contemporains* (Paris: Ancienne Maison Quantin, 1894), for instance, has sections on can-can dancers, actresses, artists' models, and four different kinds of prostitute. No wonder then that 'Thanks to the Parisienne, the streets of Paris become, for all artists and lovers, a fairy-tale Eden of hidden desires, lightning attractions, strange adventures. The heart starts and leaps with every step, the eyes are endlessly delighted, and the stroll is completely taken over by delicious sensations' (p. 7). Réjane, said Filon, represents 'the type that one meets constantly on Paris pavements when the shop girls are going to lunch' (*The Modern French Drama*, p. 153). Yet, according to Robert Sherard, when Réjane's young daughter

accompanies her mother to the theatre she 'likes to look at the audience and to be looked at, for she is already a Parisienne'.

47 First performed in Paris in 1900, and in London in 1902.

48 *Star*, 6 June 1902. Or, more mutedly, *The Times*, 5 June 1902: 'Madame Réjane is the wife, hot-headed, and "instinctive" creature, in the end a wild beast; and in that sort of part this versatile actress can do just as well as in the coquetry of *Ma Cousine* or in the *canaillerie* of *Zaza*.'

49 Or, as Porto-Riche complained in 1896: 'her habit of acting in plays by Meilhac, with their continual repetition of the same thing, their tedious reiteration of the same idea, made her over-emphasise the comic and the odd, as if she was always addressing an unintelligent public.' Quoted in Edmond and Jules de Goncourt, *Journal: Mémoires de la vie littéraire 1891–1896*, ed. Robert Ricatte (Paris: Fasquelle, Flammarion, 1956), 4, p. 921.

50 See 'Preface to Miss Julie', in *Strindberg: Plays*, trans. Michael Meyer (London: Eyre Methuen, 1976), p. 102.

51 'Those mules have filled very many seats – I do not mean personally', remarked Robert Hichens (reported in the *Pall Mall Gazette*, 20 June 1904).

52 Taken from the account in *The Era*, 6 January 1906.

53 *The Speaker*, 6 July 1895.

54 *The Speaker*, 17 June 1905. Or this, on *Sapho*, from the *Pall Mall Gazette*, 18 July 1901: 'One would like to pick her up, comfort her, kiss her if need be, and explain it to the wife afterward'.

55 *The Speaker*, 22 June 1901.

56 *Star*, 9 July 1901.

7 PEACOCKS AND PEARLS: OSCAR WILDE AND SARAH BERNHARDT

1 [Jean Paul Raymond] and Charles Ricketts, *Oscar Wilde: Recollections* (Bloomsbury: The Nonesuch Press, 1932), p. 16.

2 H. Montgomery Hyde, *Oscar Wilde: A Biography* (London: Methuen, 1976), p. 40.

3 *Gaiety Chronicles*, 1898, p. 366.

4 *My Double Life: Memoirs of Sarah Bernhardt* (London: William Heinemann, 1907), pp. 297–8.

5 Robert H. Sherard, *The Life of Oscar Wilde* (London: T. Werner Laurie, 1906), p. 181. All subsequent references are to Sherard.

6 *Ibid.*, p. 293.

7 Richard Ellmann, *Oscar Wilde* (London: Hamish Hamilton, 1987), p. 113. All subsequent references are to Ellmann.

8 *The Complete Works of Oscar Wilde Vol. 1: Poems and Poems in Prose*, ed. Bobby Fong and Karl Beckson (Oxford: Oxford University Press, 2000), p. 116. All subsequent references are to Fong and Beckson.

9 E. H. Yates, *Celebrities at Home*, 3rd ser. (London: Office of 'The World', 1879), p. 161.

10 *Pall Mall Gazette*, 10 July 1879.
11 Joseph Knight, *Theatrical Notes* (London: Lawrence and Bullen, 1883), p. 262.
12 Wilde, *Complete Letters*, p. 101. The first visit was probably on his way to Italy in 1875.
13 *Les Misérables* (Paris: Bibliothèque de la Pléiade, Gallimard, 1951), p. 690.
14 Fong and Beckson, *Complete Works*, p. 149.
15 In another poem, 'Louis Napoleon' (*Poems*, 1881), an elegy for the son of Napoleon III who died in Zululand in 1879 at the age of twenty-three, Wilde addresses the dead man with 'thou shalt not flaunt thy cloak of red', and celebrates a France 'free and republican'. Fong and Beckson, *Complete Works*, pp. 117 and 277.
16 Sherard, *Life*, p. 232.
17 *Galignani's Messenger* (Paris), 14 May 1883.
18 'The English Renaissance of Art', in *Miscellanies*, ed. Robert Ross (London: Methuen, 1908), p. 255.
19 2nd edn (Paris: Charpentier, 1874), pp. 90–108. All subsequent references are to Gautier, *Romantisme*.
20 Hyde, *Oscar Wilde*, p. 165.
21 Gautier, *Romantisme*, p. 90.
22 'L'Envoi', in Wilde, *Miscellanies*, p. 30.
23 François Coppée, 'La Bataille d'*Hernani*', *Œuvres complètes de François Coppée. Théâtre 1869–1889* (Paris: Alphonse Lemerre, 1890), p. 229.
24 Gautier, *Romantisme*, p. 100.
25 Graham Robb, *Victor Hugo* (London: Picador, 1998), p. 134.
26 'The French Play in London', *The Nineteenth Century*, August 1879, reprinted in *The Complete Prose Works of Matthew Arnold*, ed. R. H. Super, 11 vols. (Ann Arbor: University of Michigan Press, 1960–71), 9, 1973, pp. 64–85, esp. 75 and 76.
27 Sherard, *Life*, p. 229.
28 *Galignani's Messenger* (Paris), 4 March 1883.
29 *Complete Works of Oscar Wilde*, ed. Merlin Holland (Glasgow: Harper Collins, 1994), p. 613. All subsequent references are to Wilde, *Works*.
30 Wilde, *Works*, p. 646.
31 *Ibid.*, p. 637.
32 Wilde, *Complete Letters*, p. 179.
33 *Ibid.*, p. 197. Also see Kelver Hartley, *Oscar Wilde: L'Influence française dans son œuvre* (Paris: Librairie du Recueil Sirey, 1935).
34 Wilde, *Works*, p. 621.
35 Wilde, *Complete Letters*, p. 203.
36 Victor Hugo, *Théâtre complet* (Paris: Bibliothèque de la Pléiade, Gallimard, 1963), 1, pp. 1082 and 1144.
37 Wilde, *Works*, p. 899; also see letter to Ross about the *Ballad* in Wilde, *Complete Letters*, p. 993.
38 Wilde, *Works*, p. 1161.
39 *Ibid.*, p. 1168.

40 *Théâtre complet*, I, p. 1795.
41 In 1924 an obscure volume of *Oscar Wilde's Letters to Sarah Bernhardt* was published in the US. I agree with the most recent editor of Wilde's letters that 'although some of them may have been partially based on genuine originals as Wilde almost certainly corresponded with her' they are mostly 'spurious'. See Wilde, *Complete Letters*, p. xv.
42 Wilde, *Works*, p. 1173.
43 A notable exception is Lawrence Danson, *Wilde's Intentions: The Artist in his Criticism* (Oxford: Clarendon Press, 1997), p. 60. Also see my 'Shopping in Byzantium: Oscar Wilde as Shakespeare Critic', in *Victorian Shakespeare. Volume 1. Theatre, Drama and Performance*, ed. Gail Marshall and Adrian Poole (Basingstoke and New York: Palgrave-Macmillan, 2003), pp. 178–91.
44 E. H. Mikhail, *Oscar Wilde: Interviews and Recollections* (London and Basingstoke: Macmillan, 1979), I, p. 249.
45 Kerry Powell, *Oscar Wilde and the Theatre of the 1890s* (Cambridge: Cambridge University Press, 1990), pp. 33–54.
46 *Bibliothèque de Mme. Sarah Bernhardt* (Paris: Librairie Henri Leclerc, 1923), Première partie, p. 105. Item 404.
47 Knight, *Theatrical Notes*, p. 278.
48 Wilde, *Works*, p. 590.
49 It seems that even in 1895, at the time of the trials, Wilde still had faith that Bernhardt would take it up. See Merlin Holland, *Irish Peacock and Scarlet Marquess: The Real Trial of Oscar Wilde* (London and New York: Fourth Estate, 2003), pp. 35, 46, 307.
50 'A Chat with Mdme. Sarah Bernhardt at her "Hôtel"', *Pall Mall Gazette*, 15 April 1889.
51 Sherard, *Life*, pp. 362–3.
52 Wilde, *Letters*, p. 116.
53 'Rue des Beaux Arts', in Derek Mahon, *The Yellow Book* (Oldcastle, County Meath: The Galley Press, 1997), p. 41. Compare 'If personality is an unbroken series of successful gestures . . .' (F. Scott Fitzgerald, *The Great Gatsby* (Harmondsworth: Penguin Books, 1961, p. 8).
54 *Cécile Sorel: An Autobiography* (London: Staples Press, 1953), p. 57.
55 *Ibid.*, pp. 58–9.
56 Fong and Beckson, *Complete Works*, p. 173.
57 'The Remarkable Rocket', in Wilde, *Works*, pp. 299–300.
58 See my *Oscar Wilde: Myths, Miracles and Imitations* (Cambridge: Cambridge University Press, 1996), p. 18.
59 *The White Peacock*, ed. Andrew Robertson (Cambridge: Cambridge University Press, 1983), pp. 30–1.
60 For the relation of theatre to early film see Richard Abel, *The Ciné Goes to Town: French Cinema 1896–1914*, updated and expanded edn (Berkeley: University of California Press, 1998) and Ben Brewster and Lea Jacobs, *Theatre to Cinema* (Oxford: Oxford University Press, 1997). Bernhardt's involvement with new media is surveyed in David W. Menefee's excellent *Sarah Bernhardt in the*

Theatre of Films and Sound Recordings (Jefferson, NC, and London: McFarland & Company, Inc., 2003).

8 THE GREATEST ACTRESS IN THE WORLD: EDWIGE FEUILLÈRE AND HER ADMIRERS

1 In *Plays: Five* (London: Methuen, 1983), p. 292.
2 8 September 1946, p. 2. The play was translated by Ronald Duncan and directed by Cocteau himself; it opened at the Lyric on 4 September 1946, transferred to the Haymarket on 12 February 1947. The essential sources for any study of Hobson are two books by Dominic Shellard: *Harold Hobson: Witness and Judge* (Keele, Staffordshire: Keele University Press, 1995) and *Harold Hobson: The Complete Catalogue 1922–1988* (Keele, Staffordshire: Keele University Press, 1995).
3 *Indirect Journey: An Autobiography* (London: Weidenfeld and Nicolson, 1978), p. 24.
4 *Sunday Times*, 7 October 1951.
5 Harold Hobson, *The Theatre Now* (London: Longmans, Green and Co., 1953), p. 79.
6 *Sunday Times*, 11 September 1955.
7 *Sunday Times*, 5 May 1968.
8 *Plays and Players*, 2 (September 1955), p. 12.
9 *Sunday Times*, 7 October 1951.
10 *Indirect Journey*, p. 244.
11 Paul Claudel, *Théâtre* (Paris: Bibliothèque de la Pléiade, Gallimard, 1947), 1, p. 915.
12 Jean-Louis Barrault, *Theatre of Jean-Louis Barrault* (London: Barrie and Rockliff, 1961), p. 189.
13 *Sunday Times*, 5 May 1968.
14 Edwige Feuillère, *Les Feux de la mémoire* (Paris: Albin Michel, 1977), p. 193.
15 Edwige Feuillère, *A vous de jouer* (Paris: Albin Michel, 1998), p. 150.
16 *Ibid.*, p. 23.
17 *The Spectator*, 5 October 1951, repr. *Curtains* (London: Longman's, 1961), p. 384, in collected vols.
18 *Eroticism*, trans. Mary Dalwood (1962, London: Penguin, 2001), p. 9.
19 Alternatively, one might compare Hobson's idealisations with Simone de Beauvoir's devastating attack on Claudel's representation of woman as destroyer in *The Second Sex*, first published in France in 1949.
20 *Sunday Times*, 11 September 1955.
21 2 October 1955, also see 18 September 1955.
22 *Sunday Times*, 18 September 1955.
23 *Christian Science Monitor*, 24 September 1955.
24 *Ibid.*, 23 March 1957.
25 *Sunday Times*, 11 September 1955.
26 *Curtains*, pp. 398–9.

27 *Christian Science Monitor*, 24 September 1955.
28 4 (April 1957), p. 11.
29 *Evening Standard*, 19 March 1957.
30 Peter Daubeny, *My World of Theatre* (London: Jonathan Cape, 1971), pp. 176–7.
31 Feuillère, *A vous de jouer*, p. 181.
32 John Dexter, *The Honourable Beast: A Posthumous Autobiography* (London: Nick Hern Books, 1993), p. 21.
33 Brian Aherne quoted in Alan Dent, *Vivien Leigh: A Bouquet* (London: Hamish Hamilton, 1969), p. 51. Dent himself complimented her on 'giving a beautiful performance of the Lady of the Camellias' (p. 180).
34 See Christiane Issartel, *Les Dames aux camélias de l'histoire à la légende* (Paris: Chêne Hachette, 1981).
35 See Nicholas de Jongh, *Not in Front of the Audience* (London: Routledge, 1992), pp. 56–7, and Alan Sinfield, *Out on Stage: Lesbian and Gay Theatre in the Twentieth Century* (London and New Haven: Yale University Press, 1999), pp. 161 ff.
36 Sheridan Morley, *John G.: The Authorised Biography of John Gielgud* (London: Hodder and Stoughton, 2001), p. 291.
37 London: Penguin, 1962, p. 177.
38 Edwige Feuillère, *Moi la Clairon* (Paris: Albin Michel, 1984), pp. 62–3.
39 *Sunday Times*, 24 March 1951.
40 *Plays and Players*, 4 (May 1957), p. 13.
41 *Curtains*, pp. 399–401.
42 *New Statesman and Nation*, 30 March 1957.
43 Daubeny, *My World of Theatre*, pp. 196–7.
44 *Sunday Times*, 13 March 1960.
45 *Sunday Times*, 17 November 1957.
46 *Observer*, 17 November 1957.
47 Margaret Rawlings Papers.
48 *The Dramatic Works of Jean Racine: A Metrical English Version*, trans. Robert Bruce Boswell, 2 vols. (London: George Bell and Sons, 1889).
49 Jean Racine, *Phèdre*, trans. Margaret Rawlings (London: Faber, 1961), preface, pp. 9–16, esp. p. 9. All subsequent pages are within the text.
50 *The Honourable Beast*, p. 52.
51 Christopher Ricks, 'Racine's Phèdre, Lowell's Phaedra', in *Essays in Appreciation* (Oxford: Clarendon Press, 1996), pp. 245–59, esp. p. 248.
52 Peter O'Toole, *Loitering with Intent* (London: Macmillan, 1996), p. 20.
53 See, for example, William Gaskill, *A Sense of Direction* (London: Faber, 1988), p. 5.
54 Lindsay Anderson, 'Get Out and Push', in *Declaration*, ed. Tom Maschler (London: MacGibbon and Kee, 1957), pp. 154–78, esp. p. 172.
55 *1956 and All That: The Making of Modern British Drama* (London and New York: Routledge, 1999), p. 143.
56 *Almost a Gentleman: An Autobiography Vol. II: 1955–1966* (London: Faber, 1991), p. 166.

57 Jean-Louis Barrault, *Memories for Tomorrow* (London: Thames and Hudson, 1974), p. 309.

58 *Les Feux*, p. 212.

59 Claire Bloom, *Leaving a Doll's House* (London: Virago, 1996), p. 112.

60 *Ibid.*, p. 70.

61 Claire Bloom, *Limelight and After* (London: Weidenfeld and Nicolson, 1982), p. 150. (This is Bloom's earlier autobiography.) Leigh later played the part in US with Mary Ure. See Tony Richardson, *Long Distance Runner: A Memoir* (London: Faber and Faber, 1993), p. 117, and Joan Plowright, *And That's Not All* (London: Weidenfeld and Nicolson, 2001), p. 71. Even Osborne was persuaded by Leigh's US performance: 'defiant, desperate and moving' (*Almost a Gentleman*, p. 166). Rachel Roberts and Jill Bennett also considered reviving *Duel of Angels* – to be directed, rather surprisingly, by Lindsay Anderson. See Rachel Roberts, *No Bells on Sunday* (London: Pavilion, Michael Joseph, 1984), p. 131.

62 Elaine Dundy, *Life Itself* (London: Virago, 2001), p. 198.

63 See Joel H. Kaplan and Sheila Stowell, *Theatre and Fashion: Oscar Wilde to the Suffragettes* (Cambridge: Cambridge University Press, 1994).

64 See Michelene Wandor, *Post-War British Drama: Looking back in Gender*, rev. edn (London and New York: Routledge, 2001).

65 See Rebellato, *1956 and All That*.

Select bibliography

Abraham, Emile, *Les Acteurs et les Actrices de Paris* (Paris: Michel Lévy Frères, 1861)

Ambrière, Francis, *Mademoiselle Mars et Marie Dorval au théâtre et dans la vie* (Paris: Seuil, 1992)

Anderson, Lindsay, 'Get Out and Push', in *Declaration*, ed. Tom Maschler (London: MacGibbon and Kee, 1957)

Anon., *An Englishman in Paris* (London: Chatto and Windus, 1892)

Antoine, André, *Mes Souvenirs sur le Théâtre Libre* (Paris: Fayard, 1921)

Antona-Traversi, Camillo, *Réjane* (Paris: Editions le Calame, 1930)

Appleton, William W., *Madame Vestris and the London Stage* (New York and London: Columbia University Press, 1974)

Archer, Frank (pseudonym of Frank Bishop Arnold), *An Actor's Notebooks* (London: Stanley Paul, 1912)

Archer, William, *The Theatrical World of 1894* (London: Walter Scott, Ltd., 1895)
William Charles Macready (London: Kegan Paul, 1890)

Arnold, Matthew, *The Poems of Matthew Arnold*, ed. Kenneth Allott (London: Longmans, 1965)
The Complete Prose Works of Matthew Arnold, ed. R. H. Super, 11 vols. (Ann Arbor: University of Michigan Press, 1960–77, 9, 1973)

Aston, Elaine, *Sarah Bernhardt: A French Actress on the English Stage* (Oxford: Berg Publishers, 1989)

Augier, Emile, *L'Aventurière*, new edn (Paris: Michel Lévy, 1870)

Austen, Jane, *Emma* (Harmondsworth: Penguin, 1966)

Baldick, Robert (ed.), *Pages from the Goncourt Journal* (Oxford: Oxford University Press, 1978)

Bancroft, Squire, *Empty Chairs* (London: John Murray, 1925)

Bapst, Germain, *Essai sur l'histoire du théâtre* (Paris: Hachette, 1893)

Barrault, Jean-Louis, *Memories for Tomorrow* (London: Thames and Hudson, 1974)
Theatre of Jean-Louis Barrault (London: Barrie and Rockliff, 1961)

Bartholomeuz, Dennis, *The Winter's Tale in Performance in England and America 1611–1976* (Cambridge: Cambridge University Press, 1982)

Bashkirtseff, Marie, *The Journal of Marie Bashkirtseff* (London: Virago, 1985)

Bataille, Georges, trans. Mary Dalwood, *Eroticism* (London: Penguin, 2001)

Baudelaire, Charles, *Œuvres complètes* (Paris: Aux éditions du Seuil, 1968)

Baudot, François, *Réjane: la reine du boulevard* (Paris: Editions 7L/Steidl, 2001)

Beizer, Janet, *Ventriloquized Bodies: Narratives of Hysteria in Nineteenth-Century France* (Ithaca and London: Cornell University Press, 1993)

Benedetti, Jean, *David Garrick and the Birth of Modern Theatre* (London: Methuen, 2001)

Berlanstein, Lenard R., *Daughters of Eve: A Cultural History of French Theater Women from the Old Regime to the Fin de Siècle* (Cambridge Mass.: Harvard University Press, 2001)

Bernhardt, Sarah, *Bibliothèque de Mme. Sarah Bernhardt* (Paris: Librairie Henri Leclerc, 1923)

My Double Life: Memoirs of Sarah Bernhardt (London: William Heinemann, 1907)

Bloom, Claire, *Leaving a Doll's House* (London: Virago, 1996)

Limelight and After (London: Weidenfeld and Nicolson, 1982)

Borgerhoff, J.-L., *Le Théâtre anglais à Paris sous la restauration* (Paris: Librairie Hachette, 1913)

Boudet, Micheline, *Mademoiselle Mars l'inimitable* (Paris: Terres des Femmes, Perrin, 1987)

Bouffé, *Mes Souvenirs 1800–1880* (Paris: E. Dentu, Editeur, 1880)

Brander Matthews, J., *The Theatres of Paris* (New York: Charles Scribners and Sons, 1880)

Brontë, Charlotte, *Villette*, ed. Mark Lilly (Harmondsworth: Penguin Books, 1979)

Brooks, Peter, *The Melodramatic Imagination* (New Haven and London: Yale University Press, 1995)

Brownstein, Rachel M., *Tragic Muse: Rachel of the Comédie-Française* (Durham, NC, and London: Duke University Press, 1995)

Cain, George, *Anciens théâtres de Paris* (Paris: Librairie Charpentier et Fasquelle, 1906)

Carlson, Marvin, 'French Stage Composition from Hugo to Zola', *Educational Theatre Journal*, 23 (1894), 363–78.

The French Stage in the Nineteenth Century (Metuchen, NJ: The. Scarecrow Press, Inc., 1972)

Carlyle, Carol Jones, *Helen Faucit: Fire and Ice on the Victorian Stage* (London: The Society for Theatre Research, 2000)

Cima, Gay Gibson, *Performing Women: Female Characters, Male Playwrights, and the Modern Stage* (Ithaca and London: Cornell University Press, 1993)

Clarétie, Jules, *La vie moderne au théâtre. Causeries sur l'art dramatique* (Paris: Georges Barba, 1869)

Profils de théâtre (Paris: Gaultier-Magnier, 1902)

Claudel, Paul, *Théâtre*, 2 vols. (Paris: Gallimard, 1947)

Collins, Herbert F., *Talma: A Biography of an Actor* (London: Faber and Faber, 1964)

Comyns Carr, J. *Coasting Bohemia* (London: Macmillan and Co., 1914)

Mrs. J. Comyns Carr's Reminiscences, ed. Eve Adam (London: Hutchinson, 1926)

Stray Memories by his Wife (London: Macmillan, 1920)

Coppée, François, *Œuvres complètes de François Coppée. Théâtre 1869–1889* (Paris: Alphonse Lemerre, 1890)

D'Heylli, Georges, *La Comédie-Française à Londres (1871–1879)* (Paris: Paul Ollendorf, 1880)

Journal Intime de la Comédie-Française (1852–1871) (Paris: E. Dentu, Editeur, 1879)

Madame Arnould-Plessy: 1834–1876 (Paris: Tresse, Editeur, 1876)

Danson, Lawrence, *Wilde's Intentions: The Artist in his Criticism* (Oxford: Clarendon Press, 1997)

Daubeny, Peter, *My World of Theatre* (London: Jonathan Cape, 1971)

Davis, Tracy, *Actresses as Working Women* (London and New York: Routledge, 1991)

The Economics of the British Stage 1880–1914 (Cambridge: Cambridge University Press, 2000)

de Beauvoir, Roger, *Mémoires de Mademoiselle Mars*, 2 vols. (Paris: Gabriel Roux et Cassanet, Editeurs, 1849)

de Beauvoir, Simone, *Le Deuxième Sexe* (Paris: Gallimard, 1949)

de Bury (née Stuart), Madame Blaz, *Molière and the French Classical Drama* (London: Charles Knight, 1846)

de Goncourt, Edmond and Jules, ed. Robert Ricatte, *Journal: Mémoires de la vie littéraire 1891–1896* (Paris: Fasquelle, Flammarion, 1956)

Germinie Lacerteux (Paris: Charpentier, 1864)

de Mirecourt, Eugène, *Mme Arnould-Plessy* (Paris: Chez Achille Faure, 1867)

Plessy-Arnould, in *Les Contemporains* (Paris: chez l'auteur, 1858)

de Molènes, Emile, *Desclée. Biographie et Souvenirs* (Paris: Tresse, 1874)

de Renzis, Rienzo, *Aimée Desclée: artista e amante* (Rome: Cremonese Editore, 1935)

Dent, Alan, *Vivien Leigh: A Bouquet* (London: Hamish Hamilton, 1969)

Descotes, Maurice, *La drame romantique et ses grands créateurs (1827–1839)* (Paris: Presses Universitaires, 1955)

Les grands rôles du théâtre de Marivaux (Paris: Presses Universitaires de France, 1972)

Les grands rôles du théâtre de Molière (Paris: Presses Universitaires de France, 1960)

Deutsch, L., *Déjazet* (Paris: Editions du Laurier, 1928)

Dexter, John, *The Honourable Beast: A Posthumous Autobiography* (London: Nick Hern Books, 1993)

Diamond, Elin, 'Realism and Hysteria: Towards a Feminist Mimesis', *Discourse*, 13 (1990–91), 59–92

Disraeli, Benjamin [The Earl of Beaconsfield, K.G.], *Tancred or The New Crusade*, in *The Collected Edition of the Novels and Tales of the Right Honourable B. Disraeli*, 4 (London: Longmans, Green and Co., 1886)

Downer, Alan S., *The Eminent Tragedian: William Charles Macready* (Cambridge, Mass.: Harvard University Press, 1966)

Dumas *fils*, Alexandre, *Entr'actes*, 2nd ser. (Paris: Calmann-Lévy, 1878)

La Femme de Claude (Paris: Michel Lévy, 1873)

Nouvelle lettre sur les choses du jour (Paris: Michel Lévy, 1872)

Une Lettre sur les choses du jour (Paris: Michel Lévy, 1871)

Théâtre complet, 4 (Paris: Calmann-Lévy, 1922)

Duncan, Barry, *The St James's Theatre: Its Strange and Complete History 1835–1957* (London: Barrie and Rockliff, 1964)

Dundy, Elaine, *Life Itself* (London: Virago, 2001)

Dunn, Leslie, and Nancy A. Jones (eds.), *Embodied Voices: Representing Female Vocality in Western Culture* (Cambridge: Cambridge University Press, 1994)

Duplan, Paul (ed.), *Lettres de Aimée Desclée à Fanfan* (Paris: Calmann-Lévy, 1895)

Duval, Georges, *Virginie Déjazet* (Paris: Tresse, 1876)

Dyer, Richard, *Stars* (London: British Film Institute, 1979)

Edwards, Stewart (ed.), *The Communards of Paris, 1871* (London: Thames and Hudson, 1973)

Eliot, George, 'Arts and Belles Lettres', *Westminster Review*, 65 (1856), 625–50.

   Adam Bede, ed. Stephen Gill (London: Penguin, 1985)

   Daniel Deronda, ed. Barbara Hardy (Harmondsworth: Penguin Books, 1967)

Ellmann, Richard, *Oscar Wilde* (London: Hamish Hamilton, 1987)

Evans, Martha Noel, *Fits and Starts: A Genealogy of Hysteria in Modern France* (Ithaca and London: Cornell University Press, 1991)

Falk, Bernard, *Rachel the Immortal* (London: Hutchinson, 1935)

Faucit, Helen (Lady Martin), 'Shakespeare's Women: By One who has Impersonated Them: Hermione', *Blackwood's Edinburgh Magazine*, 149 (1891), 1–37

Febvre, Frédéric, *Journal d'un comédien*, 2 vols. (Paris: Paul Ollendorf, 1896)

Ferris, Lesley (ed.), *Crossing the Stage: Controversies on Cross-dressings* (London and New York: Routledge, 1993)

Feuillère, Edwige, *A vous de jouer* (Paris: Albin Michel, 1998)

   Les Feux de la mémoire (Paris: Albin Michel, 1977)

   Moi la Clairon (Paris: Albin Michel, 1984)

Filon, Augustin, *The Modern French Drama* (London: Chapman and Hall, 1898)

Finney, Gail, *Women in Modern Drama* (Ithaca and London: Cornell University Press, 1989)

Fitzgerald, Percy, *Principles of Comedy and Dramatic Effect* (London: Tinsley Brothers, 1870)

Fletcher, Kathy, 'Planché, Vestris and the Transvestite Role: Sexuality and Gender in Victorian Popular Theatre', *Nineteenth-Century Theatre*, 15 (1987), 9–33.

Freud, Sigmund, 'On the Universal Tendency to Debasement in the Sphere of Love', in *The Penguin Freud Library*, 7, trans. James Strachey (London: Penguin Books, 1991)

Fussell, Edwin Sill, *The French Side of Henry James* (New York: Columbia University Press, 1990)

Garber, Marjorie, *Vested Interests: Cross-dressing and Cultural Anxiety* (New York and London: Routledge, 1992)

Gaskill, William, *A Sense of Direction* (London: Faber, 1988)

Gautier, Théophile, *Histoire du Romantisme*, 2nd edn (Paris: Charpentier, 1874)

Gordon D. J., and John Stokes, 'The Reference of *The Tragic Muse*', in *The Air of Reality: New Essays on Henry James*, ed. John Goode (London: Methuen, 1972)

Halévy, Ludovic, *Notes et souvenirs* (Paris: Calmann-Lévy, 1889)

Hartley, Kelver, *Oscar Wilde. L'Influence Française dans son œuvre* (Paris: Librairie du Recueil Sirey, 1935)

Hays, Michael, *The Public and Performance: Essays in the History of French and German Theater, 1871–1900* (Ann Arbor, Mich.: UMI Research Press, 1981)

Hazlitt, William, *The Complete Works of William Hazlitt*, ed. P. P. Howe, 21 vols. (London: J. M. Dent, 1930–34)

Hedgcock, Frank A., *David Garrick and his French Friends* (London: Stanley Paul & Co., 1911)

Hemmings, F. W. J., *The Theatre Industry in Nineteenth-Century France* (Cambridge: Cambridge University Press, 1993)

Hervey, Charles, 'Madame Arnould Plessy', *The Theatre*, 9 (1 April 1887), 194–200

The Theatres of Paris (Paris: Galignani and Co.; London: John Mitchell, 1846)

Hobsbawm, E. J., *The Age of Revolution, 1789–1848* (London: Weidenfeld and Nicolson, 1962)

Hobson, Harold, *French Theatre since 1830* (London: John Calder, 1978)

Indirect Journey: An Autobiography (London: Weidenfeld and Nicolson, 1978)

The Theatre Now (London: Longmans, Green and Co., 1953)

Hollingshead, John, *Gaiety Chronicles* (London: Archibald Constable and Co., 1898)

My Lifetime, 2 vols. (London: Sampson Low, Marston and Co., 1895)

Plain English (London: Chatto and Windus, 1880)

Hooker, Kenneth Ward, *The Fortunes of Victor Hugo in England* (New York: Columbia University Press, 1938)

Horne, Philip (ed.), *Henry James: A Life in Letters* (Allen Lane: The Penguin Press, 1999)

Hugo, Victor, *Les Misérables* (Paris: Bibliothèque de la Pléiade, Gallimard, 1951)

Théâtre complet, 2 vols. (Paris: Bibliothèque de la Pléiade, Gallimard, 1963–4)

Hyde, H. Montgomery, *Oscar Wilde: A Biography* (London: Methuen, 1976)

Issartel, Christiane, *Les Dames aux camélias de l'histoire à la légende* (Paris: Chêne Hachette, 1981)

J. P. [Juliet Pollock], 'The French Stage', *Macmillan's Magazine*, 21 (1870), 400–4.

James, Henry, *Autobiography*, ed. F. W. Dupee (London: W. H. Allen, 1956)

Parisian Sketches, ed. with an introduction by Leon Edel and Ilse Dusoir Lind (London: Rupert Hart-Davis, 1957)

The Complete Plays of Henry James, ed. Leon Edel (London: Rupert Hart-Davis, 1949)

The Complete Tales of Henry James, vol. 5 1883–1884, ed. Leon Edel (London: Rupert Hart-Davis, 1963)

The Scenic Art (London: Rupert Hart-Davis, 1949)

The Tragic Muse, ed. Philip Horne (London: Penguin Classics, 1995)

The Tragic Muse (London: Hart-Davis, 1948)

Janin, Jules, *Rachel et la tragédie* (Paris: Amyot, 1859)

Kaminsky, Alice, *George Henry Lewes* (Syracuse: Syracuse University Press, 1968)
Kaplan, Joel H., and Sheila Stowell, *Theatre and Fashion: Oscar Wilde to the Suffragettes* (Cambridge: Cambridge University Press, 1994)
Kaye, Richard, *The Flirt's Tragedy: Desire Without End in Victorian and Edwardian Fiction* (Charlottesville and London: University of Virginia Press, 2002)
Keates, Jonathan, *Stendhal* (London: Minerva, 1995)
Kemble, Frances Ann, *Records of Later Life*, 3 vols. (London: Richard Bentley, 1882)
    Record of a Girlhood (London: Richard Bentley and Son, 1878)
Knepler, Henry, *The Gilded Stage* (London: Constable, 1968)
Knight, Joseph, *Theatrical Notes* (London: Lawrence and Bullen, 1883)
Labarthe, Gustave, *Le Théâtre pendant les jours du siège et de la commune* (Paris: Fischbacher, 1910)
Lady Pollock, 'The Comédie-Française', *The Contemporary Review*, 18 (1871), 43–55
Lambert, Albert, *Sur les planches* (Paris: Flammarion, 1894)
Lawrence, Dan H. (ed.), *Bernard Shaw: Collected Letters 1874–1897* (London: Max Reinhardt, 1965)
Lawrence, D. H., *The White Peacock*, ed. Andrew Robertson (Cambridge: Cambridge University Press, 1983)
Leathers, V., *British Entertainers in France* (Toronto: University of Toronto Press, 1959)
Lecomte, L. Henry, *Une Comédienne au XIXe siècle: Virginie Déjazet* (Paris: Léon Sapin, 1892)
    Virginie Déjazet: D'après ses papiers et sa correspondance (Paris: Librairie Illustrée, Montgredien et Cie, 1902)
Legouvé, Ernest, *Sixty Years of Recollections*, trans. with notes by Albert D. Vandam (London and Sydney: Eden, Remington and Co., 1893)
Lewes, G. H., 'The State of Criticism in France', *British and Foreign Review*, 16 (1844), 327–62
    'The French Drama: Racine and Victor Hugo', *Westminster Review*, 34 (1840), 287–324
    Dramatic Essays: John Forster and George Henry Lewes, Reprinted from the "Examiner" and the "Leader", with notes and an introduction by William Archer and Robert W. Lowe (London: Walter Scott Ltd., 1896)
    Ranthorpe, ed. Barbara Smalley (Athens, OH: Ohio University Press, 1974)
    Rose, Blanche and Violet (London: Smith, Elder and Co., 1848)
    On Actors and the Art of Acting (London: Smith, Elder and Co., 1875)
Lissagaray, Prosper Olivier, trans. E. M. Aveling, *History of the Commune of 1871* (London: Reeves and Turner, 1886)
Litvak, Joseph, *Caught in the Act: Theatricality in the Nineteenth-Century Novel* (Berkeley, Los Angeles and Oxford: University of California Press, 1992)
Lyonnet, Henry, *Dictionnaire des Comédiens Français*, 2 vols. (Paris: E. Jorel, 1908)
Maas, Henry, L. Duncan and W. G. Good (eds.), *The Letters of Aubrey Beardsley* (London: Cassell, 1970)

Macready, William Charles, *Macready: Reminiscences and Selections for his Diaries and Letters*, ed. Sir Frederick Pollock, 2 vols. (London: Macmillan and Co., 1875)

Mahon, Derek, *The Yellow Book* (Oldcastle, County Meath: The Galley Press, 1997)

Marshall, Gail, *Actresses on the Victorian Stage* (Cambridge: Cambridge University Press, 1998)

Martin, Sir Theodore, *Helena Faucit (Lady Martin)* (Edinburgh and London: William Blackwood and Sons, 1900)

Marx, Karl, and Frederick Engels, *Marx and Engels: Selected Works* (London: Lawrence and Wishart, 1968)

Mathews, Charles J., *Letter from Mr Charles Mathews to the Dramatic Authors of France* (London: J. Mitchell, 1852)

Maurois, André, *Three Musketeers: A Study of the Dumas Family* (London: Cape, 1957)

McIntyre, Ian, *Garrick* (London: Penguin Books, 2000)

Meilhac, Henri and Ludovic Halévy, *Froufrou* (Paris: Calmann-Lévy, 1885)

Meisel, Martin, *Realizations: Narrative, Pictorial and Theatrical Arts in Nineteenth-Century England* (Princeton: Princeton University Press, 1983)

    Shaw and the Nineteenth-Century Theatre (Princeton and London: Princeton University Press, 1963)

Menefee, David W., *Sarah Bernhardt in the Theatre of Films and Sound Recordings* (Jefferson, NC, and London: McFarland & Company, Inc., 2003)

Meunier, Dauphin, 'Madame Réjane', *The Yellow Book*, 2 (1894), 197–206.

Mikhail, E. H. (ed.), *Oscar Wilde: Interviews and Recollections*, 2 vols. (London and Basingstoke: Macmillan, 1979)

Mix, Katherine Lyon, *A Study in Yellow* (Lawrence, Kan.: University of Kansas Press, and London: Constable, 1960)

Moers, Ellen, *Literary Women* (London: W. H. Allen, 1977)

Molènes, Emile de, *Desclée biographie et souvenirs* (Paris: Tresse, 1874)

Moody, Jane, *Illegitimate Theatre in London, 1770–1840* (Cambridge: Cambridge University Press, 2000)

Moraud, Marcel, *Le Romantisme Français en Angleterre de 1814 à 1848* (Paris: Librairie Ancienne Honoré Champion, 1933)

Morgan, Lady Sydney, *France in 1829–30*, 2 vols. (London: Saunders and Otley, 1830)

    France, 3rd edn, 2 vols. (London: Printed for Henry Colburn, 1818)

    Passages from My Autobiography (London: Richard Bentley, 1859)

Morley, Henry, *The Journal of a London Playgoer* (Leicester: Leicester University Press, 1974)

Morley, Sheridan, *John G.: The Authorised Biography of John Gielgud* (London: Hodder and Stoughton, 2001)

Nicoll, Allardyce, *A History of English Drama 1660–1900*, 4 (Cambridge: Cambridge University Press, 1955)

O'Toole, Peter, *Loitering with Intent* (London: Macmillan, 1960)

Osborne, John, *Almost a Gentleman: An Autobiography Vol. II: 1955–1966* (London: Faber, 1991)

Paulin, Tom, *The Day-Star of Liberty: William Hazlitt's Radical Style* (London: Faber and Faber, 1998)

Pemberton, T. Edgar, *Charles Dickens and the Stage* (London: George Rodway, Covent Garden, 1888)

Phillips, Adam, *On Flirtation* (London: Faber and Faber, 1994)

Pierron, E., *Virginie Déjazet* (Paris: Bolle-Lasalle, 1856)

Planché, J. R., *The Extravaganzas of J. R. Planché, Esq.*, 5 vols. (London: Samuel French, 1879)

Plowright, Joan, *And That's Not All* (London: Weidenfeld and Nicolson, 2001)

Pollitzer, Marcel, *Trois reines de théâtre* (Paris: La Colombe, 1958)

Pollock, Lady, *Macready as I Knew Him* (London: Remington and Co., 1884)

Pougin, Arthur, *Dictionnaire historique et pittoresque du théâtre* (Paris: Librairie de Firmin-Didot, 1885)

Powell, Kerry, *Oscar Wilde and the Theatre of the 1890s* (Cambridge: Cambridge University Press, 1990)

Pruner, Francis, *Les Luttes d'Antoine* (Paris: Lettres Modernes, 1964)

Racine, Jean, *The Dramatic Works of Jean Racine: A Metrical English Version*, trans. Robert Bruce Boswell, 2 vols. (London: George Bell and Sons, 1889)

 Phèdre, trans. Margaret Rawlings (London: Faber, 1961)

Rebellato, Dan, *1956 and All That: The Making of Modern British Drama* (London and New York: Routledge, 1999)

Richardson, Joanna, *Rachel* (London: Max Reinhardt, 1956)

Richardson, Tony, *Long Distance Runner: A Memoir* (London: Faber and Faber, 1993)

Ricketts, Charles [Jean Paul Raymond], *Oscar Wilde: Recollections* (Bloomsbury: The Nonesuch Press, 1932)

Rimbaud, Arthur, *Œuvres complètes* (Paris: Gallimard, 1972)

Roach, Joseph R., *The Player's Passion: Studies in the Science of Acting* (Newark: University of Delaware Press, 1985)

Robb, Graham, *Victor Hugo* (London: Picador, 1998)

Roberts, Rachel, *No Bells on Sunday* (London: Pavilion, Michael Joseph, 1984)

Robinson, Crabb, *The London Theatre 1811–1866, Selections from the Diary of Henry Crabb Robinson*, ed. Eluned Brown (London: Society for Theatre Research, 1966)

Sarcey, Francisque, *Comédiens et Comédiennes*, 2 vols. (Paris: Librairie de Biblio-philes, 1884)

 Paris during the Siege (London: Chapman and Hall, 1871)

Sardou, Victorien, *Théâtre complet*, 15 vols. (Paris: Albin Michel, 1950)

Schechner, Richard, *Performance Studies: An Introduction* (London and New York: Routledge, 2002)

Schlegel, Augustus William, *Course of Lectures on Dramatic Art and Literature*, trans. John Black, Esq., Revised according to the last German edn (London: Henry G. Bohn, 1846)

Scott, Clement, *The Drama of Yesterday and Today*, 2 vols. (London: Macmillan and Co., Ltd, 1899)

Senelick, Laurence, *The Changing Room: Sex, Drag and Theatre* (London and New York: Routledge, 2000)

'The Evolution of the Male Impersonator on the Nineteenth-Century Popular Stage', *Essays on Theatre*, 1 (1982), 31–44

Shaw, Bernard, *Our Theatres in the Nineties*, 3 vols. (London: Constable, 1948)

Shellard, Dominic, *Harold Hobson: The Complete Catalogue 1922–1988* (Keele, Staffordshire: Keele University Press, 1995)

Harold Hobson: Witness and Judge (Keele, Staffordshire: Keele University Press, 1995)

Sherard, Robert H., *The Life of Oscar Wilde* (London: T. Werner Laurie, 1906)

Showalter, Elaine, *The Female Malady* (London: Virago, 1987)

Silverman, Kaja, *The Acoustic Mirror* (Bloomington: Indiana University Press, 1988)

Sorel, Cécile, *Cécile Sorel: An Autobiography* (London: Staples Press, 1953)

Stendhal [Beyle, Marie-Henri], 'Racine et Shakespeare' in *Œuvres complètes*, 37 (Geneva: Edito-Service, 1970)

Chroniques pour l'Angleterre, 4 vols. (Grenoble: Publications de l'Université des langues et lettres de Grenoble, 1982–5)

Correspondance, 3 vols. (Paris: Gallimard, 1962–8)

Love, trans. Gilbert and Suzanne Sale (Harmondsworth: Penguin, 1945)

Œuvres intimes, 2 vols. (Paris: Gallimard, 1981)

Stephens, John Russell, *The Profession of the Playwright: British Theatre 1800–1900* (Cambridge: Cambridge University Press, 1992)

Stokes, John, 'Aspects of Bernhardt', *The Yearbook of English Studies*, 11 (1981), 143–60

'Rachel Félix', in Michael Booth, John Stokes and Susan Bassnett, *Three Tragic Actresses* (Cambridge: Cambridge University Press, 1996)

'Sarah Bernhardt', in John Stokes, Michael Booth and Susan Bassnett, *Bernhardt, Terry, Duse: The Actress in her Time* (Cambridge: Cambridge University Press, 1988)

'Shopping in Byzantium: Oscar Wilde as Shakespeare Critic', in *Victorian Shakespeare, Volume 1. Theatre, Drama and Performance*, ed. Gail Marshall and Adrian Poole (Basingstoke and New York: Palgrave-Macmillan, 2003)

Oscar Wilde: Myths, Miracles and Imitations (Cambridge: Cambridge University Press, 1996)

Taranow, Gerda, *Sarah Bernhardt: The Art Within the Legend* (Princeton: Princeton University Press, 1972)

The Bernhardt Hamlet: Culture and Context (New York: Peter Lang, 1996)

Taylor, George, *Players and Performances in the Victorian Theatre* (Manchester: Manchester University Press, 1989)

The French Revolution and the London Stage 1789–1805 (Cambridge: Cambridge University Press, 2000)

Thomas, Edith, *The Women Incendiaries* (London: Secker and Warburg, 1967)

Townsend, Joanna, 'Elizabeth Robins: Hysteria, Politics and Performance', in *Women, Theatre and Performance: New Histories, New Historiographies*, ed. Maggie B. Gale and Viv Gardner (Manchester: Manchester University Press, 2000)

Trollope, Mrs, *Paris and the Parisians in 1835*, 2 vols. (London: Richard Bentley, 1835)

Tynan, Kenneth, *Curtains* (London: Longman's, 1961)

Uzanne, Octave, *La Femme à Paris. Nos Contemporains* (Paris: Ancienne Maison Quantin, 1894)

Vandam, Albert D., 'The Real Madame Sans-Gêne', *New Review*, 62 (1894), 24–34

Vigneron, Robert, 'Stendhal et Hazlitt', *Modern Philology*, 35 (1937–8), 375–414

Walker, Pierre A., *Reading Henry James in French Cultural Contexts* (Dekalb: Northern Illinois University Press, 1995)

Wheatley, Katherine E., *Racine and English Classicism* (Austin: University of Texas Press, 1956)

Wilde, Oscar, *Complete Works of Oscar Wilde*, ed. Merlin Holland (Glasgow: Harper Collins, 1994)

  Miscellanies, ed. Robert Ross (London: Methuen, 1908)

  The Complete Letters of Oscar Wilde, ed. Merlin Holland and Rupert Hart-Davis (London: Fourth Estate, 2000)

  The Complete Works of Oscar Wilde Volume 1: Poems and Poems in Prose, ed. Bobby Fong and Karl Beckson (Oxford: Oxford University Press, 2000)

Witemeyer, Hugh, *George Eliot and the Visual Arts* (New Haven: Yale University Press, 1979)

Yates, E. H., *Celebrities at Home*, 3rd ser. (London: Office of 'The World', 1879)

Zeldin, Theodore, *An Intimate History of Humanity* (London: Sinclair Stevenson, 1994)

  France 1848–1945, 2 vols. (Oxford: Clarendon Press, 1973)

Zola, Emile, *Le Naturalisme au théâtre* (Paris: Charpentier, 1923)

  The Downfall (London: Chatto and Windus, 1892)

Index